Disposing of Modernity

Published in cooperation with the Society for Historical Archaeology

UNIVERSITY PRESS OF FLORIDA

Florida A&M University, Tallahassee
Florida Atlantic University, Boca Raton
Florida Gulf Coast University, Ft. Myers
Florida International University, Miami
Florida State University, Tallahassee
New College of Florida, Sarasota
University of Central Florida, Orlando
University of Florida, Gainesville
University of North Florida, Jacksonville
University of South Florida, Tampa
University of West Florida, Pensacola

DISPOSING OF MODERNITY

The Archaeology of Garbage and Consumerism during Chicago's 1893 World's Fair

REBECCA S. GRAFF

University Press of Florida
Gainesville · Tallahassee · Tampa · Boca Raton
Pensacola · Orlando · Miami · Jacksonville · Ft. Myers · Sarasota

Copyright 2020 by the Society for Historical Archaeology
All rights reserved
Published in the United States of America

First cloth printing, 2020
First paperback printing, 2026

31 30 29 28 27 26   6 5 4 3 2 1

Library of Congress Cataloging-in-Publication Data
Names: Graff, Rebecca S., author.
Title: Disposing of modernity : the archaeology of garbage and consumerism
  during Chicago's 1893 World's Fair / Rebecca S. Graff.
Description: Gainesville : University Press of Florida, [2020] | Includes
  bibliographical references and index.
Identifiers: LCCN 2020001903 (print) | LCCN 2020001904 (ebook) | ISBN
  9780813066493 (hardback) | ISBN 9780813057552 (pdf) | ISBN 9780813081618 (pbk)
Subjects: LCSH: World's Columbian Exposition (1893 : Chicago,
  Ill.)—History. | Refuse and refuse disposal—Social
  aspects—Illinois—Chicago. |
  Exhibitions—Illinois—Chicago—History—19th century. | Chicago
  (Ill.)—History. | Chicago (Ill.)—Social life and customs.
Classification: LCC T500.B1 G73 2020 (print) | LCC T500.B1 (ebook) | DDC
  907.4/77311—dc23
LC record available at https://lccn.loc.gov/2020001903
LC ebook record available at https://lccn.loc.gov/2020001904

The University Press of Florida is the scholarly publishing agency for the State University System of Florida, comprising Florida A&M University, Florida Atlantic University, Florida Gulf Coast University, Florida International University, Florida State University, New College of Florida, University of Central Florida, University of Florida, University of North Florida, University of South Florida, and University of West Florida.

University Press of Florida
PO Box 140239
Gainesville, FL 32614
floridapress.org

GPSR EU Authorized Representative: Mare Nostrum Group B.V, Doelen 72, 4831 GR Breda, The Netherlands, gpsr@mare-nostrum.co.uk

For Ryan J. Cook and Alexander Elias Cook

CONTENTS

List of Figures ix

List of Tables xi

Acknowledgments xiii

1. Introduction: The Vanishing Fair and the Enduring Home 1
2. Situating the Sites in Chicago: Elite Networks and Archaeology 10
3. Temporalities as Ideologies 54
4. Domesticity and Social Life 82
5. Consumption and Conspicuous Disposal 119
6. Conclusion: At the Center of the World, Again 160

References 173

Index 195

FIGURES

2.1. The Y-shaped Chicago municipal device 14

2.2. Map of Chicago's 1893 World's Columbian Exposition 30

2.3. View from the 1893 World's Columbian Exposition's South Canal 31

2.4. French's Statue of the Republic after the Peristyle fire 32

2.5. Survey map of Jackson Park 35

2.6. Performing shovel tests in Locus 2 in Jackson Park 36

2.7. Jackson Park, Locus 2 37

2.8. The first day of excavation in Jackson Park, April 2008 37

2.9. Site map of the Jackson Park Archaeological Project 38

2.10. Plan view of Excavation Units (EUs) 40

2.11. The Ohio Building 40

2.12. Plaster volute with detail of the Ohio Building 41

2.13. Base of plaster urn with detail of the Ohio Building 41

2.14. Map of Chicago showing the Gold Coast and Jackson Park 43

2.15. James Charnley residence, Chicago, Illinois, ca. 1890s 45

2.16. View of the Charnley-Persky House Archaeological Project 50

2.17. Charnley-Persky House Archaeological Project Site Map 51

2.18. Bottles and a teacup from the Charnley-Persky House 52

3.1. James Charnley residence, Chicago, Illinois 73

3.2. Plan of James Charnley residence 74

3.3. The atrium and first floor hall of the Charnley-Persky House 75

3.4. Transportation Building, Golden Door, 1893 77

3.5. Alarm clock from the Charnley-Persky House 78
4.1. The Ohio Building at the 1893 World's Columbian Exposition 92
4.2. Approved design for the Ohio Building 97
5.1. Cruet or decanter tops from the 2008 Jackson Park Archaeological Project 128
5.2. Minton cat plate, ca. 1873–1891 135
5.3. Chicago Artifact Map 136
5.4. World Artifact Map 136
5.5. Partial dentures 142
5.6. Yacht Club salad dressing 144
5.7. Cover of *Yacht Club Manual of Salads* 145
5.8. MacLaren's Roquefort cheese 146
6.1. *The Adventures of Uncle Jeremiah and Family at the Great Fair* 170

TABLES

4.1. Materials ordered for constructing the Ohio Building   94
4.2. Furnishings ordered for the Ohio Building   95
4.3. Charnley House renters and owners   107
4.4. Employers and employees at the Charnley House   116
5.1. World's fairs products   126
5.2. Identified pottery companies   134
5.3. Identified brands and products   138

ACKNOWLEDGMENTS

I finished this manuscript inside my rented home on the campus of Lake Forest College (LFC), a small liberal arts college located on the North Shore of Chicago. Architect Howard Van Doren Shaw designed my temporary home in 1916 for the use of college faculty. It, and its three identical neighbors on the campus, have siblings on the Indiana side of Lake Michigan. In the corporate city of Marktown, Shaw used a similar plan for the house of the Mark Company overseer. The collegiate domesticity evoked by my house was translated with very little revision into a corporate paternalism. Shaw, employed by Jenney and Mundie, also worked on the White City of the 1893 fair. Entangled connections like these are all too common in the archaeology of the contemporary past, as this volume shows.

The book I envisioned when I began my research on the archaeology of the Chicago's 1893 World's Columbian Exposition is very different from the dual site research you see presented here. Trying to think of whom I need to thank for their assistance for one season of a survey project, three excavation seasons, three field schools for three different academic institutions, two laboratory courses—and all this is for the archaeological side of this work alone—I feel overwhelmed and humbled by the scale of undertaking and the work of all those who lent a hand or a trowel over the last decade. This list seems as immense as World's Columbian Exposition itself, and the work it represents certainly lasted longer (so much longer!). I am not so bold as to think that I can list all of those who contributed without inadvertently leaving someone out. Instead, I will highlight as I can.

Archaeological fieldwork is driven by labor from many people. Thanks to all of my field school students who pitched in at both Jackson Park and the Charnley-Persky House, including students from the University of Chicago, DePaul University, and LFC. My field school students were absolutely essential to this project and made it both more joyful and more challenging by their participation as they learned about the practice of archaeology. I am also immensely grateful to all those people who volunteered at these sites. By choosing to do fieldwork in the same city in which I attended graduate school meant that I had a wealth of brilliant archaeologist friends who were willing to throw in a trowel. They, and my other volunteers with different experience in archaeology, made this project possible.

Some key colleagues and co-instructors in the field deserve special mention and my heartfelt thanks. Mary Leighton worked as an instructor at the Jackson Park Archaeological Project, and then codirected the 2010 Charnley-Persky House Archaeological Project season. Megan E. Edwards Alvarez supervised excavation units in Jackson Park and undertook the analysis of the faunal materials from the site. Sarah Kautz supervised excavation units in Jackson Park and helped me relocate the extremely important Shovel Test 55. Tiffany Charles codirected the 2015 Charnley-Persky House season. Grace Krause analyzed the faunal samples from both seasons of that excavation.

My thanks to the mentors who believed in the project and in me, especially after I began a second project at the Charnley-Persky House. Thank you Shannon Lee Dawdy, Michael Dietler, Anna Agbe-Davies, and Raymond D. Fogelson. Ray is the person who first told me about the 1893 World's Columbian Exposition, and for that I am forever grateful.

I can think of no better set of partners for the Charnley-Persky House side of this endeavor than Pauline Saliga and her colleagues at the Society of Architectural Historians (SAH). They endured two summers of dust, debris, and noisy undergraduates at their workplace, not to mention having their driveway turned into an excavation site twice. The SAH's Beth Eifrig generously shared her stellar research into the Charnley family with me. I knew that Pauline's sincere interest in bringing archaeological work into engagement with architectural history was special. I was delighted when this brought her and the SAH the 2010 Public Service Award from the Illinois Archaeological Survey, recognizing their efforts to protect an archaeological site in Chicago. I hope that I can show why this project is illustrative of the ways we should collaborate across organizations and disciplines in Chicago.

LouAnn Wurst served as my editor when it was announced this work would be a co-publication through SHA. She delivered important critiques and made sure that I knew that she believed in the project (even if she also suggested a glass of wine while I read her comments). Annalies Corbin at the SHA and Meredith Babb at University Press of Florida have likewise been crucial supporters. Thanks to my three manuscript reviewers for taking their time to share their significant and helpful comments.

At LFC I am grateful for the enthusiastic support of my colleagues. Thank you to Holly Swyers, Todd Beer, David Boden, and Ahmad Sadri for being fabulous departmental colleagues. Before either of us knew we would be working together at LFC, Holly Swyers helped with the most crucial parts of the 2008 Jackson Park excavations. She, along with Ryan Cook, have shown the world that (some) sociocultural anthropologists can do archaeology very well. Davis Schneiderman and Emily Mace made the integration of my research project into our institutional Mellon Grant as seamless as possible. I owe special thanks to Emily and to Jennie Larsen for their logistical help for Charnley 2015. Emma O'Hagan made beautiful publicity materials for the excavation season, and Linda Blaser made sure the press knew what was going on. My sincere thanks to Stephen D. Schutt, who gamely took on this new archaeological facet of his presidency, and to Michael Orr, for likewise being so willing to take this on in his then-capacity as dean of faculty. My other colleagues at LFC could not have been more welcoming. Thanks to Nancy Sosna Bohm, Linda Horwitz, and Anne Thomason for their help. I also want to thank my former colleagues at Michigan Technological University, especially Tim Scarlett, for welcoming my Gilded Age gilded artifacts to the Copper Country.

I must thank the many others who supported this project with digging, an invited lecture to help me push through an idea, a read of my chapters, and more: Adela Amaral, Julia Bachrach, Andrew Bauer, Jane Eva Baxter, Zachary Chase, J. Eric Deetz, Diane Dillon, Elizabeth Fagan, Royal Omar Ghazal, Geneviève Godbout, Sarah R. Graff, M. Elizabeth Grávalos, D. Ryan Gray, Alan F. Greene, Amanda Grupp, Debora Heard, Matthew Johnson, Petra Johnson, Morag Kersel, Andrew Leith, Michelle Lelièvre, Amanda Logan, Mark Lycett, Claudine Malik, Terrance Martin, Maureen Marshall, Madeleine McLeester, Cassie O'Neill, Charles E. Orser Jr., David Pacifico, Jason Ramsey, Matthew Reilly, François Richard, Deb Rotman, Frances Vandervoort, Kathryn O'Neill Weber, Jessica Westphal, Vanessa Will, Brian Wilson, Kathleen Yang-Clayton, and Lauren Zych. Special thanks to go to my undergraduate research assistants at LFC who helped bring the Charnley materials into order through our website:

Anne Marie Brugioni, Rebecca Howell, and Lexie Nogulich. Thanks to Jamie Williams for piecing the Minton kitten plate back together so wonderfully, and to Deki Gyaltshen, Hannah Gurholt, and Paula Pelletier for helping check citations.

Parts of this project were supported by a fellowship from the Karla Scherer Center for the Study of American Culture at the University of Chicago and by the Lake Forest College Digital Humanities Grant (*Digital Chicago: Unearthing History and Culture*) from the Andrew W. Mellon Foundation.

My family and friends kept this project going by keeping me going. All my love to Laura Kunstler Graff, Jane Kunstler, Ben Graff, Marc Graff, Cindy and Doug Graff, Myron and Janet Cook, the Raidas, all my Chicago Graff family, and my dear Berkeley friends. To Alexander Elias Cook: thanks for arriving into the world early enough that I missed my deadline for the first version of the book, forcing me to come up with something better. You have brought me invaluable perspective and joy. Ryan J. Cook was the artifact photographer, creator of excellent stratigraphic profiles, editor, critic, primary caregiver for our very energetic child, and more. Words can't suffice. But here they are.

1

INTRODUCTION

The Vanishing Fair and the Enduring Home

Jackson Park, 1894

The World's Columbian Exposition closed its gates for the last time on October 30, 1893, and on January 1, 1894, the exposition directors officially turned the fairgrounds back to Chicago's South Park Commission. Consisting of Jackson Park and the Midway Plaisance, the 633-acre site was open once more to all who wanted to visit, not just for those who had the economic means to pay the fifty-cent entrance fee to the exposition.

Soon the site was in disarray as people flocked among the still extant structures of the 1893 World's Columbian Exposition. Those affected by the recent economic depression and related labor strikes sought refuge in Jackson Park, using and altering the invitingly empty fair structures. Several *Chicago Tribune* articles from the harsh winter of 1894 remarked on the discovery of "tramp nests" in basements of buildings (*Chicago Tribune* 1894b, 1) and destructive fires started by those trying to stay warm (*Chicago Tribune* 1894c, 1). And there was free sustenance in addition to housing within the fairgrounds. Hungry people ate leftovers from food displays abandoned in the buildings, including "boxes of canned meat, sardines, prepared soups, choice pickles, wines of the most popular brands and articles of confectionary" (*Chicago Tribune* 1894b, 1).

Other visitors wandered the former fairgrounds with commemorative goals in mind. Eager to maintain a tangible and personal memory of the

White City, some people pried off bits of buildings to fashion their own souvenirs. In one afternoon, an estimated ten thousand "relic hunting vandals" went on a rampage, removing mementos that included pieces of the fair buildings as well as virtually destroying the Midway's Javanese Village. They took these "bits of glass, pieces of staff, sticks, tin cans, and bottles," which, according to one reporter, they "cherished as objects of much value" (*Chicago Tribune* 1894d, 11). The grounds were rife with these "relic fiends," and the remaining Columbian Guards—the private security force of the fair—could not do much to stop them.

Yet another group of citizens was concerned with permanently memorializing the fair in Jackson Park for the larger public. Having lived alongside this "dream of beauty" for the last year, not all Chicagoans could accept it essentially vanishing from the landscape. In November 1893 local residents circulated a series of petitions and held meetings with the hope that at least the Manufactures and Liberal Arts Building could be saved (*Chicago Tribune* 1893d, 2). One such resident suggested that the buildings should be preserved in situ and covered in ivy to conceal their condition because "they would make fine ruins" (*Chicago Tribune* 1893c, 13). Some Chicagoans wished to set stone tablets or allegorical statuary at the site of each building to visually memorialize the fair (*Chicago Tribune* 1895c, 32). In a newspaper editorial, an anonymous author pleaded with the leadership of the South Park Commission, who had ultimate control of Jackson Park: "Don't tear down those majestic edifices that make the magical White City an enchanted realm. . . . Let time's fingers alone touch them" (*Chicago Tribune* 1893a, 16).

Despite all these desires, the South Park Commission went ahead with the original plan to take down the remaining structures and began seeking bids from private businesses for their removal. The Exposition Company turned over the twenty-seven main fair buildings, Daniel Chester French's Statue of the Republic, and a variety of bridges, bandstands, piers, lampposts, and other smaller features as well as their anticipated profits from sales of scrap to the South Park Commission. It would no longer be liable for any damage to Jackson Park, ending its oversight and spatial administration of the fair (Gregerson 1996, 273).

The questions of eradication, preservation, memorialization, or commercialization became moot when a series of fires destroyed the mass of remaining structures from the fair. Beginning on January 8, 1894, massive fires plagued the former fair site. The January conflagration claimed the

Peristyle, Music Hall, and Casino, and damaged several other buildings. On February 7, 1894, another fire destroyed the Agricultural Building. Labor unrest, of the same social currents as the 1892 Homestead and 1894 Pullman strikes and stemming from the economic depression of 1893–94, may have spurred arsonists to set fire to further structures on July 5, 1894. By the time the flames were extinguished on July 6, the fair's Terminal Station, Administration Building, Mines and Mining Building, Electricity Building, Manufactures and Liberal Arts Building, Agricultural Building, and Machinery Hall were gone, and many of the other buildings severely damaged (*Chicago Tribune* 1894e, 7). Upward of ten thousand tourists flocked to Jackson Park to watch these fires, showing the pervasiveness of the touristic impulse even at the end of the fair's lifecycle (*Chicago Tribune* 1894e, 7). Soon not even those in precarious straits, or hunting souvenirs, or taking final inspiration from the ruins could roam the White City. It was gone.

Astor Street, 1892

James and Helen Charnley, along with their eighteen-year-old son, Douglas, finally moved into their new home at 99 Astor Street in Chicago's burgeoning Gold Coast neighborhood. Although they had moved frequently in the last few years, only a decade earlier the family lived in an ornate Queen Anne–style house mere blocks from this new home. Designed in 1882 by Burnham and Root—the same men and firm who would eventually oversee the architectural program of the World's Columbian Exposition—their previous Gold Coast house once contained a larger number of Charnleys. In the winter of 1883, daughters Bettie and Helen, ages four and six, died from diphtheria and the family moved away. Now the Charnleys returned to the Gold Coast, in a new home designed by architects Louis Sullivan and Frank Lloyd Wright—both of them hard at work on designs for the upcoming Chicago World's Fair.

Their new house did not look like any others. With an austere façade assembled from courses of yellow Roman brick over a gray ashlar limestone base and with little ornament save a small, wooden loggia and a copper cornice, the home was smaller and simpler than those that surrounded it. Inside, it was even more starkly different from comparable, Victorian residences—more modern, in the words of Wright, who apocryphally characterized the Charnley's Astor Street home as "the world's first modern house." Entering the home, one proceeded through an intimate vestibule to an open hall bordered by a mosaic fireplace of curving geometric shapes in shades of cream, red, yellow, and blue. Demarcated only by wooden arches, the first floor's open plan had no doors to shut off one room from the next; accordingly, each room flowed into the next. Bathed in light from an atrium and skylight of a type typically found in commercial architecture, the cream-colored interior walls of the house were quite plain. This simplicity was opposed to the current vogue for elaborately decorated interior surfaces that produced small, dark rooms filled with a startling amount of highly patterned and overstuffed furniture and mass-produced bric-a-brac. So, too, was the scale of the Charnleys' new home different than the other homes in the vicinity. The entire Charnley House could fit within the art gallery of Potter and Bertha Palmer's nearby mansion, with room to spare (*Chicago Tribune* 1893f, 1; and Bluestone 2004, 41).

As for the Charnleys, little is known about how they lived in their new, modern home. Did the intricacies of their daily lives take different patterns than in their previous traditional, Victorian-style home? While living on Astor Street, did the Charnleys take a boat or train to visit the World's Fair—as did most Chicagoans in 1893—a trip spanning just ten short miles from their home? Or did they follow the fair via newspapers, magazines, or gossip for the six months that it dominated the headlines? Did they change their consumption choices and habits based on the new ideas and products presented there? Nine years after the fair, and after being rocked by family scandal and concerns about James's ill health, the Charnleys left Astor Street in 1902 for warmer climes. What else, if anything, did they leave behind?

Approaching Modernity at the Center of the World

The White City. The Magic City (Buel 1894). The Enchanted City (Burnett 1895:166). A City of Realized Dreams (*Catholic World* 1893, 566). The City of Palaces (Conkey 1894). The Phantom City (Jenks 1893, 221). The Dream City (Ives 1893). The Vanishing City (Schoch 1893, 5). These are some of the many evocative names for the 1893 World's Columbian Exposition—ones that hint at the feelings they generated in the populace. Between May and October 1893, Chicago's Jackson Park hosted an American fair even larger than the massive 1876 Philadelphia Centennial Exposition. Located seven miles south of Chicago's Loop, Jackson Park was "the center of the world" when approximately 12 to 16 million individual sightseers visited and revisited the area to experience the 1893 World's Columbian Exposition, ostensibly a celebration of the four hundredth anniversary of Columbus's voyage to the New World. At a time when the total U.S. population was approximately 63 million, over 27 million tickets were sold to the event. The fairscape presented an encyclopedic display of raw materials, manufactured goods, new inventions, fine arts, entertainments, foods, native people, and ancient and modern architecture, all held in this temporary "city" that was designed to be demolished at the fair's end. Nineteenth-century world's fairs as cultural forms emerged from the social currents of industrial capitalism, where a customer base of millions might be reached to consume the goods and ideas on display, each event characterized as a veritable "clearing-house of civilization" (Palmer 1893, 5). In the same way that the modern, unornamented façade of the Charnley House drew attention and made it a unique sight on Chicago's Gold Coast, the transformative potential of new forms and technologies for daily life drew much of the tourist gaze at the Chicago fair. Still, after millions of visitors had experienced the promises and contradictions of a new modern age on display at the fair, and as the fairground was dismantled through design and by arson, people like the Charnleys were left wondering what this future would mean for them.

The 1893 World's Fair is often cited as a watershed moment in the development of modern, industrial American society and invites further investigation to understand the myriad social and cultural processes still part of American urban experiences today. Henry Adams famously said of the fair: "Chicago asked in 1893 for the first time the question whether the American people knew where they were driving" (Adams 1907: 299). Yet in 1929, nearly thirty-five years after the World's Columbian Exposition shut its doors and as the Charnley House was being altered with an addition, Robert Staughton Lynd and Helen Merrell Lynd noted in their classic sociological study of cultural change on "Middletown" (their pseudonym for an "typical" small American city, now known to be Muncie, Indiana) that "it is not uncommon to observe 1890 and 1924 habits jostling along side by side in a family with primitive back-yard water or sewage habits, yet using an automobile, electric washer, electric iron, and vacuum cleaner" (Lynd and Lynd [1929] 1956, 97–98). In analyzing the ways that the white (they deliberately did not consider African American households) residents of Middletown worked, made and organized their domestic spaces, worshipped, and spent their leisure time, the Lynds' social survey captured information about seemingly mundane elements of material home life. That this "unevenness in the diffusion of material culture" (Lynd and Lynd [1929] 1956: 98) is described in terms of temporal dissonance calls our attention to the utility of archaeology to assess the terms of such stasis or change and to answer Adams's call as to whether Americans, amid these modern transformations, knew where they were going.

My 2007–8 archaeological and archival research focused on the ephemeral "White City" and Midway Plaisance of the 1893 Chicago fair and links the fair—as a catalyst for structural change—and its material record to the larger social structures of late nineteenth-century American modernity. Lasting for only six months before its structures "vanished," the fair's permanent impact on American consumer culture, on city planning in American urban centers, on modeling the "right" sort of citizenry for the next century, and on promulgating conceptions of people from foreign lands in terms of America's own imperial aspirations was deeply tied to and reinforced by its ephemerality. The results of the excavation in Jackson Park (site number 11CK1105) revealed the robust archaeological signature of the extensive sanitary infrastructure of the fair and, surprisingly, the delicate plaster remains of the fair's Ohio State Building. These state structures were constructed at the same scale as homes—a dramatic contrast from the rest of the monumental fairscape—and served as clubhouses for visitors to the fair.

Two seasons of excavations (2010 and 2015) of a historic artifact midden at the Charnley-Persky House (site number 11CK1248) provides a contemporaneous domestic example with which to look at home life during the time of the 1893 fair. The excavations at the Charnley House produced almost 28,000 artifacts from approximately 1880–1920, many of which represent brands that debuted at the Chicago fair and related fairs. As an assemblage, they provide data on a vast array of consumer patterns found as fragments of mineral water bottles, milk glass cheese containers, dentures, and monogrammed porcelain dinnerware. We identified over 150 different manufacturers and brands from the excavated materials, with some items produced and sold a block from the Charnley House and others manufactured on the other side of the world.

Using the results of these two projects, this volume engages with this critical period in the nation's history to address the ambivalent reactions to the changing world of 1890s urban America, pointing to these competing notions of modern and premodern, of progress and retrenchment, of confidence and anxiety. If expositions were "quintessential Victorian artifacts" (Schlereth 1991, xiv) that displayed the growing and changing material world and served a cultural mission with their architecture, art, and technological innovation, they can be understood as pedagogical moments for Americans, teaching what and how to consume and, ultimately, how to discard their consumables. How, then, were these messages themselves consumed by the tourist publics, and how did transformations in the domestic sphere reflect or refute these modernizing tendencies?

Chapter 2 introduces the two Chicago-based archaeological sites that provide the material signature of this book: Jackson Park, the former site of the 1893 World's Columbian Exposition, and the Charnley-Persky House, today the headquarters for the Society of Architectural Historians as well as an operating museum. After an introduction to Chicago's natural and anthropogenic landscapes and an overview of the Chicago fair's predecessor exhibitions and its planning, the chapter provides historical background on Chicago's Gold Coast, the Charnley family, and their home designed by the firm of Adler and Sullivan. Results from archaeological research in Jackson Park (2007, 2008) and at the Charnley-Persky House (2010, 2015) are framed with attention to the elite social networks of wealthy, white, Protestant Chicagoans in whose hands these projects were entangled. The archaeological results from the two sites provide a powerful testament to the lasting ties of commerce and concomitant ideology that suffused the forms of both fairscape and home.

Chapter 3 focuses on temporalities at both sites. For the World's Columbian Exposition, its brief, six-month lifespan and subsequent material erasure provided transformative potential within the greater narrative of America in the late nineteenth century. Here the logic of capitalist creative destruction was experienced as the sense of loss felt by tourists as the immense "city for a single summer" vanished from the landscape. The fleeting nature of the fair was an integral part of its allure and its message. By seeming to vanish materially, the White City could be mustered to further ideological agendas. Moreover, the fair incorporated architecture, exhibits, and attractions from the imagined past, present, and future, presenting ideological messages through deliberate manipulations of temporalities—ones that were consumed by many a tourist public as an unproblematic totality. Our archaeological research likewise centered upon temporalities of the fair, here with attention to the fair's monumental ephemerality, with its enormous structures made of insubstantial building materials like plaster, and its infrastructural permanence, with systems of sewerage, water, electricity, and gas that still endure within the soil of Jackson Park. Next, the chapter turns to the solid and still extant Charnley House, designed by Louis Sullivan and draftsman Frank Lloyd Wright as an aesthetically modern home. Critics noted that its spare façade looked "out of time" with the rest of the domestic architecture of the city. Finally, the discussion of a tin-can style alarm clock excavated from the Charnley midden reinforces and makes materially possible the keeping of modern, industrial time within the modern home.

Chapter 4 considers domesticity and social life within two "houses" at the center of the volume: the fair's Ohio Building and the Charnley House. The chapter begins with an overview of American ideologies of domesticity and notions of domestic spaces as understood through historical and archaeological accounts. Next discussion moves to the Ohio Building, a small structure from the fair that operated as a sort of clubhouse for fair tourists. Many conceived of the fair's quasi-domestic state buildings as domestic because of their nonmonumental scale, their intended use as spaces for informal social life, and the cutting-edge sanitary infrastructure, such as toilet facilities, that tourists to the fair could experience within them. The chapter turns from the fair to a detailed residential history of the Astor Street home, but that account moves from the expected chain of title discussion to one that reveals further interconnections and entanglements of elite social networks in Chicago. To these experiences, a look at the limited documentary record of servants from the Charnley House and the Ohio Building expands upon domestic life, architecturally, materially, and socially.

Chapter 5 refocuses attention on the archaeologically robust elements of both sites: the goods people consumed as evidenced via their garbage, the changing waste management regimes in Chicago, and what I term the "conspicuous disposal" practices that typified turn-of-the-twentieth-century America. The sites are profoundly tied by the consumer goods themselves: many of the products recovered and identified from the Charnley-Persky House excavations as well as from the Jackson Park excavations first debuted at world's fairs and expositions. An overview of the ways world's fairs and related institutions were used as marketplaces for new products is followed by a close look at the brands, advertising, and point-of-sale or manufacture of the products recovered from the Charnley House and how these shed light on a suite of conceptions of health, hygiene, grooming, foodways, and culinary choices. Next the chapter looks at the historic lack of waste disposal infrastructure in Chicago and other urban centers and how that created the conditions for the accrual of the Charnley midden. The midden seems mightily at odds with the sanitary future of waste disposal that the fair demonstrated, yet it also echoes the phenomena of world's fairs themselves as exemplars of conspicuous disposal by their very design.

Chapter 6 concludes by deliberately returning to present-day, presentist concerns—ones explicitly engaged through the archaeology of the contemporary. Here Jackson Park's current reappearance on the world stage as the future home of the Obama Presidential Center is reckoned with, along with the Charnley House and related contemporary archaeological and architectural preservation efforts. By looking at these "strangely familiar" experiences of time, domesticity, consumption, and disposal of the recent past through the frame of contemporary archaeology, I argue that these historical trends that impact the present are, in fact, of the present itself.

This volume is essentially a microhistory of two urban structures and the people who lived their lives within them to understand the broader sociocultural trends of modernity that we continue to experience today. Separated by ten miles, the Charnley's Astor Street home and the structure created to represent, house, and boost the reputation of the state of Ohio at the World's Fair both operated within the same sociocultural milieu. One home endures as a house museum and landmark, actively used by an international architectural organization and toured by numerous visitors; the other exists as unearthed fragments now boxed in another museum's storage space. Both allow for an investigation into this time and its place in our narratives of what it means to be modern at a time of rapid change and disenchantment. With Jackson Park entering the latest phase of its lifecycle as the site and home of the Barack Obama Presidential Center, it will be fascinating to see the ways in which the fair is remembered, politicized, forgotten, or erased as new tourists flock to a small stretch of land on the South Side of Chicago.

2

SITUATING THE SITES IN CHICAGO

Elite Networks and Archaeology

Separated by ten miles, Chicago's Jackson Park and the Charnley-Persky House maintain a historic as well as contemporary connection that belies their spatial segregation. From a cursory view, both sites clearly share a status as local tourist destinations. For Jackson Park, this frequently includes visits to the Museum of Science and Industry, an institution located in the former Palace of Fine Arts from the 1893 World's Columbian Exposition. The Charnley-Persky House, part of the Astor Street Historic District and a member of the Chicago Historic House Museum consortium, receives architecture enthusiasts eager to see that unusual example of Louis Sullivan and Frank Lloyd Wright's domestic design.

Materially, the sites share another present-day commonality—one all too rare in Chicago—of having been archaeologically excavated and researched. In 2007 and 2008 we surveyed and then excavated in Jackson Park, ultimately revealing both the plaster remnants of the 1893 Ohio Building and the extensive infrastructural network that supported the immense undertaking of the World's Columbian Exposition (Graff 2011a, 2011b, 2012). In 2010 and again in 2015 we excavated within a rich midden of historic materials alongside the eastern face of the Charnley-Persky House, recovering almost 28,000 domestic artifacts representing over 150 identified brands and products from the turn of the twentieth century.

Ideologically, the sites share connections both to the elite social networks that created them and to the notions of modernity, domesticity, and consumption for which events like the 1893 fair laid the groundwork.

The links between the wealthy, white, Protestant Chicago elite are numerous and seem to call for a social network analysis to truly see the extent of these interconnections. The shared the visions of modern domesticity and consumption practices made material at the two sites similarly show the ways that the 1893 fair marketed goods and concomitant ideologies far beyond the boundaries of Jackson Park. A few examples suffice to sketch the connections between the sites, with other threads discussed in the chapters that follow.

From the outset, the built environment of elite nineteenth-century Chicago unites Jackson Park and the Charnley House via Daniel H. Burnham, director of works for the 1893 World's Columbian Exposition. Burnham, charged with hiring and creating a board of architects to design the main buildings of the fair, selected ten prominent American firms, deliberately choosing five from Chicago and five from elsewhere to promote a national, rather than solely Chicagoan, sense of the enterprise: Richard M. Hunt (New York), George B. Post (New York), McKim, Mead and White (New York), Peabody and Stearns (Boston), Van Brunt and Howe (Kansas City, Missouri), Burling and Whitehouse (Chicago), Jenney and Mundie (Chicago), Henry Ives Cobb (Chicago), Solon Spencer Beman (Chicago), and Adler and Sullivan (Chicago) (Higinbotham 1898, 29). While working on 1893 fair plans in Chicago, many of these architects accepted private commissions in the up-and-coming Astor Street District of the Gold Coast. There they designed extravagant homes for the very men who, again, not coincidentally, swelled the ranks of the World's Columbian Exposition's governance committees. For example, in 1891 Stanford White of the firm McKim, Mead and White designed the still-extant Elinor Patterson–Cyrus H. McCormick Jr. House at 1500 North Astor Street, coinciding with his time in town for the fair (Stone 2005, 87). Also notable for their work in both Jackson Park and in the Gold Coast is the firm of Adler and Sullivan, who designed the Transportation Building for the fair during the same time period as they designed the Charnley House.

Social life on Astor Street also illuminates these elite networks and the ways the socioeconomic connections entangled with the 1893 fair. A memoir by Edith Ogden Harrison—daughter-in-law of Chicago mayor Carter H. Harrison Sr., whose October 1893 assassination tainted the end of the World's Fair—sheds light on these personal and familial relationships within the powerful networks. Her chapter "Columbian Exposition Days" is immediately followed by the chapter "Astor Street Days," linking the two locations through her reminiscence of the sociality and friendships she found when she moved to that desirable Astor Street District at the close of the fair (Harrison 1949). Furthermore, the Harrisons lived at the same intersection of Schiller and Astor Streets as James and Helen Charnley, although, strikingly, the Charnleys are never mentioned in the cavalcade of who's whos that Harrison otherwise provides in her memoir. These other neighbors, many of whom served various capacities in World's Fair governance and planning committees, would return daily from Jackson Park to their residences on Astor Street and to the elite social worlds they inhabited, dining with each other, worshipping together, intermarrying, and forming new business associations among themselves.

Most revealingly a reminder of the relationships between Chicago's business elite, their Gold Coast homes, and the 1893 fair—as well as the particular forms of consumption that typified them (see chapter 5)—is the infamous story of Bertha Honoré Palmer's snub by Spain's Infanta Eulalia. Bertha and Potter Palmer's mansion—or "Castle," as they called it—loomed over the Charnley's house to its southeast and was the site of significant World's Fair socializing. Potter Palmer (1826–1902) made his fortune as a dry goods merchant, hotelier, and real estate magnate and was a member and a second vice president of the board of directors of the World's Columbian Exposition, serving on its Committee on Grounds and Buildings and its Committee on Fine Arts. But his established socialite and philanthropist wife, Bertha Honoré Palmer (1849–1918), was the more visible and socially active of the two both before and after the fair. Bertha served as the president of the fair's "Board of Lady Managers" and, as a result, functioned as the default "hostess" of the fair. The Palmers would throw some of the most elaborate parties in the city the following year, including the notorious reception for the *infanta* of Spain, a royal representative of the other nation vested in the story of the Columbian discovery from which the fair took its inspiration. But when the *infanta* learned of the service-adjacent occupations of her hosts, she declared that she would not attend an event held by an "innkeeper's wife," a statement that rankled the Gold Coasters and other Chicagoans alike. One wonders if James and Helen Charnley, who lived on the same block as the Palmers, were similarly miffed at this characterization.

In this chapter, anecdote is joined by material connection as the two sites, their history, and a brief overview of our archaeological investigations weave them together in a manner that might not come as a surprise to the "intimate set" of business and social acquaintances who had a hand in both projects on numerous levels (Harrison 1949, 77). That these social networks have voids, as will be discussed in the Charnley case, is clear; still, the material remains at these two sites provide a powerful testament to the lasting ties of commerce and concomitant ideology that suffused the forms of both fairscape and home. Because Chicago's history ranges far beyond its nineteenth-century preeminence as the seat of the fair, the choices that created the conditions for the World's Columbian Exposition and the rise of the elite enclave of the Gold Coast need brief exposition and context.

Chicago, before the Fair and House

Landscape and Human Settlement

Landscape transformation and the choices past and present Chicagoans made regarding their modification of the flat, glacial plain along Lake Michigan threads Jackson Park and the Gold Coast together. "Chicago" is a transliteration of an Algonquian word commonly translated as "skunk," possibly referring to a strong odor. Some scholars attribute the source of the smelly name to *Allium tricoccum*, a variety of wild garlic or ramp whose scent permeated the area in the spring (Swenson 1991, 235). The wild garlic–filled Chicago region had swampy terrain that necessitated a variety of interventions to surmount its muck. Those challenged by this landscape include the indigenous inhabitants of the area, French fur traders and missionaries, British military personnel, American settlers, and, eventually, the architects and planners of the World's Columbian Exposition and the Gold Coast.

Chicago is located alongside an inland sea, Lake Michigan, within the Great Lakes geographic region. Lake Michigan dominates the shoreline, and Chicago's river systems connect it to the Mississippi River and ultimately the Gulf of Mexico with the help of infrastructural projects like the Illinois and Michigan Canal (constructed 1836–48) (Conzen and Carr 1988). Chicago's municipal "device" (the official term given to the symbol of the city) is a riverine "Y," chosen via an 1892 *Chicago Tribune* contest. Found on decorative cornices, old subway tokens, bridges, and the like, the "Y" depicts the center of the city, where the Chicago River divides into its north and south branches at Wolf Point (Figure 2.1). This symbolic

Figure 2.1. The Y-shaped Chicago municipal device, as seen in the second "C" of the Chicago Theatre's marquee. Photograph by Ryan J. Cook.

choice highlights the importance of river traffic and transportation in the birth of the city. Moreover, the selection of the symbol was yet another set of local preparations for the 1893 World's Fair, and Francis Davis Millet, the fair's director of decoration, was in charge of the judging (*Chicago Tribune* 1892b:1). For both its prehistoric and historic period inhabitants, the swampy area was best traveled by these water routes and short portages symbolized in the Y. The most noteworthy was the Chicago Portage located between the Des Plaines River and the south branch of the Chicago River, used by Native Americans and documented by Père Jacques Marquette and Louis Jolliet during their travels in 1673.

Archaeological investigations and oral traditions of the Chicago area have produced materials accounting for ten thousand years of aboriginal occupations, with the documentary record beginning in 1634 with French exploration in Green Bay, Wisconsin (Lace 2002, 23). Because of poor drainage, the area that became the city of Chicago was not the site of any major prehistoric or early historic period occupation. Early peoples instead located their villages, such as the Grand Village of the Kaskaskia, farther inland (Tanner and Pinther 1987). The early Native American inhabitants of the Chicago area favored the rise of the drier tops of sandy ridges and moraines; these made the best surfaces, along with other ridges and elevated beach areas, for travel by foot, by animal, and, today, by automobile, throughout all seasons of the year. All the major "Indian trails" of the Chicago area run atop these moraines at a diagonal to the mouth of the Chicago River, roughly where Michigan Avenue meets the river (and, in 1803, the site of Fort Dearborn). These trails, mapped by Albert Scharf, a German cigar storeowner turned amateur archaeologist, are today traversed as Lake Street, Archer Avenue, Portage, Clybourn Avenue, Green Bay Road (or Clark Street), Barry Point Road, Milwaukee Avenue, Elston Avenue, Vincennes Avenue, and Cottage Grove Avenue (Scharf 1900; Shapiro 1929). Note, however, that Chicago was already a central place in terms of both geography and social life. While people did not choose to live in what is now the city center of Chicago, they regularly would have camped, traveled there via the trail systems, and even traded in the area.

The Chicago area was indeed a major entrepôt in prehistoric times, ever if it was not a preferred place for permanent domestic settlement until the turn of the nineteenth century. The indigenous people who lived in Chicago through the European contact period include the Illinois (also called Illini or Illiniwek); Miami (and associated Wea and Piankeshaw); the Potawatomi, Ojibwa, and Odawa—collectively the Anishinaabeg; the Meskwakie, often referred to as the Sauk or Sac and Fox; and the Kickapoo. These Indian nations can be divided into three categories: the resident people, such as the Illinois, who had lived in the area for thousands of years; refugee populations from the Atlantic seaboard, like the Miami, who fled their homeland to escape war and encroaching European settlement; and temporary allies or opponents from areas south or west of the Great Lakes (Tanner and Pinther 1987). Although the lingua franca of the area was Ojibwa, the Native American historic period inhabitants of Chicago spoke Algonquian, Iroquoian, and Siouan languages. But again, this linguistic and cultural diversity did not center spatially in the area of Chicago itself because of its topography. Records from a French trader, Nicolas Perrot, state that Chicago was only a semipermanent settlement of some Miami people by 1672 (Balesi 1996, 24). Instead, the French recorded large Illinois villages at Starved Rock, Peoria Lake, and Utica (Shapiro 1929).

The historic period of the Chicago area is typically divided into its French, British, and American occupations and resultant changes in sovereignty over the area. French settlers, many of whom were either itinerant fur traders or Jesuit missionaries, officially controlled the area until the 1763 Treaty of Paris concluded the Seven Years' War in Europe (known as the French and Indian War in North America), ceding the area to the British. The British remained in control of the region, bounded by Spanish possessions to the west of the Mississippi River, until the end of the American Revolutionary War and the second Treaty of Paris in 1783, which ceded the area to the new United States. While an American territory, the area that became Chicago was at various times part of Connecticut (ceded in 1786), Indiana Territory (1800), Illinois Territory (1809), and eventually, the state of Illinois (1818).

With the 1787 Northwest Ordinance providing the structure for the region's settlement and governance, the United States began a period of intense treaty making in the area. These include multiple and often contradictory treaties with members of Native American tribes for control of the Chicago area. At the signing of the 1768 Fort Stanwix Treaty, which established the Ohio River as the line between white and Indian settlements in the southeastern Great Lakes region, the Potawatomi were the dominant Indian nation in the Chicago area. They claimed much of the coastal area of Lake Michigan in what is now Wisconsin, Illinois, Indiana, and Michigan; however, villages of Odawa, Ojibwa, and Sauk people existed in Chicago contemporaneously with the Potawatomi (Tanner and Pinther 1987).

The United States effectively gained control of Chicago with the 1795 Treaty of Greenville. This treaty, signed by twelve Indian nations, ceded an area six by six miles in size centered around the mouth of the Chicago River, an area that would become the site of Fort Dearborn in 1803. Other treaties that specifically mention the area of Chicago include the Treaty of St. Louis (1816), the Treaty of Chicago (1821), the Treaty of Prairie du Chien (1829), and the second Treaty of Chicago (1833), signed a year after the Black Hawk War—a battle where the Sauk leader, Black Hawk, returned to northwestern Illinois with one thousand people to take back his ancestral home village (Lurie 1988, 165).

Chicago's permanent population grew with the increasing dominance and profit of the fur trade in the Great Lakes region. Between 1816 and 1834 Chicago was a growing, culturally diverse, and multiracial settlement, "a community of such middlemen traders and their employees—clerks, voyageurs, and engagés of French, British, American, Indian, and mixed extraction" (Peterson 2002, 37). Individuals of note in the histories of the area include Jean Baptiste Point du Sable, a man of Haitian and African ancestry who ran a trading post until 1800 (see Graff 2005); the Beaubien family, métis owners of the Sauganash Tavern at Wolf Point; and the British-American Kinzie family, many of whom were multilingual in indigenous languages as a result of living with different nations. In 1830 James Thompson created the plat for Chicago while working for the Illinois and Michigan Canal Commissioners, and the town was officially organized in 1833. When the city of Chicago was officially incorporated in 1837, it had a population of more than four thousand people. It was still small and located far from the established American cities of the east, but it was on the rise.

Landfill, Industry, and Ashes

The landscape of Chicago, like that of similar urban centers, was significantly altered through construction, demolition, and related episodes of landfill. Using urban refuse as fill to raise low-lying areas and to create new land is an essential component in the growth of cities (Colten 1994). The practice of using garbage to produce new land impacted and created conditions for both Jackson Park and the Gold Coast, including the Charnley House's artifact-filled midden. Such use of waste was a creative process that made more space for the city. Yet these cycles of construction, demolition, and landfill in Chicago as part of the logic of "creative destruction" under capitalism were often driven by Chicago elites who destroyed the old to make way for the new (Schumpeter 1942). An example of this process was the effort around installing a sewerage system in Chicago in 1855. Because the area was too low to install a typical gravity-fed sewage system, city sanitation workers laid the pipes in the middle of the streets and then raised their grade with refuse (Colten 1994, 130). While some buildings were raised up to the level of the new street surface—the raising of the exclusive Tremont House hotel in 1861 is one famous example—the rest of the population was literally left in the muck (*Chicago Tribune* 1861, 1). In certain neighborhoods like Bridgeport, Bucktown, and Pilsen, one can still see homes in Chicago that sit significantly below street level.

The lacustrine and riverine landscapes of Chicago also changed with the use of fill. Beginning in the 1830s Chicago's lakefront shoreline edged eastward as new land cast as "improvements" were made from both natural accretion (sandbars) and from dumping events (landfills). Landfill not only create additional land; this practice found a place to put municipal waste. For example, debris from the 1871 Great Chicago Fire was used to create new land, eventually moving the boundary of the shore eastward from Michigan Avenue, thereby creating Lakefront Park (now Grant Park). In 1886 George Wellington "Cap" Streeter's boat was purportedly stranded in Lake Michigan during a storm, after which he left the damaged ship in situ and declared the area his own sovereign territory, "The District of Lake Michigan" (Ballard 1914, 215–16; Seligman 2005b). The site continued to grow from the natural accumulation of sand and from Streeter's practice of charging people for the privilege of dumping their refuse at his site (Ballard 1914, 218, 221). During the 1893 Chicago fair, Streeter repaired his boat and used it to ferry people to and from the fair site (Ballard 1914, 220). Today the area is known as Streeterville, a neighborhood just southeast of the Gold Coast.

Frederick Jackson Turner famously declared the frontier closed at Chicago's 1893 meeting of the American Historical Association, held in tandem with the World's Columbian Exposition. But William Cronon's *Nature's Metropolis* notably situated the emergent industrial city of Chicago as the place "were the west began," reading Turner backward by arguing that cities were the beginning of the frontier rather than its end (Cronon 1991, 91, 46). He argued that by looking at the complex interconnections and interdependencies between urban centers and rural hinterlands, one could see the ways that the city and the county are inextricably linked and mutually constitutive. Chicago, "nature's metropolis," had "natural advantages" in terms of water transportation, as discussed above, and this same landscape created the possibilities for its nineteenth-century role as nexus of major railroads. The railroads would move grain, lumber, and meat through this central American marketplace, converting the products into capital and back again (see Graff and Edwards 2018 for a discussion of the Chicago stockyards and meat provisioning at the 1893 World's Fair). Here one can see what imaginative force the idea of "Chicago" had as an essential part of the American economic system. Cronon ends his study by acknowledging the pivotal role of the 1893 fair in Chicago history, calling it "the fulfillment of the city's destiny" (Cronon 1991, 31).

But before the phoenix of the World's Fair could arise to signal the triumphant peak of Chicago's material progress, it had to have ashes from which to merge: the 1871 Great Chicago Fire. On the evening of October 8, 1871, a fire started in a neighborhood south of the Chicago River, eventually wiping out over two thousand acres (almost four square miles), destroying eighteen thousand buildings, and leaving at least ninety thousand people homeless in the city's center (Pierce 1937). The fire, and Chicago's resultant rebirth, became a central motif in the Chicago boosters' campaign for hosting the 1893 fair. In the days immediately after the fire, the front page of the *Chicago Tribune* read on October 11, 1871: "In the midst of a calamity without parallel in the world's history, looking upon the ashes of thirty years' accumulations, the people of this once beautiful city have resolved that CHICAGO SHALL RISE AGAIN" (Medill 1871, 2). When the Chicago City Council passed legislation banning wooden structures in the burned-out downtown, architects poured into the city to partake of abundant commissions for new stone and brick buildings, creating the foundation for Chicago's architectural preeminence (Mayer and Wade 1969, 118). The fire was generative of a whole host of municipal projects, from a central fireproof commercial zone (Condit 1964, 19, Bluestone 1991, 112–14) to relic-laden beer halls (see Graff 2017) to the 1893 fair itself.

The City of Chicago's flag has four red stars, each one standing for a critical event in the city's history. The first memorializes the 1812 Battle of Fort Dearborn that took place between United States troops and Potawatomi people right at the spot where today's Michigan Avenue and the Chicago River meet. The second star commemorates the 1871 fire that destroyed the heart of Chicago's downtown while simultaneously creating the opportunities for architectural innovation in its rebuilding. The third star honors the 1893 World's Columbian Exposition. While the fourth and final star recalls the Century of Progress International Exposition of 1933–34—the second important international fair hosted by Chicago—it is that third star, the 1893 fair, that deserves context to find its place in the firmament, and in this story.

World's Fairs: An Overview

Historical Roots of a "Quintessential Victorian Artifact"

In a handsome souvenir booklet, the Chicago Exposition Committee listed resolutions for their great fair, replete with lofty language declaring Chicago's consummate suitability to host it: "*Resolved*: That the main object of the exposition should be to exhibit in systematic arrangement, in one immense collection, the products of all kinds of mechanical, artistic, and industrial skill and labor, including the products of manufacturers, mines, inventions, agriculture, horticulture, painting, sculpture, and all the trades and arts, together with the raw and wrought materials of commerce in all forms" (Van Arsdale and Massie 1873, 25). Moreover, the committee agreed to "provide amply for musical and other popular entertainments," to be "national and metropolitan in scope," and to make their coveted foreign visitors "assured of a warm welcome, hospitable entertainment, and equal facilities in every respect" (Van Arsdale and Massie 1873, 25).

Those familiar with Chicago's 1893 World's Columbian Exposition might find these self-aggrandizing statements to be in keeping with conventional promotions of that spectacle. Yet this resolution comes from the 1873 Chicago Inter-State Industrial Exposition, not the 1893 fair. The Inter-State Exposition was held along Michigan Avenue from Monroe to Jackson Streets from September 25 to November 12, 1873. Planned primarily as a venue for manufacturers and merchants to display their wares, generate income for Chicago's businesses, and stimulate the local economy—something especially critical after the devastating 1871 Chicago fire—the Inter-State Exposition showcased billiard tables, pianos, furnaces, bricks, harvesters, millinery goods, horseshoes, perfumes, artificial limbs, and church furniture. Its six hundred thousand visitors had the opportunity to witness a grand inaugural ceremony with speeches and music and then to view the industrial goods for which the venture was named. The 1873 exposition planners anticipated that those assembled would find that "Chicago to-night, with its industries and warehouses, its hotels and banks, and Exposition, sat like a queen on the lake, greater and more magnificent than ever—the wonder and glory of the world" (Van Arsdale and Massie 1873, 46). Planners expressed the notion that the 1873 exposition would have a lasting impact on every echelon of society, and, perhaps most importantly, it would "elevate the working classes" via object lessons derived from looking at these new, industrial goods (Van Arsdale and Massie 1873, 27–28).

Like the fairs that preceded it and those that would follow, the main building of the 1873 Inter-State Exposition was designed to be impermanent. Chicago's business leaders, still reeling from the economic consequences of the 1871 Chicago fire, did not have sufficient capital to build "adequate, permanent buildings" for their fair (Van Arsdale and Massie 1873, 26). Led by exposition president, Potter Palmer, the executive committee hired architect W. W. Boyington, designer of Chicago's famed Water Tower (1869), to create their temporary structure. Thus Potter Palmer's work at the helm of the World's Columbian Exposition governance committees was his second, not first, involvement with successfully mounting a world's fair.

Although intentionally ephemeral, the Exposition Building was nevertheless built on a grand scale. Designed in Italian style, the 232,800-square-foot building included a twelve-sided center dome, 473 windows, and eighteen doors and was popularly known as the "Crystal Palace" after its London namesake (Van Arsdale and Massie 1873, 40; Weimann 1981, 11). Built of iron, wood, brick, and glass, the impermanent Exposition Building was outfitted with plumbing, fittings for gas lighting, and sewerage. After the close of the Inter-State Exposition, the "temporary" structure hosted eighteen further expositions until 1892, when the building was torn down to make way for the Art Institute, an undertaking related to the 1893 World's Columbian Exposition (Pierce 1937, 475).

Rather than a singular event, Chicago's 1893 World's Columbian Exposition, like its 1873 predecessor, can best be understood within the larger context of the many international expositions and smaller national fairs held in Europe, Australia, and the United States during the nineteenth century. The seemingly singular elements of the 1893 Chicago fair—its dreamlike White City and "exotic" Midway Plaisance—are firmly part of this fair tradition. Likewise, the intentionally temporary structures of the 1893 fair, built from impermanent materials while still requiring robust and permanent infrastructure, are not unique to the Chicago planners of either 1873 or 1893.

The 1893 Chicago fair resembled and expanded upon the messages of its antecedents—fairs held in London (1851), Philadelphia (1876), and Paris (1889)—from their spatial design to the didactic lessons found within these temporary cities. The material results of this tradition of world's fairs are what historian Thomas Schlereth characterizes as "quintessential Victorian artifacts" (1991: xv). In one venue, tourists to fairs could take in the latest in "workplaces, housing preferences, consumer choices, recreational pursuits, eating habits, and demographic patterns" of the late nineteenth century (Schlereth 1991: xii). These transformations in the material world and their accompanying messages could be consumed and absorbed by these sightseers even as—or precisely because—the physical fair city itself had vanished.

The 1893 Chicago fair, including its exhibits, entertainments, and ephemeral architecture, must be considered within the larger tradition of international world's fairs and expositions. Between 1865 and 1925, 360 million people attended world's fairs in Europe, the United States, Australia, and New Zealand, a figure compiled from the attendance data of the major international fairs (Findling and Pelle 2008, 413–17). Fairs were venues within which to display the growing and changing material world. Serving an overt cultural mission with their architecture, art, and technological innovation, they can be understood as pedagogical moments for many Americans, teaching them what and how to consume, and to what end. It is helpful to consider the following description of modern fairs, with its particular attention to the materiality of these undertakings:

> Imagine an area the size of a small city centre, bristling with dozens of vast buildings set in beautiful gardens; fill the buildings with every conceivable type of commodity and activity known, in the largest possible quantities; surround them with miraculous pieces of engineering technology, with tribes of primitive peoples, reconstructions of ancient and exotic streets, restaurants, theatres, sports stadiums and band-stands. Spare no expense. Invite all nations on earth to take part by sending objects for display and by erecting buildings of their own. After six months, raze this city to the ground and leave nothing behind, save one or two permanent land-marks. (Greenhalgh 1988, 1)

Some scholars trace world's fairs—also called "exhibitions" (Britain), *expositions universelles* (France), and *weltausstellungen* (Austria and Germany)—to the Middle Ages, when medieval market fairs in city centers provided a space for commerce and socializing in pre-industrial Western society (Luckhurst 1951, 10). Other writers suggest a singular moment for the emergence of fairs in the biblical story of Persian king Ahasuerus, who exhibited his wealth and collections in the form of a celebratory feast for those who entered his kingdom (Luckhurst 1951, Rydell 1984, Wilson 2007). Similar gatherings within towns or villages in ancient Egypt, pre-Conquest Mexico, and twelfth-century BCE China are also categorized as fairs (Benedict 1983, 3). Still other lists of "fairs" include Doge Lorenzo Tiepolo's 1268 festival of guilds in Venice and a celebration of the Dutch East India Company's goods in 1689 Holland, with their function as gatherings for commerce, consumption, and theatrical spectacle (Wilson 2007, 10).

In the United States, agricultural fairs—part of American state and county fair traditions—can trace their origins to at least 1807 with a fair held in Pittsfield, Massachusetts (Oliver 2011). The United States also boasts a history of sanitary fairs organized by the United States Sanitary Commission to provide support for the physical health of Civil War soldiers. Northern U.S. cities hosted several sanitary fairs in the 1860s, including an 1863 fair in Chicago. A Chicago Fair Association organized horse-racing shows with some agricultural exhibits beginning in 1881 (Pierce 1937, 476). These smaller fairs share the same named category of "fairs" but not the same scale or scope as international world's fairs. This ambiguous definition makes almost every moment of mass spectacle and commerce into some sort of "fair," dispensing with their sociocultural context and any analytic relevance.

Instead, in examining the 1893 World's Columbian Exposition in terms of the "world of fairs" (Rydell 1984), I follow the more recent historiography for the development of this modern spectacle. Modern fairs—encyclopedic displays of raw materials, manufactured goods, new inventions, fine arts, entertainments, foods, native peoples, and ancient and modern architecture held in temporary "cities" that are demolished at the fair's end—trace their beginnings from two interrelated strands: the French national exhibitions and the British industrial exhibitions of the eighteenth and early nineteenth centuries. Both of these starting points emerge from the phenomenon of industrial capitalism, where a customer base of millions might be reached to consume the goods on display at the fairs (Benedict 1983, 2). And, unlike premodern fairs that also served as gatherings for trade and consumption with some entertainments thrown into the mix, this modern fair tradition differs in scale from earlier fairs. But more importantly, modern fairs promote ideologies of industrialization—both through their material undertakings and the transformational messages they deliver.

The Modern Fairs

In Britain, the modern fair tradition began in 1754 with the founding of the Society for the Encouragement of Arts, Manufactures and Commerce, or Society of Arts. Beginning in 1760, the society held exhibitions of fine arts and manufactures, all shown to "edify" the society's members as well as "farmers, manufacturers and businessmen" (Greenhalgh 1988, 8). In 1837 these events were combined with those of the Mechanics Institutes, whose goal was to advance industry in the "consciousness" of those who attended the exhibitions (Greenhalgh 1988, 8).

In France the primary goals of the first Exposition publique des produits de l'industrie française in 1798 were to provide an immediate market for goods left over from revolutionary stockpiles, to demonstrate that the French state was functioning well, and to push for the mass acceptance of what was tremendous societal change—a sort of "propagandist ceremony of state" (Wesemael 2001, 63; Greenhalgh 1988). Ten French industrial fairs followed this one, all national in scope. Initially held in previously standing structures (like the Hôtel d'Orsay in Paris), their success encouraged their planners to construct buildings solely for the purpose of hosting expositions (Wilson 2007, 10; see also Eisinger 2000 for a discussion of the rise of convention centers and similar urban entertainment venues).

Soon other nations joined England and France by instituting their own industrial fairs. The United States held its first industrial fair in 1828 (Greenhalgh 1988, 9) when the American Institute of the City of New York hosted "artisans and manufacturers from New York City, New York State[,] and New Jersey, and occasionally from New England" at its October event (New-York Historical Society 2011, n.p.). But the first international fair—in many ways, the first "modern" industrial fair—unequivocally was London's 1851 Crystal Palace Exhibition, formally called The Great Exhibition of the Works of Industry of All Nations.

Held in a single magnificent building designed by landscape architect and gardener Joseph Paxton, the exhibition ran from May 1 through October 11, 1851, in London's Hyde Park. The light-filled exhibition structure was built with technology similar to that used in green houses, and within it were displays from 17,062 exhibitors representing twenty-eight countries (Mattie 1998, 11). As part of a "modernizing agenda" that reflected recent moves toward free trade (Davis 2008), the exhibits generally featured industrial and commercial goods. In all, 6 million tourists visited Paxton's Crystal Palace to partake in the spectacle of goods that included a McCormick reaper, shawls from India, and even an easy chair that, upon closer inspection, was revealed to be made from papier-mâché (Briggs 2003, 48). Due to its easily transportable partitioned design coupled with an outpouring of public affection for the structure, the Crystal Palace was not destroyed and instead was dismantled after the exhibition ended. Removed to a site in Sydenham, South London, it was reconstructed and expanded and used to host various events until it was destroyed by fire in 1936. Although the building was destroyed, many of the industrial goods displayed at the exhibition became the founding collection of the South Kensington (now Victoria and Albert) Museum.

Although the majority of tourists to the Crystal Palace whose accounts were recorded had positive reactions to this first modern industrial fair, some did not. Fyodor Dostoyevsky called the event "the epitome of soulless materialism, this apocalyptic monster of iron and glass" (Dostoyevsky 1863, quoted in Brain 1993, 41). Such revulsion at both the new form of architecture that supported it and exhibitionist commerce, perhaps a form of antimodernism (Lears 1981) was found at this first modern fair. Even with some small minority of public dissent at these fairs, the overwhelming financial and public success of the Crystal Palace spurred governments and leading businesses all over the Western world to plan further fairs. The United States quickly followed the success of the 1851 London exhibition by holding the 1853–54 exhibition of the Industry of All Nations in New York, which had an attendance of approximately 1,150,000 people within a "Crystal Palace" made of glass and iron (Findling and Pelle 2008, 414). The first large-scale and truly international American fair took place over two decades later when the Philadelphia Centennial Exposition was launched in 1876.

Held in Philadelphia's Fairmount Park from May 10 through November 10, 1876, the International Exhibition of Arts, Manufactures and Products of the Soil and Mine of 1876 (also called the Centennial Exhibition) consisted of 249 structures, including the Main Building, a Women's Pavilion, and a small stone structure built for the state of Ohio, the latter of which remains extant in Fairmount Park (Giberti 2002, 81; Seyfert 2006).

Ten million visitors attended the exhibition, where they could see elevators, sewing machines, and typewriters, all arranged within a classificatory system of ten departments that attempted to divide up the world into its constituent parts. Even the arm and torch of the Statue of Liberty were on display, in advance of its installation in New York Harbor, and it could be toured for an additional fee.

After the success of Philadelphia, Americans were even more keenly interested in launching another grand fair. Representatives from several American cities traveled to Paris to observe the 1889 Paris Exposition Universelle with the intention of incorporating the insights gained from Paris in their own fair proposals. One of the most significant sights at the 1889 Paris Exposition was not found in the exhibits at the Champs de Mars, the Trocadéro, and the Esplanade des Invalides, or found displayed on the banks of the Seine; it was instead the technological marvel that was Gustave Eiffel's iron tower, soaring a thousand feet above the city to become a symbol of both the exposition and eventually the city of Paris itself. Buoyed by the success of the 1876 Philadelphia Centennial, and the tantalizing promises of the 1889 Paris Exposition Universelle, Americans were exceptionally interested in mounting more fairs. The Chicago fair became the next great international fair when it opened its gates in 1893.

Planning the Chicago Fair

Discussions about hosting another American world's fair began after the highly successful 1889 Paris Exposition Universelle. The United States representatives, in an effort to overcome a sense of cultural inferiority to Europe, pushed on with plans to hold a fair that would outshine that of Paris and improve upon the success of the 1876 Philadelphia Centennial Exposition. But which U.S. city would host the next American fair was still undecided. Washington, D.C., and St. Louis, Missouri, were in the running, but by 1890 only New York and Chicago were in real contention to win the right to host the fair. Chicago purportedly earned its "Windy City" nickname for the heavy-handed bragging during the heated battles between Chicago and New Yorker representatives. Chicago's boosters—mainly the business elite who would profit from hosting a world's fair—positioned Chicago as the only city fit to host the Columbian Exposition, due in large part to its central location as terminus for thirty-eight railroads (Johnson 1897, 1:10). Their self-promotion proved effective: an April

1890 act of Congress formally established Chicago as the site of the fair and created the initial financial outlay for the exposition.

An undertaking this immense necessitated similarly gargantuan bureaucratic apparatus. The official governmental structure of the 1893 fair was as complex as the fair itself, reflecting the flourishing bureaucratization of the United States, a process characterized as the "incorporation of America" (Trachtenberg 1982). Beginning in 1889 the Chicago City Council instructed a group of Chicago businessmen to form a committee and begin organizing the effort to host a world's fair (Higinbotham 1898). Their "World's Exposition of 1892" Company (renamed the World's Columbian Exposition Company in June 1890) incorporated itself in Chicago as a capital stock company to raise money for the fair. Additional financing for the fair came from stock subscriptions, bonds, and $5 million in federally minted Columbian half dollars. Overseen by a board of forty-five directors including Cyrus McCormick, Charles Yerkes, and Charles Hutchinson, members of the company met regularly, led by three consecutive presidents—Lyman J. Gage, W. T. Baker, and Harlow N. Higinbotham—all executives in local industry. Potter Palmer, once again taking a leadership role in a Chicago exposition, was elected second vice president of the World's Columbian Exposition Company (Johnson 1897, 1:17). After Congress approved Chicago as the host city in 1890, the World's Columbian Commission (also known as the National Commission), headed by Thomas W. Palmer, began to meet with a board of 108 members: two commissioners from each U.S. state and territory and the District of Columbia and eight commissioners-at-large. Thus a municipal and a federal organization began to plan the fair.

Next Congress created the Board of Lady Managers through an amendment to the initial House bill, formally sanctioning another planning committee for the fair. This was in stark contrast to the planning role of women at the 1876 Philadelphia Centennial, when a subcommittee of thirteen women organized that fair's Women's Pavilion in spite of, rather than because of, the backing of the main exposition committee (Weimann 1981). By incorporating a women's board into the executive structure of the 1893 World's Fair, the Chicago Board of Lady Managers had formal structural authority to plan the women's representation and exhibits at the fair. Led by president Bertha Honoré Palmer and supervised by the National Commission, the board had 117 members from across the United States—more than the National Commission's board (Weimann 1981).

The final major fair governance committee, the World's Congress Auxiliary, formed nineteen departments (woman's progress, public press, medicine and surgery, temperance, moral and social reform, commerce and finance, music, literature, education, engineering, art, government, science and philosophy, labor, religion, Sunday rest, religious societies, public health, and agriculture) to run the 139 conventions at the fair (Johnson 1897, 4:6). The departments were designed to be like a "university for which the fair has served as museums, laboratories and recreation grounds" (Johnson 1893, 117).

With these mammoth plans under way, it soon became clear that the opening the fair in 1892 to celebrate the quadricentennial of Columbus's voyage to the New World would not be feasible. By at least the fall of 1890, planners decided that there was not sufficient time to ready the site and coordinate the related congresses and functions. Instead of scaling back their grand plans to meet an 1892 deadline, they set the new deadline to May 1893. To observe the actual 1892 anniversary, a series of commemorative events, including numerous balls and a dedication ceremony, were planned.

Jackson Park, a partially developed park seven miles south of Chicago's central business district, was selected as the site of the fair. Initially the preferred site choice for the fair was Chicago's downtown lakefront between Randolph and Twelfth Streets, but Jackson Park proved less costly. The South Park Commissioners, the governmental body that oversaw Jackson and Washington Parks, granted permission for the use of both Jackson Park and the Midway Plaisance as long as the site was transformed back into public parkland after the close of the fair (Burnham and Millet 1894). In 1890 the Committee on Grounds and Buildings hired architects Daniel Hudson Burnham and John Wellborn Root; landscape architect Frederick Law Olmsted and his partner, Henry Codman; and engineer Abraham Gottlieb to fashion a plan to transform swampy Jackson Park into the pristine and monochromatic "White City." Francis D. Millet, the noted artist, the fair's director of decoration and the person who selected the Chicago "Y" symbol, oversaw the selection of exterior color treatments for the fair buildings and was thus responsible for the "whiteness" of the White City.

Burnham, hired as chief of construction and director of works for the fair, created a board of architects to design the main buildings. Burnham's partner, John Wellborn Root, was appointed architect for the fair.

Root died unexpectedly and suddenly from pneumonia in 1891 after planning the broad scheme of the fair. After Root's death, Burnham took over the entirety of planning (Johnson 1897, 1:42). Determined to make the architectural program of the fair a national undertaking, Burnham selected architects mainly from outside the Midwest, a choice that garnered him ample criticism from his fellow Chicago architects. Burnham picked the firms of Richard M. Hunt (Administration Building); George B. Post (Manufactures and Liberal Arts Building); McKim, Mead and White (Agriculture Building); Peabody and Stearns (Machinery Building); Van Brunt and Howe (Electricity Building); Burling and Whitehouse (the unbuilt Venetian Village); Jenney and Mundie (Horticulture Building); Henry Ives Cobb (Fisheries Building); Solon S. Beman (Mines and Mining Building); and Adler and Sullivan (Transportation Building). As mentioned in the opening of this chapter, many of these architects took commissions on Gold Coast homes during this same time. Novice architect Sophia G. Hayden won the design contest for the Women's Building; Charles Atwood designed the Palace of Fine Arts, the Anthropology Building, and a host of other smaller structures and light posts; and a team of Japanese builders created Masamichi Kuru's Ho-o-den Palace. Thus, for the most part, the fair was designed by similarly trained, professional, established American architects.

In comparison to the 72 acres that made up the 1889 Paris fair, the total size of the Jackson Park fairgrounds was 686 acres and was populated by over two hundred structures (de Wit 1993, 49). To prepare the site for building, construction laborers transformed the natural landscape of Jackson Park, dredging lagoons, carving an island from a peninsula, and planting trees throughout the site. With the exception of Louis Sullivan's Transportation Building, the main structures of the White City were unified examples of Beaux-Arts design—even a common cornice height of sixty feet had been set by committee to maintain this visual unity. Set up in a biaxial arrangement, the Court of Honor consisted of these main buildings and a series of lagoons, with the rest of the site dotted with smaller structures that did not have to adhere to strict stylistic guidelines. State and foreign government buildings, some built to evoke the distinct architecture of their region, were situated near the northernmost boundary of Jackson Park. The Midway Plaisance, a strip of land west of the main grounds, so-called as it was located "midway" between Jackson and Washington Parks, housed commercial concessions and was not formally

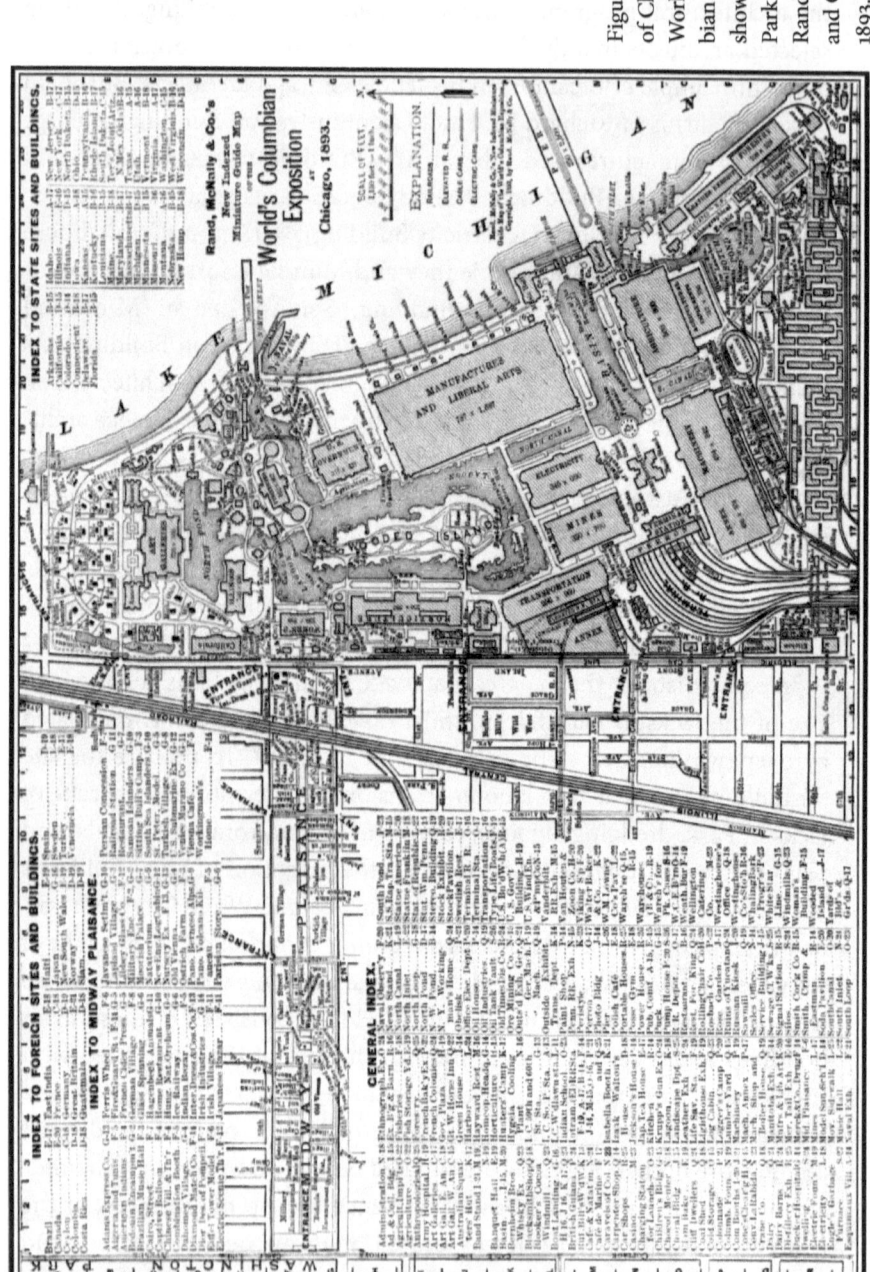

Figure 2.2. Map of Chicago's 1893 World's Columbian Exposition showing Jackson Park. From Rand, McNally and Company, 1893.

arranged with neoclassical architectural conventions (see chapter 3 for a discussion of Beaux-Arts and the City Beautiful movement).

The many maps created for fair tourists and photographs taken by them show an intricate landscape (figures 2.2 and 2.3). An island, lagoons, ponds, and a series of bridges broke up the uniform parkland, with Lake Michigan framing the fair's eastern border. The fair's main structures were clustered around the North Basin, near where visitors could disembark from their boats and glimpse Daniel Chester French's Statue of the Republic as framed through the Peristyle's column. The Republic, one of the main symbols of the fair, became even more evocative of the endeavor when the fires destroyed the structures surrounding it in 1894 (figure 2.4). To the southeast of the Republic and the Court of Honor were large buildings including Forestry, Leather, and Anthropology along with the massive stock exhibits. The Terminal Railway brought goods directly to

Figure 2.3. View from the 1893 World's Columbian Exposition's South Canal looking northeast. The Machinery Building, the Columbian Fountain, and the Electricity Building are on the left, with the Agriculture and the Manufactures and Liberal Arts Buildings on the right. The Illinois State Building's dome is in the center, and the flatter dome of the California State Building is to its left. Image is by an anonymous photographer, 1893. From the Smithsonian Institution Archives.

Figure 2.4. Daniel Chester French's Statue of the Republic after the 1894 Peristyle fire. From the Chicago History Museum. ICHi-025106.

the southwest of the fairgrounds, adjacent to Sullivan and Adler's golden Transportation Building. Heading north along Stony Island Avenue, where further entrances were scattered, took visitors past the Horticulture Building and then the Women's Building, which stood sentinel to the east of the Midway Plaisance's mile-long phantasmagoria.

Catching a glimpse of the roofs of the Ho-o-den Palace on Wooded Island to the east, a visitor could head northward to see the smaller state and foreign government buildings set around the Palace of Fine Arts. These state buildings often functioned as informal "clubhouses" for their visiting citizens, offering a place for weary visitors to rest or to catch up with their neighbors. Still other structures filled the spaces in between the major fair buildings for similar purposes of rest and sustenance: public comfort stations, soda pavilions, and restaurants. Finally, the numerous smaller-scale exhibit and concession buildings (e.g., the White Star Line, the Hunters' Camp, Chocolat Menier) brought a different scale of visual interest against the massive main structures. Add to all of this an elevated train that looped around the fairgrounds, the sounds of tourists talking mixed with band concerts, sights of "Little Egypt" performing the *danse du ventre* or children doing gymnastics in the model kindergarten, smells of baking bread from the French bakery exhibit or beer and wurst from the German Village, and one starts to get a small sense of the teeming character of the 1893 fair. It was immense, crammed to the brim with structures, people, and experiences but designed to be temporary—an exercise in planned obsolescence that so characterizes twentieth and twenty-first-century mass culture (see London 1932; Vance 1960).

A massive amount of primary (Bancroft 1893; Handy 1893; White and Igleheart 1893; Higinbotham 1898), secondary (Burg 1976; Badger 1979; Rydell 1984; Harris et al. 1993), and tertiary literature (i.e., bibliographic guides to the literature of the fair; see Dybwad and Bliss 1992; Bertuca, Hartman, and Neumeister 1996; Findling and Pelle 2008) has been written on the 1893 World's Columbian Exposition alone, and on world's fairs in general. There is an immense and seemingly unremitting interest in world's fairs that abounds across academic disciplines. New studies are published each year from history (e.g., Reed 2000), architecture and city planning (e.g., Wesemael 2001), anthropology (e.g., Benedict 1983; Hinsley and Wilcox 2016), musicology (e.g., Mazzola 1985)—essentially any discipline has a claim to some aspect of the fair.

An increasingly popular and generalist interest in the 1893 fair also flourishes alongside an academic one. This interest was particularly encouraged by Erik Larson's *The Devil in the White City: Murder, Magic, and Madness at the Fair That Changed America* (2003), a novelistic treatment of the creation and building of the 1893 fair punctuated with the story of a gruesome string of murders. Popular fiction centered on the 1893 fair includes at least twenty-six book-length publications (Yandell and Hayes 1892; Holley 1893; Jenks 1893; Neville 1893; Stevens 1893; Burnham 1894; Butterworth 1894; Finley 1894; Burnett 1895; Lawson 1957; Mark 1992; Hoobler and Hoobler 1993; Lawlor 2001; Peck 2001; Croft 2003; Michod 2004; Walker 2006; Austin 2007; Ransom 2007; Bemis 2011; Hockensmith 2011; Gist 2013, 2014; Newport 2013; Gray 2014; Martin and Martin 2016). *The World's Columbian Exposition Centennial Bibliographic Guide* lists eighty-two entries of fiction, prose, general literature, and poetry (Bertuca et al. 1996, 234–40). Some of these were published immediately after the 1893 fair by authors who visited it themselves, while the creation of other works sits firmly in the twenty-first century. Many of the contemporaneous novels aimed at juvenile and young adult audiences, instilling a fascination with the 1893 fair in the next generation, with prices suggesting that they were marketed to middle-class households who could afford them as souvenirs or gifts (Kitzmiller 2013, 37). More books are likely in the works as this volume goes to press, perhaps along with the long-awaited filmic adaptation of the *Devil in the White City*. That there is still a flourishing academic and popular interest in these fairs suggests that their significance continues to endure because of their material erasure.

Given the mammoth volume of textual and photographic documents from and on the fair, it nevertheless remains crucial to note that the archaeological record of the fair provides a separate and different evidentiary line than these records. But what, then, would the archaeological record of such an immense but briefly occupied site look like, and where would one start to explore it?

Fair Archaeology in Jackson Park

Until our work in 2007, there had been no archaeological excavation of the World's Fair site, save a mitigation project on the Midway in 2000 that revealed, during construction of a skating rink, the footings of the world's first Ferris wheel (Moffett 2000). In choosing to archaeologically explore Jackson Park, a site that extends over six hundred acres, I used the documentary record of the 1893 fair in tandem with current maps of the park to select potential sites for excavation. I did not consider some areas of Jackson Park because of significant topographical changes (e.g., landscaping, the deposition of fill, and the creation of new features such as roads) or because of current uses that would prohibit excavation (e.g., golf course, athletic track). Informal pedestrian reconnaissance and survey of the park made it possible to hone in on areas of particular interest that also had the promise of archaeological productivity. I selected four loci for subsurface testing (figure 2.5): Locus 1, Wooded Island, the former site of the Ho-o-den Palace (11CK1104); Locus 2, land around North Pond and the former site of the Ohio, Michigan, Wisconsin, Indiana, and Illinois State Buildings to the west and south, and the former site of the Brazil, Turkey, Venezuela, and Guatemala Foreign Government Buildings to the east (11CK1105); Locus 3, the former site of the Women's Building and an area of movement of people in and out of the fairgrounds near two official fair entrances, 59th Street and Stony Island Avenue and 60th Street and Stony Island Avenue (11CK1106); and Locus 4, the former site of the Anthropology Building, the Forestry Building, and the Engle

Figure 2.5. Survey map of Jackson Park showing Locus 1 (Wooded Island), Locus 2 (North Pond), Locus 3 (Women's Building), and Locus 4 (Garbage and Anthropology Building). Map by author.

Figure 2.6. Performing shovel tests in Locus 2 in Jackson Park, August 2007. Photograph by author.

Sanitary Garbage Cremator (11CK1107). In total, we performed over 150 shovel tests at these loci in 2007 (Figure 2.6).

After laboratory analysis, I plotted and mapped the densities of nineteenth-century artifacts for each locus to create a series of spatial *termini post quem* for the four loci and selected the areas of highest density of nineteenth-century materials as good sites for open excavation. All four loci had potentially productive sites within them, but because I planned to excavate the site as an archaeological field methods course for undergraduates at the University of Chicago, I selected Locus 2 for excavation (Figure 2.7). Its advantages were, first, its logistical ease for hosting the undergraduate field school, being located near our equipment storage area in the Museum of Science and Industry and an easy walk from the University of Chicago campus. Second, it had the benefit of being highly visible within the landscape, performatively demonstrating the presence and viability of archaeology in Chicago.

Fieldwork began on April 4, 2008, and was completed on July 27, 2008, for a total of thirty-five days of work (Figure 2.8). Excavation units (EU) were judgmentally placed adjacent to clusters of shovel tests that had high

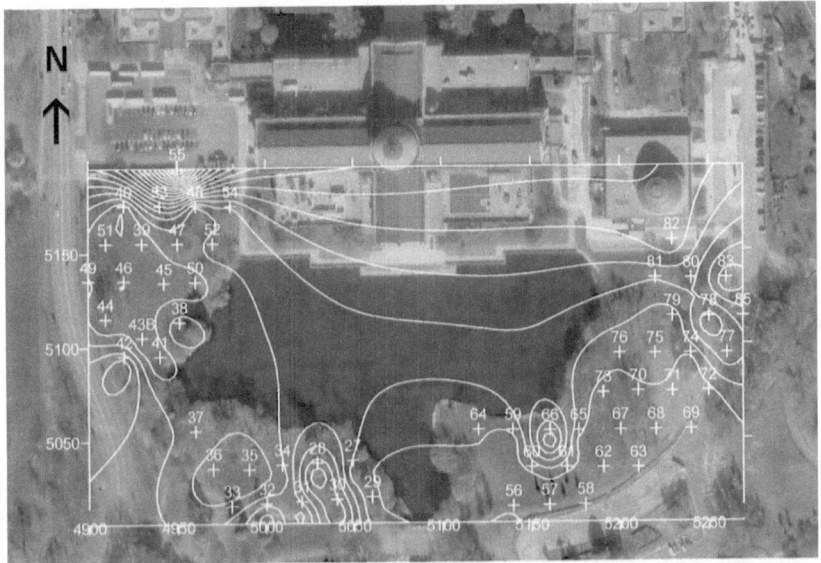

Figure 2.7. Jackson Park, Locus 2 with SURFER map overlay showing locations of shovel test probes (marked with their number and a "+"). The areas with more closely aligned lines depict the highest densities of nineteenth-century artifacts. Note in particular Shovel Test 55, the location of EUs 3 and 5. Map by author.

Figure 2.8. The first day of excavation in Jackson Park, April 2008, with the Museum of Science and Industry in the background. Photograph by the author.

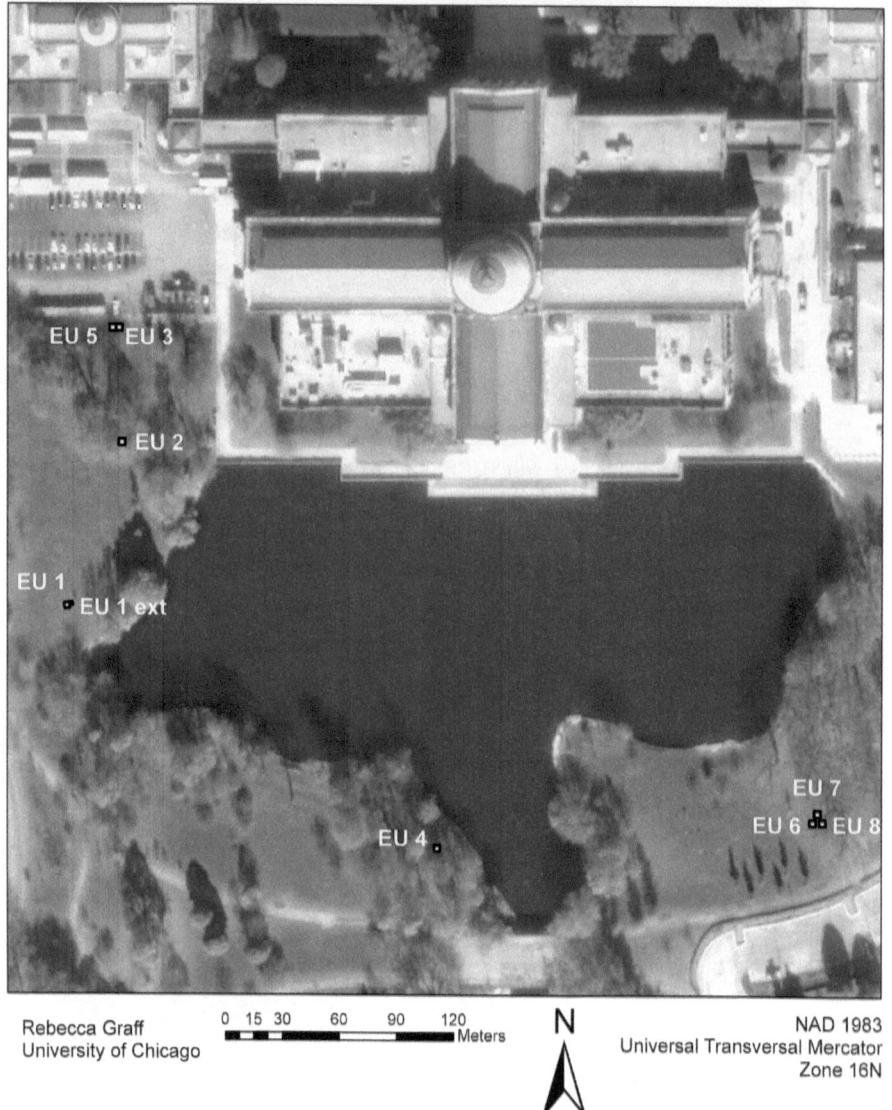

Figure 2.9. Site map of the Jackson Park Archaeological Project showing excavation units. Map by author.

densities of nineteenth-century materials (Figure 2.9). In total, seven 2 m × 2 m excavation units, one 1 m × 2 m extension unit, and a 1 m × 1 m extension unit were excavated, representing a total of 21.214 m³ of soil. Vertical control of the excavation was maintained through the use of contexts (ctx), using arbitrary 10-centimeter levels until we encountered natural levels and features. When these natural layers were encountered, excavation proceeded through the use of natural stratigraphic contexts rather than arbitrary ones. No context, natural or arbitrary, exceeded a depth of 10 cm. All contexts were integrated using the Harris Matrix for stratigraphic sequencing.

Due to more than a century of constant landscaping and relandscaping, much of the top strata of Jackson Park consist of redeposited soils and artifacts from several centuries. Despite this, there were intact deposits of materials from the 1893 World's Columbian Exposition, including sealed deposits (EUs 3 and 5). EUs 1, 1ext, 2, 3, 4, and 5 all contained remnants of the infrastructure built for the 1893 World's Columbian Exposition. These include features like the sewerage and water system in EU 1 and EU 1ext, the pipe and pipe trench in EU 2, and the utility trench as related sewer pipes in EUs 3 and 5. Artifactual evidence of this infrastructure is found in the form of electrical pipe (EUs 3, 4, and 5), electrical porcelain insulators (EUs 3, 4, and 5), arc lamp carbons (EUs 3, 4, and 5) and a railroad spike that is most likely from one of the pre-fair period's temporary railroads (EU 4, ctx 47).

Most surprisingly, over fifty large fragments of plaster columns, urns, and volutes recovered in EUs 3 and 5 have been positively identified as part of the 1893 fair's Ohio Building by comparisons with historic photographs (figures 2.10, 2.11, 2.12, and 2.13). Uncovered in what appears to be a utility or builder's trench at a depth of 76 to 115 cm below the ground surface, the plaster pieces and their associated artifacts provide a glimpse into daily life in the nineteenth century. In addition to these architectural fragments, there is evidence of food and drink consumption within the Ohio Building, as interpreted from the artifacts found amid the plaster fragments. These include ceramic tableware (whiteware, porcelain), a lone piece of lead glass tableware, and two glass cruet tops from ctx 61 (see chapter 5).

Interpreting the meaningfulness of the ephemeral 1893 Ohio Building becomes clearer when coupled with a consideration of the enduring 1893-era Charnley House. While the Ohio Building was a short-term,

Figure 2.10. Plan view of EUs 3 and 5 showing plaster columns from the Ohio State Building (ctx 85 and 87), July 2008. Photograph by author.

Figure 2.11. Plaster columns and terra cotta roof tiles with detail of the Ohio Building. Photographs by author with details from a historic photograph from the Museum of Science and Industry.

Figure 2.12. Plaster volute with detail of the Ohio Building. Photograph by author with details from a historic photograph from the Museum of Science and Industry.

Figure 2.13. Base of plaster urn with detail of the Ohio Building. Photograph by author with details from a historic photograph from the Museum of Science and Industry.

quasi-domestic space built of flimsy construction materials (although with permanent and robust infrastructures—see chapter 3) its form, use, and meanings connect it to longer-term residential, domestic spaces like the Charnley House. The next section gives an historical overview of the Charnley House and a sketch of our archaeological research to provide another facet of the quintessential Victorian artifacts that formed the materials and ideologies of the World's Fair.

Chicago's Gold Coast: An Overview

The area today referred to as the "Gold Coast" is situated on the Near North Side of Chicago, with Lake Michigan bounding it to the east, Clark Street to the west, Oak Street to the south, and North Avenue to the north (Figure 2.14; Seligman 2005a). Known as a desirable residential neighborhood for the white upper class by the 1880s, its location—adjacent to the "slum" featured in Harvey Zorbaugh's 1929 ethnography, *The Gold Coast and the Slum: A Sociological Study of Chicago's Near North Side*—meant that socioeconomic difference did not map to geographical distance. Indeed, far from the area being monolithically upper class and white Protestant, the neighborhood that included the Charnley House also housed students, artists, and recent Irish and Sicilian immigrants. Coupled with the fact that the people who provided the labor for the mansions on the Gold Coast came from farther afield and with varied European immigrant backgrounds, the area and its domestic residences was far more diverse than its reputation might suggest. Zorbaugh characterizes the mixed social landscape: "The Near North Side is an area of high light and shadow, of vivid contrasts—contrasts not only between the old and the new, between the native and the foreign, but between wealth and poverty, vice and respectability, the conventional and the bohemian, luxury and toil" (Zorbaugh 1929, 4). Close to the mansions of the Gold Coast was the neighborhood variously known as "Little Hell," "Kilgubbin," "the Patch," "Swede Town," "Smoky Hollow," "Little Italy," "Little Sicily," and "Black Hollow." The area's name changes over time map to the various ethnic and racial groups who consecutively colonized the area—Irish, Swedish, Italian, and African American (Vale 2014, 22).

An elite setting on the South Side preceded this Gold Coast: Prairie Avenue, "Chicago's First Gold Coast" (Commission on Chicago Historical and Architectural Landmarks 1973: n.p.). Beginning in the 1870s, wealthy

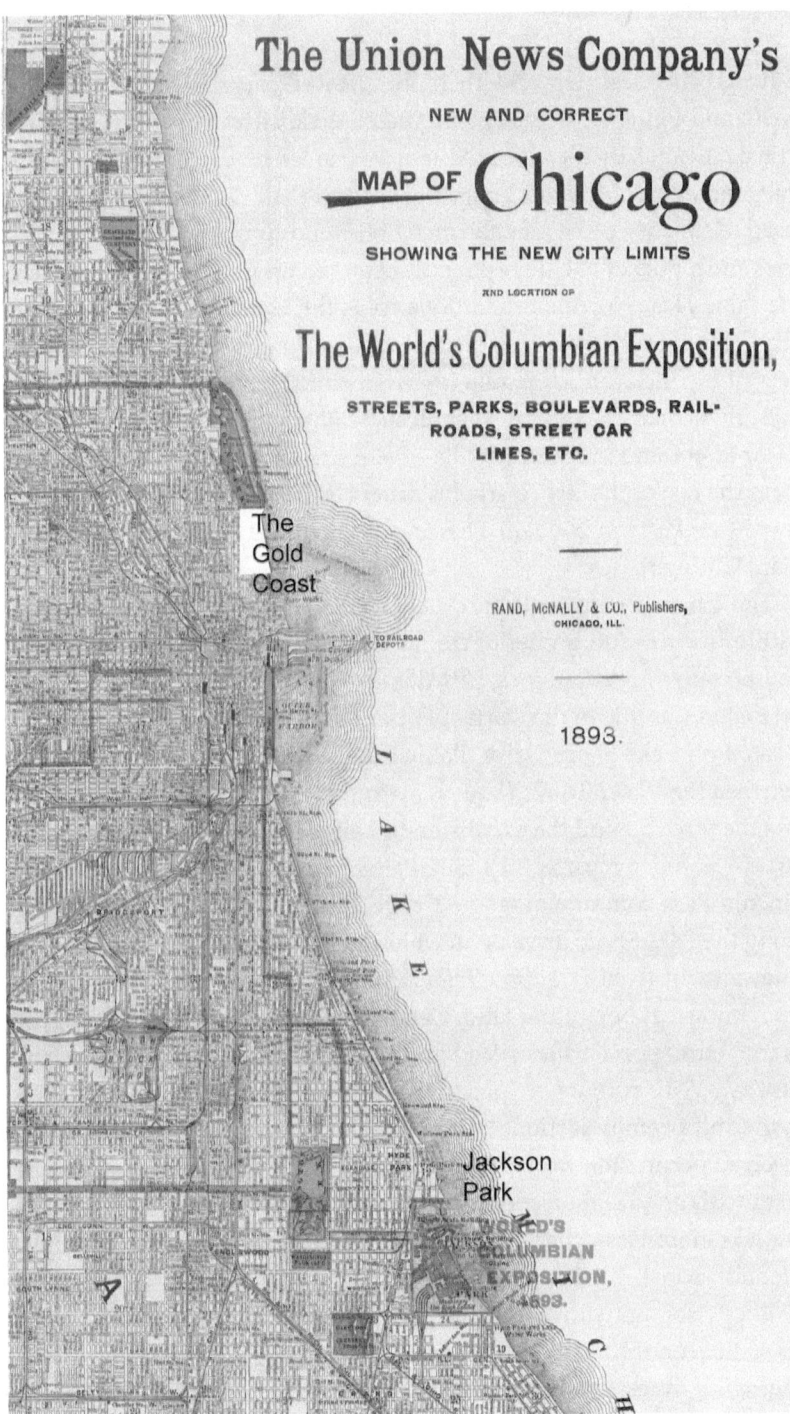

Figure 2.14. Map of Chicago showing the Gold Coast and Jackson Park. Map modified by author from the Union News Company's 1893 map. From Rand, McNally and Company, 1893. Harvard Map Collection, Harvard Library.

Chicago businessmen and their families—George Pullman, Marshall Field, and Philip D. Armour—moved to the district near 18th Street and Prairie Avenue. By the 1890s the area was no longer as desirable as the initial generation of founders began to die and their children moved northward (Reiff 2005). The new elite neighborhoods were the Astor Street District and a pocket of elite residences centered on Rush and Erie Streets in the same Near North community area as the Gold Coast (Stamper 1991: xix). This smaller area, McCormickville, was named for the many members of the McCormick family (of McCormick Reaper Works fame) who built their mansions there. That all these elite enclaves—Prairie Avenue, Astor Street, and McCormickville—were attempts to be spatially bounded from the rest of the city clearly inscribes class status on the Chicago landscape (see Pearson 2009 on class and the architectural landscape of Pullman, Chicago).

The Charnley House (figure 2.15) sits block from Lake Michigan but within the pre-1830 border of the lakefront, although by 1882 this border had already moved a block east due to landfill activity. That particular extension was due to the work of Potter Palmer, whose own mansion was located on Lake Shore Drive. Palmer owned most of the street frontage between the Water Tower (806 N. Michigan Avenue) and Oak Street and was the force behind the expansion of Lake Shore Drive north from Pine Street (Stamper 1991, xx). In 1882 Palmer received permission from the Lincoln Park commissioners to dredge "sand from the lake to fill up lots along the Lake Shore drive upon which he proposes to build" and to place sidewalks in front (*Chicago Tribune* 1882a, 8). Previously the area had been known as boggy and fetid: Captain Streeter referred to it specifically as the "stink pond" where dead animals were often tossed (Ballard 1914, 222–23). With rumors of "plague-spots" or possible malarial conditions in the still swampy sections of Lake Shore Drive, other area homeowners received permission from the city to dredge the lake and fill in low-lying areas with up to eight feet of material (*Chicago Tribune* 1882b: 9). In 1900 the lakeshore was expanded half a block more, and again in 1930 (McClendon 2005).

Boggy soil notwithstanding, by the 1880s Potter Palmer chose to lure his socioeconomic equals to the area by selling them plots of land and encouraging the establishment of another North Side elite enclave. Palmer's own Gold Coast mansion, known as the "Castle" (designed by Cobb and Frost; 1882–5) was set on a large piece of property on Lake Shore Drive

Figure 2.15. James Charnley residence, Chicago, Illinois, ca. 1890s. Historic Architecture and Landscape Image Collection, Ryerson and Burnham Archives, The Art Institute of Chicago. Digital File #19811.

between Schiller and Banks Streets. Besides selling parcels to his peers, Palmer commissioned and built homes throughout the neighborhood that he would then sell or rent to other upper-class families (Bluestone 2004, 41). Historian Daniel Bluestone describes the block bounded by Lake Shore Drive, Schiller, Astor, and Banks Streets—where Palmer's Castle stood and the Charnley House remains—as "arguably the most prominent one in Chicago's late-nineteenth-century residential landscape" (Bluestone 2004, 37).

The 1890s were a productive time for building elaborate residences on the Gold Coast, due in part, as noted earlier in the chapter, to the presence of additional firms and individual architects in town to work on the architectural program of the 1893 World's Columbian Exposition. While fulfilling their Columbian duties, these architects designed many of the homes that gave the area its architectural significance, making the neighborhood "a showcase for a precious, tightly woven architectural fabric of immensely varied texture, color, and detail" (Gapp 1974, 7).

Although many of these mansions were torn down in the 1970s, the area remains affluent and influential. The Astor Street District was eventually recognized as a Chicago Landmark (1975; see City of Chicago 2018), and the Gold Coast District is part of the National Register of Historic Places (1978). As an operating museum, the Charnley-Persky House hosts tourists to the area who are interested not only in the architectural achievements of Sullivan and Wright but in the mysterious lives of the eponymous owners of the home: the Charnleys.

Astor Street Days

The Charnleys of Astor Street

James Charnley (1844–1905) arrived in Chicago in 1866 after a privileged childhood in Philadelphia, Pennsylvania, and New Haven, Connecticut, and following his graduation from Yale University (Longstreth 2004, 5). In Chicago Charnley made a living in lumber and several other industries, listing himself as a "capitalist" in the city directories from 1893 to 1896. His first business in the city was in lumber—Bradner, Charnley and Company (1866–71)—founded with his brother, (the later scandalous) Charles, and their brother-in-law, Lester Bradner (Longstreth 2004, 5–6; Hotchkiss 1894, 452). James's other businesses include Charnley Bros. and Company (with Charles Charnley and Charles Mather Smith, 1871–81), James Charnley and Company (with John M. Douglas, 1881–84), the James Charnley Lumber Company, and the Mesaba Lumber Company (Duluth, Minnesota)—all later versions of the original lumber business— as well as the Garden City Wire and Spring Company and the American Cooperage Company (Hotchkiss 1894, 452–53; Day 1907, 263).

James married Helen Douglas (1854–1930) in 1872. Helen was the daughter of his former partner, John Madison Douglas (1819–91), and Amanda Marshall Douglas (1819–90). John Douglas was a prominent member and later president of the Illinois Central Railroad. Helen was born in Galena, Illinois, but grew up in Chicago (NARA 1921). James and Helen's own connections between lumber interests and railroads show the very coordination and control of capital investments that characterized Chicago's role as described in *Nature's Metropolis* (Cronon 1991).

James and Helen, their two daughters—Helen (1876–83) and Elizabeth "Bettie" (1878–83)—and their son, Douglas (1874–1927) lived in several locations near their eventual Astor Street house. These residences include their first architect-designed home, blocks away from Astor Street at 1200–83 Lake Shore Drive. Daniel Burnham and John Wellborn Root—two men who became the architectural directors of the World's Columbian Exposition—designed that Queen Anne–style home in 1882. On February 26 and March 4, 1883, while living on Lake Shore Drive, daughters Helen and Bettie died from diphtheria, one of the deadliest diseases for children at that time, with 51 deaths per 1,000 in Illinois in 1882 attributed to it (Illinois State Board of Health 1884, 83). In 1883, the year that both Charnley daughters died, 50.84 percent of the year's 11,555 total deaths consisted of children age five and under (Chicago Department of Health 1885, 63–64). Of those, 529 deaths were due to diphtheria (Chicago Department of Health 1885, 65). Several years after the tragic deaths of the youngest Charnleys, James, Helen, Douglas, and their servants moved to a series of other locations before moving to what is now 1365 N. Astor Street.

Sullivan and Wright on Astor Street

James and Helen knew Dankmar Adler and Louis Sullivan well before they hired their firm, Adler and Sullivan, to design their new home. This social relationship may have begun through a familial and business connections. Sullivan's brother, Albert Sullivan, and Helen's father, John Douglas, may have already known each other since both worked for the Illinois Central Railroad (Longstreth 2004, 8). Society of Architectural Historians comptroller Beth Eifrig recently located a newspaper account that shows Dankmar Adler, then with Burling and Adler, designing homes for John Douglas and James Charnley at the corner of Erie and State Streets in 1873 (*Chicago Tribune* 1873, 1). And in 1890 the Charnleys hired Sullivan to build their beach house in Ocean Springs, Mississippi, and even encouraged Sullivan to purchase a piece of land adjacent to theirs, making him their Gulf Coast neighbor well in advance of their Gold Coast project. Perhaps because of these preexisting social relationships, the Charnleys were able to commission this unique, noncommercial building from Adler and Sullivan, a firm that focused on commercial architecture.

Only a few months after buying their new Gold Coast property on the same block as Potter Palmer, the Charnleys sold off several additional parcels of the new land, leaving only a small corner lot on which to build and with a party wall agreement just to the east (Bluestone 2004, 53–54). A "party wall" is a term used to describe a common wall that two buildings adjoin. The Charnley House party wall was never joined to another structure, so its plain brick façade still faces east, next to the driveway where we excavated the historic midden. The Charnleys sold that lot to Sarah K. Otis and Ephraim Otis but neither they nor any subsequent owners ever built on that land—notable as the very area where the oddly placed Charnley midden was discovered in 2003.

The design and construction of the small Astor Street house ran from 1891 to 1892. Frank Lloyd Wright, then twenty-four years old and only recently hired by Adler and Sullivan, served as Sullivan's chief assistant on this project. With previous work including the Auditorium Building (1889, Adler and Sullivan), Sullivan's genius, according to premier Sullivan scholar Hugh Morrison, was the ability to "integrate romanticism and realism, to achieve a synthesis both in theory and practice, completely expressive of modern life," making him "the first modern architect" (Morrison 1935, xiii). Modernity and modern aesthetics also describe the house itself. The house has been characterized as "the first modern house in America," a statement often attributed to Wright, although thus far there is no documentary evidence. The earliest that the concept appears in print, described by the authors, not Wright, as "America's first modern house," is in an editorial in the *Prairie School Review* (Sprague and Vinci 1975, 4).

Much of today's interest in the house focuses on its architectural significance: scholars and laypeople alike try to identify the hand of Sullivan or Wright in the house design. The records from Adler and Sullivan's firm were lost in a fire, making this process difficult but nevertheless well-documented and analyzed by architectural historians (see Longstreth 2004). Looking at the detail of the house, it is clear that both architects influenced the design, combining "Sullivan's decoration with a relatively austere exterior that seems to presage Wright's later work" (Kamin 2015, 6). Still, Wright made claims in the years after Sullivan's death that suggest he alone designed the home:

> The city house on Astor Street for the Charnleys, like the others, I did at home evenings and Sundays in the nice studio draughting room upstairs at the front of the little Forest Avenue home. . . . In the Charnley city-house on Astor Street I first sensed the definitely

decorative value of the plain surface, that is to say, of the flat plane as such. The drawings for the Charnley house were all traced and printed in the Adler and Sullivan offices, but by preparing them for this purpose at home I helped pay my pressing building debts with "overtime" and paid out. (Wright 1977, 132)

Many recapitulated this idea (see Morrison 1935, 102), although contemporary publications list only the firm of Adler and Sullivan as architects. It is important to note that is was not uncommon for Wright to take credit for the work of other architects as part of his showmanship (see Gill 1987).

Despite its architectural importance, the Charnleys did not live in their modern home for very long. In 1902 the family left, and a series of renters, and then owners, moved in. Yet so too were these subsequent Charnley House tenants intricately tied into the elite social networks of the area (discussed in greater depth in chapter 4). For example, the daughter of an owner (Ellen Waller) and the daughter of a renter (Rue Winterbotham) both married the same man (John Alden Carpenter), although not at the same time (Barton 1987, 24).

Although social networks exist between people, the material things that form their social worlds reflect, mediate, and act upon these relationships. The artifacts from the Charnley House Archaeological Project reveal these connections between individuals, networks, institutions, and events like the world's fairs at the turn of the twentieth century, often in ways that the oral historical and documentary records do not capture.

Archaeology at the Charnley-Persky House

Owned by the Society of Architectural Historians (SAH), today the Charnley House operates as the headquarters for the SAH as well as a historic house museum. Philanthropist, preservationist, real estate investor, and attorney Seymour H. Persky (1922–2015), purchased the site in 1995. Shortly thereafter he deeded it to the SAH to serve as its new headquarters, a condition of his initial purchase (Saliga 2015). Previously headquartered in Philadelphia, the SAH agreed to Persky's conditions and moved to their new location in 1995, adding the "-Persky" to the home to recognize Persky's gift.

In the same ways the social conditions unite the World's Fair and the Charnley House, so too are the archaeological projects interrelated.

50 · Disposing of Modernity

Figure 2.16. View of the Charnley-Persky House Archaeological Project, looking south 2010. Photograph by author.

Renovations in 2003 along the eastern party wall of the Charnley House revealed a rich midden of historic refuse. While these architectural historians conveniently employed within the Charnley House collected and documented the finds during the construction project, they also wanted to have the site excavated by professional archaeologists. In 2008 the press from our Jackson Park archaeological excavations brought our work to Pauline Saliga, the executive director of the SAH, who got in touch. To date, our 2010 and 2015 archaeological work at the Charnley-Persky House (11CK1248) represents the only known systematic excavation in the area (figure 2.16). I directed the 2010 excavation season with Mary Leighton and our undergraduate students in DePaul University's Urban Historical Archaeology Field School and several volunteers from the graduate program in anthropology at the University of Chicago. Fieldwork took place from June 12 through July 23, 2010. We excavated three 1.5 m × 2 m excavation units in the driveway to the east of the house. A total of 7.43 m^3 of soil was excavated in context of no more than 10 cm—arbitrary until a natural level was reached—and screened through ¼-inch mesh. Excavations uncovered the evidence for an additional twenty-first-century construction

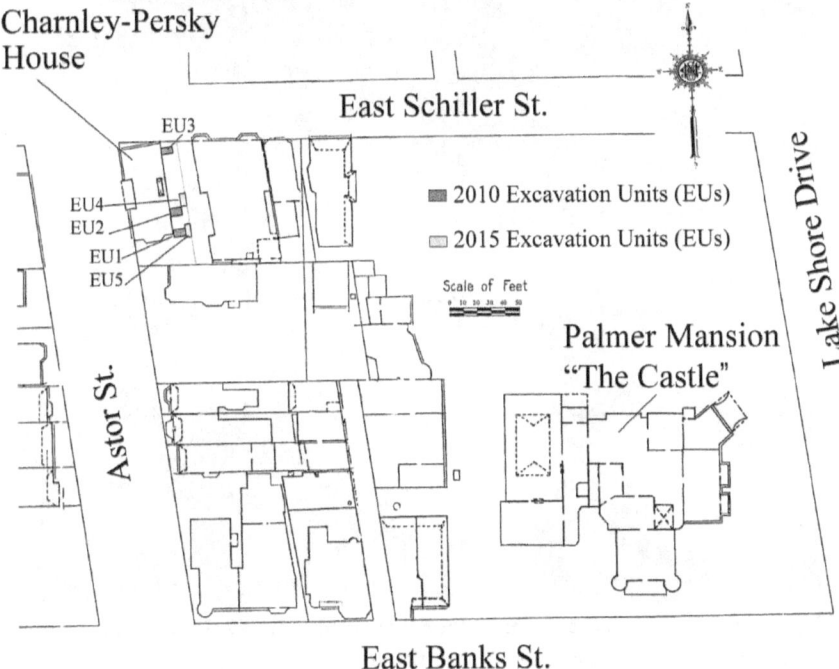

Figure 2.17. Charnley-Persky House Archaeological Project Excavation Site Map, both seasons. Map by author using a modified 1906 Sanborn Fire Insurance Map.

project that cut through at least two of the three excavation units while still revealing additional material from the late nineteenth through the early twentieth centuries.

In July 2015, under the auspices of Lake Forest College's "Unearthing Chicago" digital humanities grant from the Mellon Foundation, I directed another field school with Tiffany Charles. Here we opened an additional two 1 m × 2 m excavation units at the eastern edges of the driveway as an attempt to locate undisturbed deposits (see figure 2.17). The excavation methodology used the same as in 2010, and we removed 4.98 m³ of soil, for a site total of 12.41 m³.

We recovered almost 28,000 artifacts from both excavation seasons at the Charnley-Persky House, items that currently remain in the care of the Charnley-Persky House and the SAH. Analysis centered on the almost 150 different brands—from locally and globally distributed sites of manufacture—that we identified from the fragments of these bottles, plates, and

Figure 2.18. Bottles and a teacup from the 2010 Charnley-Persky House Archaeological Project excavation. Photograph by Mary Leighton.

other vessels from 1880 to 1920. The results of the excavation provide a glimpse into the consumer habits of the men, women, and children who lived on Chicago's Gold Coast at the turn of the twentieth century (figure 2.18; see chapter 5).

Unlike the surprise we encountered in Jackson Park when we uncovered the fragile plaster remains of the monumental World's Columbian Exposition's Ohio Building, the assemblage recovered from the Charnley House midden feature proves more typical to historical archaeological research and to the foundational place of "other people's garbage" in discipline of archaeology. Yet these ordinary items make the surprising aspects of the Ohio Building meaningful: they connect people—elite fair planners, Chicago capitalists, working-class women—back to the fair via their fair-produced consumptive and bodily experiences, as analyzed through their trash (see chapter 5).

Conclusion

The *Chicago Tribune*'s weekly "In Society News" column carried the details of social comings and goings of the city's wealthy and socially prominent elite. Like many of these society pages in the United States (Inman 1968) and abroad (e.g., Canada, Lang 1990; and the Philippines, Bulatao 1964), the column included notices of afternoon receptions, teas, card parties, church bazaars, and weddings. No gathering was too inconsequential to omit from mention, no guest too insignificant to name. The society columns also contain data about the material culture that made up these social worlds. When Helen Charnley hosted a party at her Astor Street home to introduce her niece, Nora Neef, to Chicago elites, the society column contained detail of Nora's gown (white chiffon), what she carried (American beauty roses), and the names of the thirteen invited guests (*Chicago Tribune* 1899a: 42). Such reporting could have been a boon to those seeking to climb the social ladder by emulating elite dress or dining practices captured in these columns.

Not surprisingly, these social and artifactual descriptions from society columns or from many other documentary accounts are but superficial glimpses into daily life in the nineteenth century and leave out details not only of the elite they tend to focus upon but also the lives of the working class, of women, of those who were not literate, of those who did not speak or write in English, of those people whose skin color denied them full participation in every facet of American society, and more. The archaeological research presented in this volume from both the World's Columbian Exposition and the Charnley House does not even this playing field, but it provides the avenues within with to locate nuance and greater meaning. From the wrappers that surround our commercially produced foodstuffs to the infrastructure that makes our toilets flush found within an ephemeral world's fair building or a sturdy Gold Coast mansion—these are the stuff of shreds and patches that form our material and ideological worlds. The chapters that follow explore the material sides of the elite social networks that produced both the World's Fair in Jackson Park and the Astor Street neighborhood of the Charnley House—as well as the ideologies the people of the networks were vested in.

3

TEMPORALITIES AS IDEOLOGIES

When Leonard Schoch, then a medical student in Chicago, wrote to his friend Anna Mahaney on November 19, 1893, he reflected on the end of the World's Columbian Exposition with a somber and meditative tone:

> Our city seems quiet and somewhat deserted now that the Fair visitors have left us. The Dream City is, indeed[,] a vanishing city. The work of destruction goes rapidly on. It seems a pity that its life should be so brief—that so much of beauty and interest must soon be only a memory. There is so much that I had hoped to see and which for want of time I did not see, that I feel it as a personal loss to have it all disappear so quickly. (Schoch 1893, 4–5)

Like Schoch, many people during the late fall and winter of 1893 felt bewilderment at the rapid pace of the destruction of the White City. It was, after all, designed to be temporary, but with over two hundred buildings, a network of pipes and electrical lights, abundant statuary, and a series of monumental water features, it seemed too immense to materially disappear. And yet it did; by the following year most of the remaining surface structures were gone. The "Vanishing Fair" (Van Meter 1894) was, as an article in the popular *Scribner's Magazine* summed up for its readership, "a city for a single summer" (Mitchell 1893, 189).

The ephemerality of the monumental World's Columbian Exposition encourages an investigation into its place and transformative potential in the imagination of its planners, builders, and tourists. This ephemerality is captured in letters and personal accounts like Schoch's, in the intensity and volume of the official photographic record (Arnold and Higinbotham 1893; see also Gilbert 1993; Brown 1994; Hales 2005), and in contemporary literary chronicles of the fair (e.g., Yandell and Hayes 1892; Holley 1893; Neville 1893; Stevens 1893; Burnham 1894; Butterworth 1894; Finley 1894; Burnett 1895). Yet the brief lifespan of this behemoth was not simply something lamented by those who missed it: the World's Columbian Exposition *needed* to become part of the past rapidly for it to have greater impact on the narrative of American modernity in the late nineteenth century. The ideological thrust of this need was likely unintended or latent, but the planned erasure of the fairgrounds was logically necessary and legally mandated by the South Park Commission, the owners of Jackson Park. This planned loss is analytically derivable and implicit, even in the final sentences of a children's novel on the fair, *Two Little Pilgrims' Progress: A Story of the City Beautiful* (1895) written by Frances Hodgson Burnett, the author better known for *Little Lord Fauntleroy* (1886), *A Little Princess* (1905), and *The Secret Garden* (1911). The guardian of an unhappy child—unhappy because she is thinking about the impending dissolution of the White City—comforts the child as they sail on Lake Michigan away from the fair: "'No,' he said, 'it won't vanish away. It's not one of the things that vanish. Things don't vanish away that a million or so of people have seen as they've seen this. They stay—where they're not forgotten and time doesn't change them. They're put where they can be passed on—and passed on again. And thoughts that grew out of them bring other ones. . . . It won't vanish away'" (Burnett 1895, 214). As part of American collective memory (see Harris 1993, 4; Halbwachs and Coser 1992; Connerton 1989), performed and experienced during the six months of spectacle, the fair did not really vanish. But, more tangibly, as a material phenomenon—a full city made for a summer!—it persists both archaeologically and in the myriad products, inventions, and innovations that poured from its exhibits into American homes.

The fleeting nature of the colossal fair was an integral part of its allure and its message and was one of many engagements and manipulations of temporalities—both real but mostly imagined—that made it so transformative. The fair's brief, six-month existence as the White City and Midway Plaisance was a duration much shorter than that of typical cities, as well as many other urban archaeological sites, although its scale and infrastructure—particularly the infrastructure for its water and sewerage—was equivalent to a city of three hundred thousand (Burnham et al. 1989, 1:19). For example, the fair's Manufactures and Liberal Arts Building was nicknamed "Leviathan" and was the largest building in the world in 1893. That this one building occupied over 1.36 million square feet (over thirty acres) made its swift erasure from the landscape that much more startling and seemingly impossible (White and Igleheart 1893, 95–96).

The World's Columbian Exposition was a short-term social and cultural event infused with the material interpretations and imaginings of past, present, and future forms, further drawing attention to uses of temporalities for ideological ends. That the fair was erased from the landscape so quickly and thoroughly only increased its evocative power. Indeed, the Vanishing City pushed ideological agendas via its materiality and its concomitant dissolution. During the six months the fair ran, the impermanence, ephemerality, and impending erasure of the material White City was contrasted with the ideas, inventions, and innovations that tourists consumed and experienced and that were supposed to be permanently transformative for them once they returned home. These lasting experiences made the brevity of the encounter with the material fair tolerable, although they were as varied as the millions of visitors who entered into Jackson Park that summer.

While the entirety of the fair's architecture and exhibits were conduits for its ideologies, some of the fair's exhibit spaces (like the Ohio Building) seemed superficially akin to the familiar and permanent forms many tourists encountered in their own homes (like the Charnley House). But the messages that suffused the temporary city were both qualitatively different and paradoxically more lasting due to the effacement of the fair site. This chapter looks at the temporalities of the 1893 Chicago fair and the Charnley House in three senses. First, it illuminates the ways in which the fair planners used conceptions of time and temporality to push ideological agendas in their exhibits, from the Midway Plaisance's exhibits of non-Western peoples to the Manufacturers and Liberal Arts Building's industrial goods to the ways women's roles were imagined in the Women's Building. Second, as evidenced in the opening lines above, the chapter explores how ideological underpinnings of the fair were furthered by its clearance from the physical landscape—the underground archaeology notwithstanding—and how this erasure incongruously helped to make such ideologies more solid within more enduring spaces. Third, the much-heralded "modern" architectural and aesthetic style of the

Charnley House made it a small vision of the future among Astor Street's Victorian mansions. The discovery of a modern alarm clock in the Charnley midden likewise draws attention to futurity of the site and its preview of modern timekeeping practices like those on display at the fair.

Experiencing "Modernity's Frankenstein" and Temporal Ideologies at the Fair

In 1893 author Hamlin Garland wrote from his new home in Chicago to his father on the family farm in South Dakota: "Sell the cook stove if necessary and come. You *must* see this fair" (Garland 1920, 458). Whether or not any of the other 27 million visitors to the 1893 World's Columbian Exposition had to make financial sacrifices to get to Chicago, judging by the records they left, many would have echoed Garland's oft-quoted, enthusiastic sentiments. In the second chapter of William Dean Howells's serialized utopian novel cum critique of capitalism, *Letters from an Altrurian Traveller*, the traveler, Homos—thus far appalled at America's socioeconomic conditions, so different from his home—exclaimed of the White City: "Of the effect, of the visible, tangible result, what better can I say than that in its presence I felt myself again in Altruria?" (Howells 1893, 220).

Others saw the World's Fair in opposition to utopia: it was a city that reflected and instantiated the dominant racial, gender, and class hegemonies the United States, with exhibits of an America whose benefits were not dispersed equally and with promises of a future that maintained this status quo. After witnessing the concerted efforts by all levels of the exposition planners to deny African Americans representation in the exposition, Ida B. Wells wrote that the exclusion of African American leaders from planning stages at the fair created, "literally and figuratively, a 'White City,' in the building of which the Colored American was allowed no helping hand, and in its glorious success he has no share" (Wells-Barnett 1893, 79). Wells and coauthors Frederick Douglass, Irvine Garland Penn, and Ferdinand Lee Barnett sought to bring attention to that institutionalized racism in their 1893 pamphlet, "The Reason Why the Colored American Is Not in the World's Columbian Exposition" (Wells-Barnett 1893). The Chicago fair inspired something powerful in those who saw it, whether awe or outrage; very few, if any, accounts in the documentary record describe a tepid or dispassionate reaction to it.

The sheer immensity of the fairscape and its exhibits made such contradictory ideologies of utopia/dystopia possible. In one of the many guidebooks written to help tourists take in the entirety of the fair, the visual and experiential excesses of the fair's physical landscape jump right off the page. Day one of the standard, recommended week at the fair, according to the "Nut-Shell" pocket guide, included visits to the Terminal Railway Station, the Administration Building, the Mines and Mining Building, the Electricity Building, Machinery Hall, the Livestock Pavilion and Colonnade, the Anthropology Building, the Forestry Building, the Shoe and Leather Building, the Dairy Building, and the Convent of La Rabida, each of which was filled with hundreds if not thousands of exhibits (Wade 1893b). Every subsequent day was likewise filled to the brim with buildings and exhibits to see and experiences to be had. An undoubtedly hungry fairgoer could choose from over thirty-five restaurants and concessions, ranging from the Louisiana Building's Creole Kitchen to the Swedish Café as well as small stands or lunch counters offering the newly created Cracker Jack, Wrigley Juicy Fruit Gum, or Vienna Beef hot dogs (Graff and Edwards 2018, 422). Each new sight, taste, smell, sound—each new experience of space and place at the fair—was a vast multitude of disparate sensations and related narratives, all consumed as a totality.

Preeminent historian of world's fairs and expositions Robert Rydell suggests the totality by calling the Chicago fair a "cultural Frankenstein," pointing to the monstrous patchwork of exhibits that merely "reaffirm[ed] existing attitudes regarding race and gender" in the service of national and imperial self-interest (Rydell 1993, 143). Alan Trachtenberg suggests that the World's Columbian Exposition represents a working through of "contrary and diverse values," all brought together to realize the message that "a corporate alliance of business, culture, and the state" would create an ideal "incorporated" America (1982, 216–17; see also Harris 1993, 26–28). Historian Henry Adams, having attended the fair at length, wrote, "No such Babel of loose and ill-joined, such vague and ill-defined and unrelated thoughts and half-thoughts and experimental outcries as the Exposition, had ever ruffled the surface of the lakes." Two pages later into his fair recollections, he incongruously claims that this hodgepodge in Chicago was also "the first expression of American thought as a unity" (Adams 1907, 297, 299).

The cultural Frankenstein of the fair could be better conceived as "modernity's Frankenstein," where these antithetical values and ideas were understood as a unity of modern life through the contrary and diverse material depictions of multiple temporalities and their connected ideologies. These different visual depictions, exhibits, and experiences—whether architectural, human, or even culinary—were often framed as showing different times. The fair's exhibits of "past," "present," and "future" things were all mixed up together though consumed as a whole. In writing about a similar move to create a representation with elements from deep antiquity side by side with contemporary ones, historian Reinhart Koselleck notes the "achronological pungency" of these mixed histories (Koselleck 2004, 11). One would only have to look at the modern American forms of fairs found at Walt Disney World and its related theme parks to see how this particular collage of materialized temporalities and their concomitant ideologies continue be consumed as rational and totalizing commodities (Fjellman 1992). It is thus no surprise that Walt Disney's father, Elias Disney, worked as a carpenter at the 1893 World's Fair, and it is tempting to speculate what Frankensteinian influence might have been transmitted from father to son (Zornado 2000, 135).

Thus, what appear to be the multiple and conflicting ideologies in exhibitions of the past, present, and the future of American life at the fair are reflections of the totalizing, nineteenth-century American ideas of their modern selves. This very "totality" consists of fragmentary and contradictory images that still exist in tension with one another. A look at some of these temporalities, here presented out of chronological order and in the same nonsequential, serpentine route that a tourist to the fair would take, begins to connect the fair's ideologies to concerns about what it was to be "modern" at the turn of the twentieth century in spaces and places like the Charnley House.

Past Apparitions

The ideology of what it was to be a modern "American" becomes singularly evident when looking at the way that the native villages of the Midway were constructed to suggest that non-Western peoples of the time lived in a pan-human past, purposely creating a bounded difference between modern American selves and the premodern "Other." The site, where American racialized ideologies were presented spatiotemporally, set the terms for both the fair's visions of the present and the future by its portrayal of the "past." The Midway was extremely popular as well as key to the financial success of the entire fair. It was not a part of the White City proper, so Midway fairgoers had to pay an additional fee to visit this set of exhibits and entertainments, an enterprise and additional revenue stream overseen by entrepreneur Sol Bloom.

Anthropological research has considered this ideological conflation of time and space harnessed by the West to place the ethnic Other within the past. Johannes Fabian wrote of how relationships between the West and other regions of the world were understood as temporal rather than spatial when nineteenth-century evolutionary anthropologists, in effect, "*spatialized* Time" (Fabian 1983, 15); they conflated time and space by conceptualizing geographic distance as a temporal dimension. Furthermore, these temporally past Others were also cast as remaining in an unchanging world. Eric Wolf (1982) pointed this out by examining the Western perception of colonized societies as "people without history," as those people who, living outside of the West, were imagined to exist in a temporal state that is both previous to the West and permanently fixed.

Anthropologist Raymond Fogelson (1991) posed a center–periphery model of the material instantiation of this spatiotemporal message of modernity in Chicago, with the most "civilized" Others found closest to the central structures of the White City and the least civilized placed at the far edges of the Midway. The fair's Midway Plaisance was a mile-long strip of land connecting the main fair site of Jackson Park with Washington Park to its west, containing reproductions of native villages of people from Algeria, Egypt, Tunisia, Turkey, Lebanon, Sudan, Dahomey, Sumatra, Borneo, Fiji, Samoa, and Lapland, as well as a concession that displayed the cabin of the Lakota leader, Sitting Bull. The Midway's European exhibits (Old Vienna, the Irish and German villages, the French cider press, the Hungarian café and concert pavilion) were located at the eastern end of the Midway Plaisance closest to the White City, with the Middle Eastern and Asian exhibits in the middle and the African encampments at the far western end, spatially recapitulating the dominant American racial hierarchy (Rydell 1978). Within the racialized "White" City proper but still at the margins of the fairgrounds were additional "native" encampments, including a Southern Labrador Eskimo Village and Indian Villages of Penobscot, Tuscarora, Seneca, and Northwest Coast peoples. Further Native American "exhibits" could be found to the southwest of the official fairgrounds. Buffalo Bill's Wild West and Congress of Rough Riders and its more than two hundred Indians performers—mostly members of the

Oglala Sioux Nation—were not allowed to be part of the official fair, but the show found a home just outside the fairgrounds by 62nd and 63rd Streets.

Newspaper articles and other contemporaneous accounts portrayed the non-Western people on the Midway and related locations as savage, backward, and reflective of humanity's pasts. This ideological messaging was especially notable in the case of the Fon people of the African Dahomey Village, who were referred to as "savages" and "cannibals" (see Reed 2000). If Midway inhabitants were more positively described, they were demeaned as stuck in an unvarying present: "A thousand years ago their Fijian ancestors danced in just this way," read a report on the "timeless" Samoans in the *Chicago Tribune* (*Chicago Tribune* 1893g, 10). George Stocking, in considering London's 1851 Crystal Palace Exhibition—the modern world's first great fair—remarked that "the most obvious lesson of the Exhibition, however, was that in pursuing their sacred mission, not all men had advanced at the same pace, or arrived at the same point" (Stocking 1987, 3). As in the Chicago fair and others that followed it, the Crystal Palace had exhibits of goods and crafts from cultures around the world. Yet in looking at these displays, visitors were led to distinguish the "'stationary' civilizations of the East from the 'progressive' West" (Stocking 1987, 3), understanding that the apex of this progression was in Great Britain (and, later, in America). Such messaging only became more blatant when viewing actual living exhibits of people on the Midway.

The emergent discipline of anthropology was also part of this conversation about non-Western peoples and their relation to modern America. Franz Boas, often called the father of anthropology, worked to collect, research, and craft culturally holistic and antievoutionary exhibits in the fair's Anthropology Building. Through his exhibits, Boas argued against the evolutionary typological and classificatory schemes found in the fair exhibits created by the Smithsonian's Bureau of American Ethnology's Otis T. Mason and John Wesley Powell (Jacknis 1985). Today it is clear that Boasian historical particularism and cultural relativism won out over racist social evolutionism in anthropology. Boas's exhibits showed that people from different cultures did not exist in different times or at different temporal stages in a unilineal model. Anthropology was not "a collection of curious facts, telling about the peculiar appearance of exotic people" (Boas 1928, 11). The material differences were choices and responses to their sociocultural worlds, ones best understood through each group's own belief systems. Thus it was while its leading figures like Boas worked at the Chicago fair that anthropology "came of age" and "went national" (Wilcox 2016, 413).

Despite Boas's work, the dominant message of the fair, found in the other anthropological exhibits from the Midway Plaisance to the Government Building, was that modern Westerners—particularly Americans—were the ultimate examples of humanity in the present and were on track to an even more impressive future. The logical outcome of that position was that non-Westerners, like those on display in replicas of their native villages on the Midway, were part of the disappearing past. One exception to this Western/non-Western dichotomy at the fair could be found in the ambiguous status of Japan. Not only was the Ho-o-den ("Phoenix") Palace centrally located on the White City's Wooded Island, but there were also many displays of Japanese works found in the main fair buildings rather than segregated in the Midway or the Anthropology Building. The Ho-o-den had a profound and highly positive impact on the way Americans viewed Japan. Just after finishing his work on the Charnley House, Frank Lloyd Wright visited the fair and was struck by the Ho-o-den's architecture, and some historians have traced the lasting influence of Japanese architectural aesthetics in Wright's work from that encounter (see Langlois 2004).

But the non-Western peoples on display in anthropology and other exhibits were not the only groups presented as living exemplars of the premodern past: ethnic European exhibits showed the very Old World that the New World was presently eclipsing. The many European-themed amusements on the Midway had, as Columbian Exposition president Harlow N. Higinbotham stated, "a flavor of ancient times that is peculiarly pleasant" (Smith 1893, 9), a "flavor" that was racialized in a different manner than the Midway's Javanese or Dahomeyan exhibits. For example, fair tourists thronged to Old Vienna, a reproduction of the seventeenth-century city, where thirsty visitors could "travel back in time" as they enjoyed beers served by women in quaint Austrian folk costumes. These white "ethnic" themed attractions, as with the many theme restaurants at Disneyland today, drew many tourists in search of uncommon yet still familiar experiences. After touring the Midway's "human kaleidoscope" (Smith 1893, 4) of people from far-flung lands conflated as from far-flung times, visitors left the fairgrounds in the process of contrasting this narrative with ideologies of (white) American progress. It is important to note, though, that the relationship of people of Irish, Sicilian, and Slavic descent as well as European Jews to the racial category "white" was ambiguous in the late-nineteenth-century United States.

Numerous shows of nostalgic American pasts were similarly available for consumption on the Midway and in the White City, temporally distancing contemporary Americans from their ancestors. Fair tourists might visit the Midway's "Ye Olden Tyme Log Cabin," where, for a fee, a visitor could enjoy a New England-style dinner served by waitresses dressed in colonial-period clothing (Blaske 1982). While they ate, "ladies in the dress of our foremothers rocked the canoe cradles, knit yarn socks, carded wool, spun yarn, drank from gourds, and gossiped like Priscilla about their John Aldens" (Buel 1894, n.p.). Another nostalgic option beyond the Midway was a visit to the Convent of La Rabida, filled with Columbian artifacts that were curated by anthropologist and folklorist J. G. Burke. La Rabida was a replica of the structure in Palos, Spain, where Columbus retreated from 1486 until 1492 to plan his Atlantic voyages and today serves in modified form as a children's hospital. These exhibits, along with the replicas of Columbus's three caravels (the *Niña*, *Pinta*, and *Santa Maria*) and the very name of the fair itself, served to link the Columbian myth to the present American exceptionalism (see Schlereth 1992). In close proximity to La Rabida, Anglophile tourists could visit the Great White Horse Inn, a reproduction of an old inn in Ipswich, England, where Charles Dickens set some scenes from *The Pickwick Papers*. The structure had a restaurant and a bar "attended by genuine English bar-maids," continuing the process of linking Anglo and Anglo-American cultures but with one residing firmly in the past (Buel 1894, n.p.). This substantiates David Lowenthal's argument on heritage movements: "If the past is a foreign country, nostalgia has made it 'the foreign country with the healthiest tourist trade of all'" (Lowenthal 1985, 4). In all of these examples we can see that the experience of the fair was permeated by multiple racialized "pasts," both ethnographic and nostalgic, all imaginary. These histories, made spatiotemporal, created the foundation for the ideologies of the present and future also on display.

Future Visions

Amid all the didactic exhibits of supposedly premodern peoples and things, the exposition held a blueprint for the imagined American future, most particularly seen in its architecture and, to a lesser extent, the portrayal of women found there. Shortly before his assassination at the 1901 Buffalo Pan-American Exposition—the next large-scale American fair after the World's Columbian Exposition—President William McKinley announced: "expositions are the timekeepers of progress" (Brain 1993, 33). This future-oriented viewpoint was clearly found in 1893 Chicago. Even negative assessments of the fair had an eye to the potentialities of its future influence. Louis Sullivan famously stated, specifically regarding its architectural program: "the damage wrought by the World's Fair will last a half century from its date, if not longer" (Sullivan 1956, 325).

The main architectural style of the fair was Beaux-Arts, with its unmistakable reference to ancient Greco-Roman and Renaissance architecture, but it was simultaneously a vision of the future. Beaux-Arts (literally "fine arts") is the term given to an academic architectural style taught at the École des Beaux-Arts in Paris, an institution with origins dating to 1671 (Twombly 1986, 58). The Beaux-Arts style emphasized symmetry, grandeur, and explicit classical borrowings in an effort to create rational public spaces. The style is often referred to as classical revival, a later form of eighteenth-century neoclassicism, signaling the iterative popularity of Greco-Roman style in the West through the 1890s. Louis Sullivan was one notable alumnus of the École des Beaux-Arts, although he rejected its veneration of ancient and Renaissance architectural style. In fact, while he was denouncing the dominant paradigms at the école, Sullivan formulated his famous and architectural philosophy: "form follows function," (Twombly 1986, 74–75). While the fair did have structures that departed from the Beaux-Arts academic style, such as the Spanish mission revival style of the California Building or Adler and Sullivan's Transportation Building, the significance of the Beaux-Arts fairscape to future municipal building projects nationwide cannot be understated.

The fair "legitimized" neoclassicism (Twombly 1986, 402) and in doing so created the ideological conditions for the City Beautiful movement and its legacy of neoclassical-style municipal buildings (post offices, banks, railway stations) that persist in the American landscape. The City Beautiful movement—where refined architecture and city planning could create the proper sort of citizenry—traces its roots directly to the fair, although its other important precursor was in the work of the future landscape architect for the 1893 fair, Frederick Law Olmsted (Wilson 1989). Olmsted, having previously worked in on a design for Jackson Park with partner Calvert Vaux, oversaw the landscape design for Jackson Park for the fair, with partner Henry Sargent Codman providing another fair-based origin point for this architectural ideology (Wilson 1989, 9). The fair's White City was the first place that demonstrated what became typical City Beautiful concerns: "sanitation; aesthetics; rationalized urban functions; women's involvement in culture, civic improvement, and urban reform; building design; artistic collaboration; architectural professionalism; and civic spirit" (Wilson 1989, 60). In 1902 fair architects Daniel Burnham and Charles McKim, fair sculptor Augustus Saint-Gaudens, and fair landscape architect Frederick Law Olmsted, along with U.S. senator James McMillan and his secretary, Charles Moore, produced the 1902 McMillan Plan for Washington, D.C., which is considered the first realization of the City Beautiful program (U.S. Congress, Senate, Committee on the District of Columbia 1902). And in 1907 Burnham, along with Edward Bennett, returned to Chicago to work on the ultimate expression of the City Beautiful: the Chicago Plan (Commercial Club of Chicago et al. 1909).

Along with its Beaux-Arts architectural style, the White City's demonstration of rational urban planning was future-oriented. Influenced by Baron Georges-Eugène Haussmann's mid-nineteenth-century restructuring of Paris, this use of urban planning to mold social experiences was a modern and increasingly influential idea, something perceived as "desirably new" by visitors to the fair during this time of rapid urbanization (Appelbaum 1980, 13). In a sentiment prefiguring that found in the White City, Haussmann spoke of his work in Paris as giving urban areas "space, air, light, verdure and flowers, in a word, with all that dispenses health" (Donald 1999, 57). The bourgeois sensibility of Haussmann's new boulevardized Paris proved to be conducive to the capitalist enterprises of railroads, commerce, and banking, making it "the great center of consumption, tourism and pleasure—the cafes, the department stores, the fashion industry, the grand expositions all changed the urban way of life in ways that could absorb vast surpluses through crass consumerism" (Harvey 2012, 8). As in Paris, much of the Chicago fair's new experiences of future city life were made possible by a vast sanitary infrastructure that introduced fair tourists to a sanitary, hygienic, and garbage-free future (see chapters 4 and 5).

In the confines of this architecturally monumental and rationally planned city, the fair's exhibits and infrastructure fostered its forward-looking ideologies. The main exhibit halls of the fair held over "65,000 exhibits of human progress" (Badger 2008, 120) with displays of electrically incubated chicks, gargantuan electrical dynamos, cutting-edge fire-fighting apparatus, and the immense Yerkes telescope, then the largest telescope in the world, although it would not be fitted with its forty-inch lens until 1895. In the Electricity Building, tourists could see exhibits of new inventions like Japanese seismographs, American telegraphs, and German clocks or, should they wish, head to the "backstage" parts of the fair and tour the very dynamos that produced the fair's "lavish" artificial illumination (Platt 1991, 61; White and Igleheart 1893, 325). Female tourists were quoted as being especially taken by what the promises of electrical appliances and inventions for cooking with electricity held for their future domestic duties (see chapter 4 for more on domesticity at the fair).

Indeed, many exhibits at the fair demonstrated how future changes in the material forms of daily life would necessarily be accompanied by a manifest change in the familiar roles of people, most notably for American women and their future domestic lives. The culmination of the work by the fair's Board of Lady Managers—led by Bertha Honoré Palmer, neighbor to the Charnleys—was the Woman's Building, but it was not a coincidence that this structure was situated where the "wilds" of the Midway met up with western edge of the White City, a spatial location that made "geographic neighbors" of "women and savages" whose "mental abilities often linked by leading anthropometrists of the day" (Trump 1998, 216; see also Ortner 1972). The structure contained exhibits meant to "arouse the majority of women, who were not emancipated, to an awareness of the achievements of which women were capable" (Weimann 1981, 260–61). Yet the vast majority of the building's exhibits emphasized past domestic roles of women rather than promises of a different future (Miller 1981). While there was a library full of female-authored books, exhibits from American "female" colleges, and the stunning "Modern Women" mural by Mary Cassatt in the building, there was a model kindergarten, model hospital, and cooking exhibits on its main floor that furthered the dominant ideological conception of nurturing motherhood as woman's main role.

As president of the Board of Lady Managers, Bertha Palmer was given the privilege of making summary remarks on women and their future at the fair. She said, "Each woman shut up in her household is out of touch, in practical matters, with the rest of her race," suggesting the perils of remaining defined by traditional domestic spheres (Corn 2011, 183). Contrast this with the conclusions of Otis T. Mason, curator of the Smithsonian's

Bureau of Ethnology, in his neo-evolutionary *Women's Share in Primitive Culture* (1894), based on exhibits in the Women's Building. He determines that the "share" in question was for women to remain the nurturers, the instructors of morals, and keepers of the hearth, although he noted: "it only remains to be seen how far the future will add to its lustre" (Mason 1894, 286).

Present Illusions

While the architectural forms and women-centered exhibits at the fair provided a glimpse of imagined future prospects, more than anything else, the fair displayed the contemporary world. More to the point, absent a time machine, the tourist to the fair would only experience present interpretations of other temporalities. And the fair's physical place was similarly limited; there may have been people and things from the world over on display, but that world was set in Chicago. Yet these conflations of time and space were the key foundation for the present illusions of the fair. Spatial distance from the civilized Western nations was exhibited and consumed as temporal distance, a common trope in racist cultural evolutionary schema. Artificial creations of nostalgic pasts were conflated with authentic pasts so that one might indeed "go back in time" while at the fair. And the future that arose with every timber and plaster coating of the fair's two hundred structures was materially in the present—more of a preview, perhaps, for those who did not yet have access to its promises, but one invented and built for 1893.

What was shown as "present" as refracted through the fair was a "sanitized view of the world with no poverty, no war, no social problems and very little nature"—in essence, a falsely utopian "perfect city" (Benedict 1983, 5; see Gilbert 1991). The summer and fall 1893 exhibits and messages at Chicago's World's Columbian Exposition may have been consumed positively or negatively depending on how much the individual tourists saw themselves in the narratives and participated in touristic experiences. By way of example, wealthy philanthropist Frances Glessner frequently journeyed to the fair from her Prairie Avenue mansion. While there she had the chance to take in intellectually stimulating exhibits and sup with her high-powered friends like Daniel Burnham (Gilbert 1991, 76–77). Contrast Glessner's experience of the fair with that of its workforce, whose largely anonymous numbers were made up of "tramps" (urban itinerant workers), white ethnic minorities, and college students (Silkenat 2011). Overall, working conditions at the fair were so poor that a total of fifty workers died during its duration. African American laborers had the additional prospect of experiencing racial violence while working at the fair. William Broda, a fair day laborer, was almost lynched by his fellow workingmen (Silkenat 2011, 281–82). Further consider, then, the Native Americans whose participation at the fair was mostly exhibitionary rather than touristic. The Inuit men, women, and children exhibited at the fair's Eskimo Village could not always explore the fairgrounds they lived in, as many of them were kept virtual prisoners for offenses such as refusing to wear heavy fur clothing during warm-weather days (Rinehart 2012, 415). No doubt the vast majority of fair tourists had experiences of a different character entirely from Mrs. Glessner's. Still other experiences at the fair were just not captured in the documentary record. To provide a personal example, Morris Graff—my paternal great-grandfather and a newly arrived immigrant—worked as a laborer at the fair. While the family tradition recounted this employment, no one knows what his working conditions were like or whether he actually attended the fair as a tourist to see the fruits of his labors.

Like the White City's imitative plaster columns that tricked the tourist into believing they were seeing ancient marble, the thin veneer of these materials and their parallel ideologies found at the World's Columbian Exposition "made itself relevant almost exactly to the extent that the world outside its gates did not conform to its symmetry" (Trachtenberg 1982, 216). Elsewhere I have argued that the use of imitative construction materials like plaster at the 1893 Chicago fair as a form of illusion and artifice was itself the defining characteristic of the Gilded Age (Graff 2012). Mark Twain coined the era's appellation to emphasize the avarice and greed of the era, as made material though excessive consumption of newly "cheap, quick, and easy" mass-manufactured goods (Twain and Warner 1873; Simpson 1999). I would add that the contemporary world inside the fair's gates was likewise distorted and was unequally experienced by the populace. Twain himself journeyed to Chicago intent on visiting the 1893 fair but instead spent the entirety of his trip sick in his hotel room (Thoreson 1980, 289). Given his previous writing on Gilded Age superficiality, one wonders how he would have appraised the present on display at the fair.

If, like Twain, a person missed the chance to visit the fair between May and October 1893, they still might consume plenty of lasting ideologies, be they messages of racialized hierarchies presented as "pasts," models for future urban experiences via architecture, or concepts of how American women might find their present roles beyond the domestic sphere. Considering nineteenth-century fairs in general, Curtis Hinsley writes: "None lasted more than six months; collectively their ideological impact was profound and permanent" (Hinsley 1991, 344). The physical and material fair endured for only six months of 1893. As discussed in chapters 4 and 5, the present fair ideologies of domesticity, consumption, and trash-making may have been the most resounding and enduring messages of its exhibits.

It is crucial to note that the mechanism behind the successful dispersal of both material goods and immaterial ideas from world's fairs was the short-term life and rapid erasure of the monumental fairscape. The material reality of the Vanishing City and the suite of material practices—both temporary and permanent—that the fair's planners, architects, and builders used was central to its spectacle and messaging.

Monumental Ephemerality and Infrastructural Permanence at the Fair

The ephemeral nature of monumental world's fair architecture merits significant attention for harnessing the fair's ideological possibilities, regardless of which temporalities they purported to show. While the temporary architecture of Jackson Park is the focus of the archaeological project of this volume, this architectural practice was not unique to the 1893 Chicago fair (e.g., it was used in Paris in 1889) but was heretofore singular in its scale and its reception.

The intentionality of constructing an impermanent structure is what makes the architecture of international world's fairs distinctive from other architectural and city planning projects. Like sandcastles or ice sculptures or a hut used for seasonal hunting, these buildings were not built to withstand the harshness of the elements or, most importantly, the march of time. But unlike sandcastles, ice sculptures, or huts used for seasonal hunting, the intentionally ephemeral architecture of world's fairs was constructed on a monumental rather than a quotidian scale.

The temporary nature coupled with the monumental scale of fairs created the conditions for the development of both innovative and spectacular buildings, where builders were forced to "solve awkward architectural problems" while at the same time impressing the tourist publics (Greenhalgh 1988, 150). Moreover, as in the case of Chicago's 1873 Inter-State Exposition, financial considerations forced fair architects to use the cheapest materials and employ the most cost-effective solutions in creating their dream cities. The solution to this dilemma lay in an unassuming material called "staff," a material that, somewhat surprisingly, remains archaeologically in Jackson Park.

Alternately described as "counterfeit marble" (Cawelti 1968, 343), a "sham" (Pettit 1874 in Giberti 2002, 42), or "pompous" (Greenhalgh 1988, 158), plaster mixtures like staff were employed to form the façades of exposition buildings at least by 1883. The Main Building of the 1883 Amsterdam Exposition was covered with plaster, and a section of canvas—another less than permanent material—hung between two towers to evoke an Oriental shawl (Mattie 1998, 62). The particular recipe for "staff" was purportedly developed for the 1889 Paris Exposition Universelle, consisting of plaster, jute fibers, horsehair, and any number of additional ingredients. Other sources note that staff "has been used for more than one hundred years as a covering for buildings, notably in South America" (Department of Publicity and Promotion 1892, 36). Staff could be carved and sculpted into any architectural fantasy, resulting paradoxically in structures that look ancient but were newly built to last for mere months (Eco 1986, 299).

Yet these structures made of plaster and plaster-faced wood were attached to infrastructure that was equivalent to, if not better than, that of corresponding buildings in American urban centers. While the lasting image of the fairs was the aboveground, impermanent architecture, the majority of the archaeologically discernable material is the underground, robust infrastructure. Moreover, the experiences created by this infrastructure were the most modern of the fair's offerings. The sewerage, gas, lighting, and water systems constructed for these temporary structures were often the best the current technology could create, and their prices and amount of labor resources testify to that fact. Beginning with the 1851 Crystal Palace, which had "very elaborate drainage, and substantial new sewers, in the innovative oval shape" (Hobhouse 2002, 80), fair builders created an underground world of pipes and conduits—all the latest technology—that was typically left in situ at the close of each exposition.

In planning the great international fairs, builders needed to use the same or improved versions of technologies, on the same scale, as for any urban center. In fact, the estimates for creating the sewage, water, gas, and electricity infrastructure for the 1893 fair were based on cities of comparable scale. During the life of the fairs, this infrastructure made the best technologies accessible to the fair tourists in the forms of water fountains, electric lighting, and even toilet facilities. Once the fairs ended, the underground elements of these temporary cities remained, left to be covered with soil as the fairscape made way for a new purpose.

At the close of world's fairs, most aboveground structures were destroyed, although some were eventually reconstructed with more durable materials to make them permanent. In most cases, the art buildings were the token edifices saved from destruction, including Philadelphia's Memorial Hall (1876, now the Please Touch Museum), Chicago's Palace of Fine Arts (1893, now the Museum of Science and Industry), and San Francisco's Palace of Fine Arts (1915, now the Exploratorium). Although some of this is due to the durability of the fireproofing these buildings required in order to carry insurance for the paintings they displayed, this alone is not the reason for their preservation. For example, Chicago's Fine Arts Palace, though somewhat fireproofed, needed to be entirely rebuilt before it could be reused as the Museum of Science and Industry in 1933. Its plaster façade was not impervious to the elements, and, apocryphally, the plaster skirts of the caryatids that festooned its sides were said to sway in the wind when stirred by the lakefront breeze. It seems that these art palaces—smaller than the grandest, main exposition buildings but larger than the state buildings, with some amount of durable materials used for fire insurance purposes—were particularly well-suited to maintain as a part of a lasting material reminder of each fair. However, like the rest of the aboveground fair structures, these buildings were never intended to last beyond the active period of the fair. When they did survive, it was in spite of the ephemeral materials, rather than because of them.

While the temporary buildings of the fair ceased their monumental dominance on the landscape of Chicago, the work of Chicago architects continued to draw the world's attention. The innovative tall office buildings—the early skyscrapers—of the 1880s gave way to what became known as the Chicago school of architecture, a mainly commercial technological and aesthetic style, making Chicago "the world center of architectural experimentation" (Miller 1996, 305; Condit 1964). Many guides to the

Chicago fair recommended that fair tourists also visit the Chicago school marvel that was Dankmar Adler and Louis Sullivan's Auditorium Building (1889)—an architectural combination of theater, office space, and hotel, which was recommended as a good place to stay for the duration of the fair. Unlike the fair, the Auditorium Building is still extant, making it, like the likewise extant Charnley House, another type of "timekeeper of progress" (Brain 1993, 33).

Keeping (Modern) Time at Charnley House

The Charnley House, built from solid brick, stone, and timber, still stands on Astor Street, its longevity in stark contrast to the temporary and ephemeral plaster architecture of the 1893 fair and any of the other expositions that characterized the nineteenth century. This intentional building with durability in mind is not distinct from the other residences of the neighborhood; indeed, it is probably more common than not for domestic structures in nineteenth-century urban sites to be constructed from materials purposely selected for their durability.

What continues to differentiate the Charnley House from its neighboring structures is its design, and it is no surprise that nineteenth-century-era responses to its unornamented façade, its symmetry, and its simple "rectilinear massing" heralded and also reviled it as the future of domestic architecture (Kruty 2004, 95; figure 3.1). Such progressive design also extended to its infrastructure: the Charnley House had electric and gas lighting along with central heating and five bathrooms—two each on the second and third floors by the bedrooms, and one in the basement laundry room (Cromley 2004, 106, 123; figure 3.2). Its atrium was also an unusual decorative and functional element for a home, heretofore only used in commercial structures like department stores (figure 3.3).

The Charnley House is often cited as one of the inspirations for Wright's famed Prairie-style homes built for wealthy Americans in the first decades of the twentieth century. One of the most well-known Prairie homes was Wright's house for Frederick C. Robie (1908), which is still extant and located near Jackson Park. The Robie House has an "interior spaciousness" not unlike the open-plan Charnley House (Upton 1998, 51). The Robie House's "main (second) floor, the living and dining space focused on a central hearth—an emblem of family togetherness in the Victorian tradition—that was open to both rooms, allowing one to see through it,

Figure 3.1. James Charnley residence, Chicago, Illinois, *Inland Architect* 18 (August 1891). Historic Architecture and Landscape Image Collection, Ryerson and Burnham Archives, The Art Institute of Chicago. Digital File #IA18XX_0771.

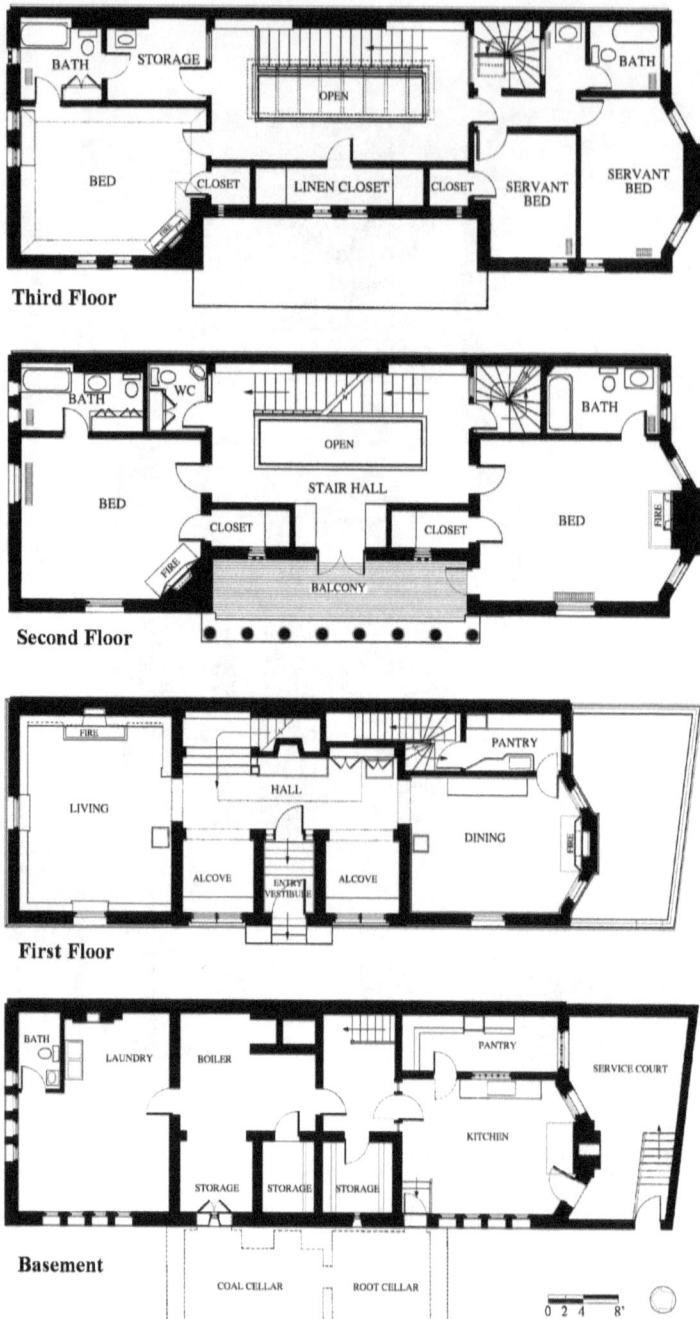

Figure 3.2. Plan of James Charnley residence, S.009 in *The Frank Lloyd Wright Companion* by William Allin Storrer © 1993 the Frank Lloyd Wright Foundation.

Figure 3.3. The atrium and first floor hall of the Charnley-Persky House, looking toward the dining room. Photograph by Ryan J. Cook.

thus creating the illusion of a single open space" (Upton 1998, 52). Such a moral focal point is similar to the central mosaic fireplace in the Charnley House. At the same time, the use of cantilevered roof eaves, horizontal bands of Roman brick, and entrances via narrow vestibules created a fortress-like exterior that preserved "the Victorian ideal of the family insulated from the outside world but thrown into each other's presence" (Upton 1998, 52). Like the open prairies that inspired the style, Wright's Prairie homes and the Charnley House have modern, undivided interior floor plans. While creating interior spatial conditions that put their inhabitants into close social proximity, these homes still adhere to older architectural practices of cloistering their inhabitants from the outside world.

Regardless of whether Sullivan or Wright designed the home (see chapter 2), the Charnley House stands as a harbinger of modern architecture and of both Sullivan and Wright's modernist legacies. Again, Adler and Sullivan was one of ten architectural firms chosen to design the main structures for the 1893 fair. Adler and Sullivan's Transportation Building, with its "Golden Doorway," stood in contrast to the derivative Beaux-Arts confections of their peers (figure 3.4). Sullivan worked by himself on the structure, creating a notable entrance one hundred feet wide by seventy feet high, covered with intricate patterns, gold leaf, and polychrome detail (Twombly 1986, 263–264). Wright echoed his *lieber Meister* ("Beloved Master"—Wright's nickname for Sullivan, see Wright 1977) when providing his take on the non-Sullivan parts of the fair's architecture: "flori[d] countenance of theoretical Beaux-Arts formalisms; perversion of what modern building we had achieved by negation; already a blight upon our progress. A senseless reversion" (Wright et al. 1960, 29).

Curiously, the reaction to the aesthetically modern Charnley House, both positive and negative, was, like reactions to the Transportation Building, couched in temporal dissonance. Montgomery Schuyler, an influential architecture critic who had previously described the architecture of the state buildings from the 1893 fair in dismal terms (Schuyler 1893; see chapter 1), wrote that the modern style of the Charnley House was an "admirable example of the value of simplification" (Schuyler 1895, 40). He explained that, with the exception of the colonnade of the second-floor balcony, the house had "no direct suggestion from the *antique*" (Schuyler 1895, 41, emphasis added). Indeed, as Frank Lloyd Wright apocryphally characterized it, the Charnley House was "the first modern house"; that is,

Figure 3.4. World's Columbian Exposition, Transportation Building, Golden Door, Chicago, Illinois, 1893. Historic Architecture and Landscape Image Collection, Ryerson and Burnham Archives, The Art Institute of Chicago. Digital File #80056.

it looked distinctive—and somewhat out of time—as compared with the urban Chicago built environment that surrounded it.

So, too, do the artifacts recovered from the excavations of the Charnley House provide a glimpse at modern temporalities and sensibilities associated with the turn of the twentieth century. Prior to the early nineteenth century, people living in cities had few personal timekeeping objects. One of the artifacts recovered from the 2010 excavation offers a particularly clear example of a material change in time-reckoning: an alarm clock (figure 3.5). Set on two feet and featuring a single bell, the clock would have assisted its user in regulating their disciplined waking.

Anthropologists and other scholars have focused on the notions of time that pervade human experience including "time-reckoning, calendric patterns, cultural constructions of the past, time as a medium of strategy or

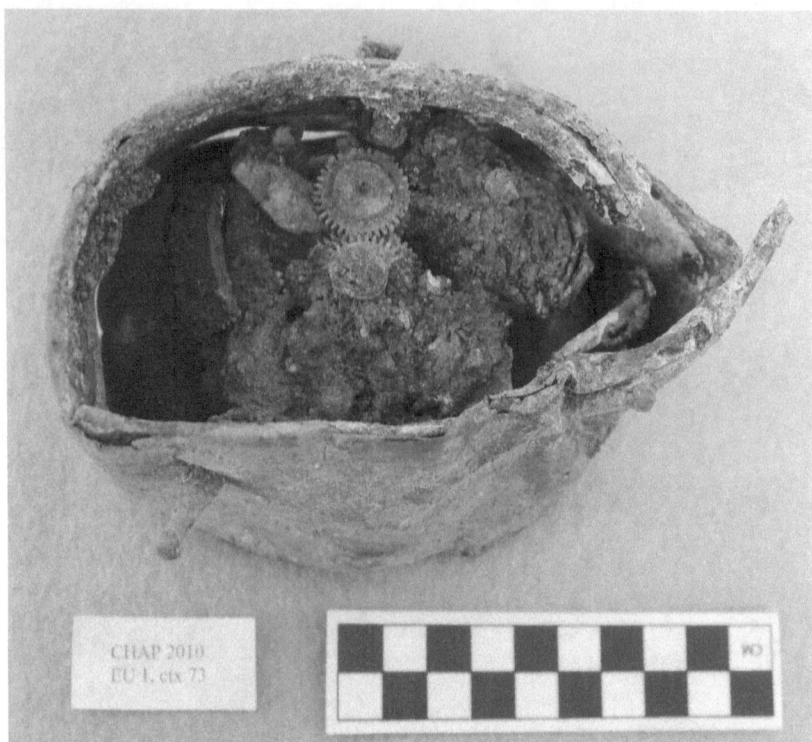

Figure 3.5. Alarm clock from the 2010 Charnley-Persky House Archaeological Project excavation. Photograph by Ryan J. Cook.

control" (Munn 1992, 116). But archaeologists in particular must consider the ways that the built environment and related timekeeping objects have shaped experiences for people, especially in urban settings. People in medieval European cities would have had the hours of religious contemplation tolled by centrally located church bells, and, after the Reformation, secularized urbanites would still require precisely reckoned time to get by in the emerging modern era (see Landes 1983; O'Malley 1990).

E. P. Thompson famously argued that, beginning in the early nineteenth century with the ramping up of industrial capitalism, Western workers developed a greater reliance on and awareness of time and temporality as their work shifted from traditional task-orientation to wage-labor (Thompson 1967). This modern time-centered "work-discipline" replaced the natural rhythms of the day and its tasks, measuring work by the clock. Consider the importance of 1880s standardized "railroad time" in growth of Chicago (Cronon 1991). Clocks were first found in town halls, churches, or factories, and then, as they became more affordable via mass production, on mantles, nightstands, watch chains, and wrists. The ideal time scale of modernity, the likes of which are also harnessed by archaeological practice, is precise, chronometric, and measured and divided by abstract units rather than by lived human experience. But while their literature reveals that nineteenth-century Americans considered themselves and their nation to be a "particularly modern place," American life maintained competing and complementary cycles of mechanized, natural, historical, and religious time and timekeeping (Allen 2008, 1–2). But regardless of the continuity of traditional temporal rhythms, as long as some people needed to reckon time more precisely, things like alarm clocks became popular and then necessary.

Seth E. Thomas, whose father founded the Seth Thomas Clock Company of Thomaston, Connecticut, patented the first mechanical alarm clock in 1876 (Thomas 1876). The Charnley House alarm clock—though far too damaged to discern its exact make and model—is a "tin-can" type manufactured by American and German firms (Israel 1993, 457). It would have been wound from a key at the back, with a spring-driven hammer sounding the interior of the single bell on its top. An 1885 advertisement from "The Fair" department store of Chicago—its name again linking department stores to the expositions that likewise presented endless consumer choices (see chapter 5)—lists a Seth Thomas Clock with an alarm for two dollars (*Chicago Tribune* 1885, 1).

While some may have had the financial means and need to purchase their own alarm clock, other Chicagoans—even into the twentieth century—employed human means for timely wakening. In an 1895 example from Chicago, a man, Patsy, served as one of these "animated alarms clocks," going from door to door with a stick, knocking until they awakened the people who hired them (*Chicago Tribune* 1895b: 42). Fifteen years later, there was still a man who worked in Chicago as a "human alarm clock" (Tarrisse 1910, E3). This slow adaptation to "modern" ways of keeping time may have been unexpected for tourists witnessing the array of public clocks atop fair structures (e.g., the U.S. Government Building) as well as exhibits of personal timepieces by companies in the Manufacturers and Liberal Arts Building (McCrossen 2013, 145–46). Certainly the modern temporalities of the Charnley House—kept by modern alarm clocks in a deceptively modern-appearing home—would have fit very well into the exhibit spaces of the 1893 Chicago fair. And yet years after the show of modern timekeeping at the 1893 fair, not everyone had the need for or access to personal timekeeping artifacts.

Conclusion

At the fair's subdued closing ceremonies, held days after the October 28 assassination of Mayor Carter Harrison, a local pastor addressed what was called the "approaching death" of the exposition: "We are turning our backs upon the fairest dream of civilization, and are about to consign it to the dust. It is like the death of a dear friend. . . . There is a call upon each one of us now. . . . It bids us to appropriate to ourselves the imperishable parts of this high feast and of the arts, industries, and sciences, and so embalm them in memory's treasure house that they may be best preserved and produce the largest fruits in generations to come" (Barrow, quoted in Higinbotham 1898, 277). But the material presence of the White City and the Midway Plaisance, as in the case of all the other great fairs and exhibitions, was produced with the intention that it would vanish.

By January 1894 another American fair opened, supplanting the World's Columbian Exposition: the San Francisco Midwinter International Exposition, held in Golden Gate Park through July 1894. What time, nature, and human destruction did not do to remove Jackson Park's White City from the frontlines of the modern imagination, modernity's progressive pace and the desire for the new did. In 1901 in Buffalo, in 1904 in St. Louis, in 1915 in San Francisco, and again and again, each temporary city was superseded by the novelty of a newer, more brilliant, more modern one.

On January 8, 1894, less than three months after the close of the fair, fire destroyed the Peristyle, the Music Hall, and the Casino and damaged the roof of the Manufactures and Liberal Arts Building (Gregerson 1996). The White City, a site so immense and so beautifully planned that it rivaled most permanent cities in the United States, was no more. Yet the 1893 World's Fair, as part of collective imagination, is still abundantly found today—not least because of Erik Larson's bestselling *The Devil in the White City* (2003). Rather than a "city for a single summer," the fair was all the cities ever in existence and all those that would come to be.

The next great Chicago fair—the 1933–34 Exposition of Progress—contained a statement on time and temporalities in its very title. In showing the progress Chicago had made since its incorporation as a city in 1833, the planners also chose to show what the future domestic spaces could look like with a series of model homes set on the fairgrounds. George Keck's twelve-sided glass and steel House of Tomorrow and eleven other homes demonstrated future-oriented technologies and domestic spaces by their very building materials, infrastructure, and architectural aesthetic (Schrenk 2007). Still, Keck's House of Tomorrow had a traditional upper-middle-class domestic interior, including a grand piano (Upton 1998, 179). Such displays were a temporal inversion of the 1893 fair's architecturally traditional state buildings with state-of-the-art utilities within them. Dell Upton notes of this temporal confusion in the 1933–34 fair structures: "Who could tell where today left off and tomorrow began?" (Upton 1998, 180). Such a question should also be asked of the 1893 fair and the Charnley House. The following chapter continues this attention to the ideologies made material in the fair's Ohio Building and Charnley House, turning to an exploration of domesticity and domestic spaces within the houses at the heart of the volume.

4

Domesticity and Social Life

In 1918 Redmond and Marion Stephens were embroiled in a bitter divorce. They had been living at the Charnley House, first as renters in 1906 and then as owners in 1911. Redmond was a successful lawyer. Marion was active in the Chicago social scene, with her sartorial choices and social engagements regularly covered in Chicago society pages. One especially unique mention during their time on Astor Street involves a daring 1911 airplane ride that Marion and a friend took, notably "without the consent of their husbands" (*Chicago Tribune* 1911, 1). At the divorce hearing, Redmond Stephens told the court: "For three years we were happy—serenely happy. . . . And then I desired to settle down. But Marion wanted to travel. *The house on Astor street could not hold her interest,* and she was away four or five months of every year" (*Chicago Tribune* 1918c, 15, emphasis added). The house on Astor Street, despite its architectural pedigree from Sullivan and Wright and regardless of its beautiful modern spatial flow and aesthetic, was still, after all, just a house. The Stephenses were granted their divorce and soon afterward sold their Chicago home.

Today the headquarters for the Society of Architectural Historians as well as an operating museum, the Charnley-Persky House was created, modified, and even partly demolished by the people who designed, lived, and worked within its walls. With its lack of architectural ornament and flowing floor plan, the Charnley House was arguably the "first modern house," as Frank Lloyd Wright purportedly termed it. It had gas and electrical lighting, central heating, and running water in multiple bathrooms—itself a very modern spatial arrangement. But even within the modern spaces, the live-in servants of the house used a back staircase that concealed and hid them as they performed their domestic labor. Having servants do their work unobtrusively as supported by the design of the built environment was definitely not a new or "modern" way of organizing domestic labor, as might befit a "modern" home, and such hidden household labor was characteristic of early industrialized households (Cromley 2004, 122–23). At the turn of the twentieth century, someone chose to throw out their household garbage—thousands of pounds, out of which over twenty-eight thousand artifacts were recovered via excavation—against the back of the Charnley House, an act nothing like the hygienic garbage disposal practices of the future on display at the World's Fair (Morse 1893; also see chapter 5 for this discussion of "conspicuous disposal"). Despite the well-studied architectural significance of the Charnley House, questions remain about the lives of the Charnleys and the subsequent renters and owners of the modern house on Astor Street; significantly, what meaning did they take from living in this structure on Chicago's Gold Coast?

Likewise, despite the massive number of academic and nonacademic works on the 1893 World's Columbian Exposition, questions have not really been raised about the uses of the Ohio Building and other nonmonumental and quasi-domestic structures of the World's Fair by the people who visited and lived within them, nor have their meanings been interrogated. As Matthew Johnson notes in his book on vernacular English houses, "houses are about human beings. Architecture is a human creation, the medium and outcome of people acting on their surroundings" (Johnson 2010, 2). I derive inspiration from Johnson's "bottom-up" rather than "top-down" approach to vernacular architecture, where he calls for returning agency to the builders and inhabitants of the houses and considering how they lived and changed within the homes (Johnson 2010, 194).

The Charnley House and the Ohio Building are not vernacular but "academic" works created by professional architects, and thus much attention and agency had been given to the "builders" but not the "dwellers"—the owners, renters, servants, tourists—of these structures. Putting the focus back upon the people who lived in the homes makes possible a claim that comes as no surprise to archaeologists but may be secondary to those solely concerned with aesthetic studies of the Charnley House and the World's Fair: *"The one true end of the study of old houses is to understand something of the ways of life and systems of thought of their builders, owners, and users*" (Johnson 2010, 3, emphasis in original). The architecture is a part, but not the totality, of the meaning in these structures; they need to be peopled to be homes.

Houses are more than architecture: they can be and can make social worlds. Within the spaces of the home and through the constitution of the household itself, the "cultural consciousness and notions of personhood are initially forged" (Beaudry 2004, 254). Comparing the Charnley House and the Ohio Building—architecturally, materially, and socially—provides an entry point to seek out the ideologies of these social worlds. How did the built environment of the old-fashioned "senseless reversion" (Wright, Kaufmann, and Raeburn 1960, 29) of the Beaux-Arts Ohio Building and the modern-styled Charnley House impact human experiences of space and place? Did these notions of "home" change with modernizing infrastructure and technology and sets of associated practices? How do we integrate and account for the all-too-typical narrative absences of the non-elite women and men whose working lives took place within these households, who made the seamless experiences of modern domesticity possible?

By examining the concept of home and ideologies of domesticity at the turn of the twentieth century, this chapter focuses the people who lived and worked in the infrastructurally modern Ohio Building and the "modern" Charnley House. And, even while focusing on the "dwellers" instead of the architect builders, experiences of servants need to be included. Here mentions of servants are found in limited ways in the U.S. census for the Charnley House, but such mentions are absent (save one mention) in fair accounts of the Ohio Building. Through this lens of domesticity and attention to peoples' social lives, the longer and enduring life history of the Charnley House contrasts with the ephemeral existence and occupation of the Ohio Building, although in many ways the two structures and their meanings made within them are startlingly alike.

Ideologies of Domesticity

There exists a substantial literature on modern, Western ideas of the home, often with a focus on the home's transformation from a site of production to a domestic, private site (see Thompson 1967). Industrialization moved production from the home workshop to the factory. Previous to that shift, the Western Anglo household *was* society, serving "functions of home, factory, school and welfare institution" (Strasser 1982, 5). As with that economic change, so too did social relations change, oftentimes creating, for example, distinct male and female spheres of influence and work and a "cult of domesticity" to ideologically maintain such boundaries (Wright 1980, 97). This domesticity, understood as "a set of norms for family life, centered on the perceived dichotomy between the private household and the world beyond the boundaries of each family's private space," is often interpreted via the built environment of the home and its furnishings (Grier 1992, 53). Yet the lived experiences of people in American homes at the turn of the twentieth century and their acceptance or rejection of ideologies of domesticity are too complex to reduce to a binary of male or female, or upper or lower class, or any other simple dichotomies. Mary Beaudry rightly cautions that "a too-ready acceptance of the nineteenth-century ideology of separate spheres leads as well to a too-ready reification of that ideology through archaeological analysis" (Beaudry 2004, 260). Archaeological research has shown again and again that the gender boundaries that were professed via ideology were not experienced in social relations or their "spatial correlates" (Rotman 2007, 94). These spatial correlates were often segregated and experienced instead along class lines, for example, upstairs (ruling class social and personal spaces) versus downstairs (domestic work areas), or, as Cromley argued regarding the Charnley House specifically, a separated "food axis" of service-oriented rooms (kitchens, pantries, dining rooms) that made a physical barrier between those serving and those being served (Cromley 2012, 19).

Moreover, the end of the use cycle of goods within a household—the final deposition of its garbage—consists of materials from men, women, children, servants, homeowners, boarder, and renters, comingled and without the physical separation that may have characterized the human actors while they used the items (Strasser 2000, 6; also see chapter 5). Each individual artifact may have been used and handled by multiple members of a household across classes, as in the case of domestic ceramics, where "they were also washed, dried, used, served, and broken by the domestics who lived and worked there," making a designation of "class" an inaccurate proxy for what are really relations across and between classes within a household (Wurst 1999, 14).

Still, particularly in the early to mid-nineteenth century, the home was widely conceived of as both a physical structure and a profoundly important imaginary. It was simultaneously perceived in architectonic and in moral terms. For many, creating a home—the building, its furnishings, and the activities hosted within it—"consumes a significant proportion of individual's incomes, preoccupies their day-dreams and their leisure time" (Chapman and Hockey 1999, xi), which again points to the home's importance as a unit of analysis. In his overview of American architecture, Dell Upton notes that "Americans are obsessed with houses—their own and everyone else's. We judge ourselves and our neighbours by where and how we live. We categorize the poorest members of contemporary society not as hungry, badly dressed, or unemployed, but as 'homeless'" (Upton 1998, 17). Some scholars argue that the "emotional resonance" (Motz 1988, 1) of the concept "home" distinguishes this period, with others claiming that the idea of home operated as the primary symbol in American lives during that time (Wright 1980, 45).

The documentary record of the nineteenth century portrays the job of making a house into a "home" as a transmutation: an alchemical process that is glorified in much of the literature from the mid-nineteenth century onward. The most famous manual to broadcast these ideologies was Catharine E. Beecher and Harriet Beecher Stowe's *The American Woman's Home* (1869), which sold an unprecedented number of copies upon its initial publication and remains in print to this day. The dedication to the book reads: "To the Women of America, in whose hands rest the real destinies of the republic, as moulded by the early training and preserved amid the mature influences of home" (Beecher, Stowe, and Tonkovich [1869] 2002). Like their famous predecessor on all things domestic, Isabella Beeton (1861), Beecher and Stowe preached that a particular set of practices, like preparing and consuming healthful foods, cleanliness, frugality, and the proper training of household servants, would result in societal (and, for them, Christian) salvation.

Such magical thinking, abundant in the nineteenth-century domestic handbooks, does powerful ideological work by placing women and their reproductive work inside the home and male productive work outside it. The powerful, but not totalizing, reception of these messages becomes clear when considering the suite of dining practices performed by the emerging American middle-class. Diana Wall's work on ceramic assemblages from two middle-class homes in mid-nineteenth-century New York shows how the "mistresses of middle-class households" controlled and shaped domestic life. With their homes and workplaces no longer integrated, middle-class women used and procured certain categories and styles of ceramics to further notions of gentility and the inviolability of the feminized domestic sphere (Wall 1991, 70). Middle-class women made the consumption of meals in the home "sacred" by selecting plain Gothic Revival ironstone tableware to be used in dining rooms with Gothic-style furniture, thereby visually, ritually, and ideologically extending Christian notions of sanctity and community to family (Wall 1991, 78; Williams 1996, 65–67). Their use of elaborate teaware for nonfamilial social gatherings, on the other hand, allowed women to "secularly" socialize with their peers while remaining safely within feminine spaces (Wall 1991).

Just as American women were "molded" via proper feminine domestic practices, so did industrialization transform the physical home with new technologies. In her book on the transformations of households and housework through technologies, Ruth Schwartz Cowan notes, like Robert Staughton Lynd and Helen Merrell Lynd in Middletown (1929), that the pace of this transformation was uneven. Some experienced gradual transformations generation by generation. For the rest, "the transition was more rapid; in these families, as the result of immigration or urbanization or sudden affluence, one generation of people may have been living and working in conditions that would have been familiar in the Middle Ages, and the very next generation may have been completely modernized— inhabitants, as it were, of a totally different world" (Cowan 1983, 3). By the late nineteenth century, technological changes like indoor plumbing, mechanized washing machines, or enclosed stoves altered the homes of urban white elites and middle-class Americans, with people from rural areas, the working class, and those from nonwhite backgrounds gaining access to these technologies far later into the twentieth century. While the notion of a nineteenth-century feminine domestic sphere as separate from masculine industrial workplaces may retain ideological weight, the technological changes with houses show that the house itself was equally industrializing and equally part of the mode of production (Cowan 1983, 4).

Even the decoration and layout of Chicago homes shifted between 1873 and 1913 from "an exuberant, highly personalized display of irregular shapes, picturesque contrasts, and varieties of ornament, supposedly symbolizing the uniqueness of the family, to a restrained and simple dwelling, with interest focused on its scientifically arranged kitchen" (Wright 1980, 3). Archaeologically recovered evidence of domestic material culture—utilitarian and decorative—as well as technological and infrastructural materials should be used to interpret these changes rather than relying solely on the personal documentary records of the individual householders who may not have deliberately recorded their mundane, quotidian experiences.

The Ohio Building and the Charnley House were built by 1893, a time of transformation and transition in American households. For the 1893 World's Fair, the enterprise was supposed to demonstrate a future ideal city through its rationally designed architectural program, but even more so through its futuristic exhibits—such as the scientific Rumford Kitchen sponsored by the Board of Lady Managers—as well as its "backstage" sanitary infrastructure that made the tourist experience so exceptional and so modern (Graff and Edwards 2018). Small state buildings such as the Ohio Building, however well visited and used by tourists, did not figure into this narrative. For the Charnley House, change was in the works in its very modern architectural style and the expectation that the lives lived within it would likewise take on a modern character, but how can one assess that without starting with the Charnleys? Considering the people of the vanished 1893 Ohio Building first, and then the former residents of the still-extant Charnley House, allows for the analysis of the social trends of the time from the now-populated "bottom up."

Social Life in an Ephemeral Home: The Ohio Building

Today the northern edge of Jackson Park contains an important remnant and reminder of the grand extent of the 1893 World's Columbian Exposition: the Museum of Science and Industry, which occupies the fair's former Palace of Fine Arts. Its monumental scale and elaborate Beaux-Arts architectural detail are the last aboveground reminders of what once filled Jackson Park. Yet this structure, occupying over 208,000 square feet (4.78 acres), was not nearly the largest at the fair and was encircled by the even smaller state and foreign government buildings (Bolotin and Laing 2002, 44). It was in this section of the fairground that tourists consumed the fair experiences in a very different manner than in the large exhibit halls or amid the thrills of the Midway Plaisance. A newspaper account of the state buildings from final month of the fair discussed these encounters: "Nowhere in the Fair grounds except at the State buildings is the social life of the visitors on exhibition. . . . It is only when he feels that he is covered by a roof he himself helped to provide, that he has a right to all the comforts by which he is surrounded, and that the good folk at his elbow are neighbors and friends—only then does he stand forth untrammeled, free, and careless" (*Chicago Tribune* 1893b, 33).

The intimate social experiences within these state buildings—often described as "clubhouses"—are not much represented in the official narratives of the fair. If the state buildings were mentioned at all, such descriptions were mostly superficial or dismissive. One architecture critic described the state buildings as a "higgledy-piggledy" result that were "strewn about promiscuously," a "pity and a misfortune" as compared to the rest of the fair (Schuyler 1893, 56). But was this what any other tourists at the fair thought about them?

Although many people—fair scholars, architectural historians, fans of *The Devil in the White City*—might heartily agree that there were far more interesting structures and events at the fair than its state buildings and the all-too-familiar social worlds within them, the connection to the primary symbol of the home underlines their ideological importance. The records of these spaces and the experiences within them are found in small and less visited or celebrated corners of the documentary record. And, as the Jackson Park Archaeological Project shows, the remnants of these buildings and the materials used by people within them have a profound material signature in the fair's archaeological record.

The state buildings, though small and architecturally unimportant, provide the spatial and experiential counterpoint to the monumental (e.g., the Manufactures and Liberal Arts Building), exhibitionary, (e.g., Boas's non-evolutionary exhibits in the Anthropology Building), and amusement (e.g., the Ferris wheel) structures of the fair, both in their scale and in their intended use. While the results of the 2008 Jackson Park excavation call for a discussion the smaller structures of the fair, the interrogation of the quasi-domesticity of the Ohio Building and its historical state building predecessors helps us more fully understand the overall meanings and object lessons of the fair.

Philadelphia 1876: State Buildings' Beginnings

It was at the 1876 Philadelphia Centennial Exhibition, the first large-scale American fair, that individual state buildings were first constructed. Located in the northwest corner of Philadelphia's Fairmount Park, twenty-four state buildings served as clubhouses for their citizens and provided a headquarters for each state's Centennial commissioner (Seyfert 2006, 9). At the Philadelphia fair, as in Chicago, the state of Ohio erected a building of its own.

Constructed from over twenty varieties of local Ohio stone, the 1876 Ohio Building was designed in a combination of Victorian Gothic revival, carpenter Gothic, and Eastlake (or stick) styles (Seyfert 2006). Each type of locally quarried stone used for the façade was duly carved with a label, creating an exhibit out of the building itself. These state buildings provided a unique opportunity to showcase the materials and industries of each state by dint of the very components from which they were constructed.

The interior space of the state buildings provided a space to present local wares and, in some cases, display small exhibits. For example, 1876 Ohio Building contained a geological map of Ohio created by the president of an Ohio college, a chandelier manufactured by the Marchand and Son Company of Cleveland, and several rocking chairs from Ohio's Delaware Chair Company (Ohio, Board of World's Fair Managers 1877, 23). Although most structures from that fair, like those that antedated it, were deliberately removed at the end of the event, today Philadelphia's Ohio Building remains in situ at the corner of Belmont and Montgomery Avenues, where it housed the Centennial Café through 2014.

With these state-produced building components, it takes no great logical leap to claim that one goal of state building design was to articulate or foster a distinct state identity that nevertheless nested within the larger national identity. While most states had additional exhibits in the main fair buildings (as they also did in 1893 Chicago), the state buildings were the only places at a fair in which the main focus of the tourist gaze was intentionally directed to the local or regional level. However, the rather bland description of the 1876 Ohio Building from a contemporary guidebook suggests the failure to bolster unique state identity and or even make it an exciting destination. The guidebook simply states, "The Ohio Building, which is a very neat and tasty edifice, [is] built of Dayton [Ohio] freestone" (Gilmore 1876, 13). While the provenance of its materials linked it to the state of Ohio—something one might have to read to know—nothing about its design or form suggested a distinctive Ohioan identity, and nothing else is mentioned in terms of public reception or use of it. Another guide also contains spare physical detail of the Ohio

Building—its building material making it the "most substantial of the State buildings"—but again this amounts to a detailed description of the Ohio quarries its stone blocks came from and not much else (Centennial Exposition 1876, 11). Importantly, the architectural materials rather than aspects of the social lives within the Ohio Building are what receive mention, and even this rather fleetingly.

State Buildings at the 1893 Chicago Fair

The more robust documentary and archaeological record of the 1893 Chicago fair provides greater insight into the ways that fair visitors used and thought about the state buildings. Formal rules and regulations for the state buildings of the 1893 fair shaped the way that these structures were designed, constructed, and used. Each state, territory, and the District of Columbia was entitled to its own building on the grounds of the fair if it could supply the funds. In 1893 there were forty-four states in the United States, and most states chose to construct individual buildings on the fairgrounds. The state delegations from Alabama, Georgia, Mississippi, Nevada, North Carolina, Oregon, and South Carolina did not construct their own buildings due to funding constraints, while the territories of New Mexico, Arizona, and Oklahoma built a joint structure, and the Utah territory constructed its own building.

The fair's director-general and its chief of the Bureau of Construction, Daniel Burnham, required states to submit their architectural plans for approval (Ohio, Board of World's Fair Managers 1891, 26). They submitted the plans to the landscape committee, and there the landscape architect Henry Sargent Codman, Frederick Law Olmsted's partner in Olmsted and Co., suggested a location; architect Charles B. Atwood "passed upon the architectural fitness of the designs presented by those who desired to build"; and Burnham himself meted out some degree of final approval (Burnham et al. 1989, 1:17). With the design approved, the fair agencies mandated that these small state buildings were "to be made of materials substantial enough for one season, but as inexpensive as possible" (Burnham et al. 1989, 1:36). In comparison to the main exhibit halls of the 1893 fair, the state buildings were small and designed by undistinguished architects. While a few were designed to architecturally evoke the specific character of their state—the California Building, for example, was constructed in the mission style—many others made do with the dominant

Figure 4.1. The Ohio Building at the 1893 World's Columbian Exposition. In Ives 1893.

neoclassical style of the main fair structures. This latter choice was the case for the Ohio Building, although there were some Ohioan architectural touches, such as the use of stucco buckeyes (nuts from the Ohio state tree) in the reception room's central decoration (*Chicago Tribune* 1893e, 26; figure 4.1).

The interior contents and attendant uses of the state buildings were also constrained by national regulations for the fair, effectively leaving space solely for their use as social hubs. State exhibits could not be competitive or showcase manufactured goods or products (Ohio, Board of World's Fair Managers 1891, 27). Unlike exhibits in the rest of the fair, there would be no chance of prizes and acclaim for state building displays. As a result, many state delegations decorated the interiors of their structures with small-scale displays of curios associated with the state. For example, Minnesota's building had "Indian relics and pipestone ornaments, a chandelier made of three elk heads and horns," while Iowa's building had a display of corn, and Ohio's contained "eight photographs of as many Columbus girls, each in Grecian robe and classic pose" (*Chicago Tribune* 1893b, 33).

The documentary record supports the practice of using the state buildings as clubhouses for the state's citizens. Wisconsin's state building—said to look like contemporaneous mansions on Milwaukee's Prospect Avenue—was a popular place for its citizens to rest and meet up with friends and neighbors (Cassell and Cassell 1984). Vermont's state building, constructed in the "Pompeian" style, was explicitly designed for use in "social purposes only" (*Chicago Tribune* 1893i, 10). Ohio tourist Alphonse Fischer decided to begin his trip to the fair by exploring all the state buildings, noting in his week-long journal of the fair that Michigan's building was "more of a club-house, or a Michigan mansion, comfortably fitted up with luxyurant [*sic*] furniture" (Fischer 1893, 10). In the world's fair novel *Sweet Clover: A Romance of the White City*, the state buildings are categorized as "dignified or dainty clubhouses" used as places for rest and socialization (Burnham 1894, 165). The novel provides glimpses of what was a common experience of the state buildings when a character visits the New York state building to rest in one of the wicker rocking chairs on its porch and, after resting, runs into a friend. Later another character goes into the New Jersey state building to rest on the "luxurious sofa" on the second floor—a similar characterization to what Fischer wrote of the Michigan building (Burnham 1894, 193–96; 354). Visitor guides to the fair buildings support this use recounted in the novel and journal: "In the northern portion of the Park the thirty State Buildings are all provided with refreshment rooms, many serving meals of elaborate character to those who care for them" (White and Igleheart 1893, 601). Although the Ohio Building is not visited by Fischer or by the fictitious characters of *Sweet Clover*, or even mentioned in the bulk of the travel guides, it nonetheless demonstrates a similar pattern of design and use as its more celebrated fellow fair structures.

Quasi-Domesticity in 1893 Ohio Building

A guide to Cincinnati, Ohio, and to the Chicago World's Fair—a strategic way of linking two spatially disparate locations—describes the Ohio State Building in the following way: "The Ohio building is colonial in style, two stories high, of wood and staff, with tile roof. The ground area is 100 feet front by 80 feet deep. The main entrance on the east side is within a semi-circular colonial portico, thirty-three feet high, the roof supported by eight great columns. The tile roof, mantels, finishing woods, and much of the visible material are the gift of Ohio producers" (Kenny 1893, 417). This description could easily match that of an upper-class residence of the era. The terra cotta roof tiles mentioned in the guidebook were manufactured in New Philadelphia, Ohio (Kenny 1893, 417), and were recovered in abundance in our 2008 excavation (in EUs 3, 4, and 5). This material was in fashion: terra cotta building materials, including tiles, drainpipes, and chimney pots, were regularly used for both public and commercial buildings in Great Britain and the other urban industrial nations from the 1870s on (Barker and Majewski 2006, 217).

The Ohio commissioners selected a group of Ohio architects to design the Ohio Building: James W. McLaughlin of Cincinnati, J. W. Yost of Columbus, George W. Rapp of Cincinnati, and F. A. Coburn of Cleveland. They ordered Ohio-produced building materials and furnishings including the terra cotta tiles from New Philadelphia. Unlike Ohio's stone 1876 structure, the exterior material of the 1893 Ohio Building was formed from wood covered with plaster staff in keeping with most structures of the White City (Ohio, Board of World's Fair Managers 1892, 3). However, a published list of building materials beyond the staff used in the structure includes durable stone, metal grates, ceramic tile, and art glass (Ohio, Board of World's Fair Managers and Alberson 1893, 7, 9; table 4.1). The art glass may have been used for a series of stained-glass windows, located in the upper story of the Ohio Building, that depicted the names of "the sixteen chief cities of the State" (Wade 1893a, 187).

A report from the board's secretary lists some of the furnishings bought to outfit the building (Ohio, Board of World's Fair Managers and Alberson 1893; table 4.2). The furnishings—tables, settees, rugs, pillows—would not be out of place in many domestic spaces, save for the letter case (a type of elaborate desk; Singleton and Sturgis 1916, 532) and the large number of

Table 4.1. Materials ordered for constructing the Ohio Building

Item Description	Cost (in 1892 dollars)	Cost (in 2017 dollars)
Art glass	824.73	22,900.00
Grates and tile	70.50	1,960.00
Stone	50.00	1,390.00
Total Expenses	**$945.23**	**$26,250.00**

Source: Data from Ohio, Board of World's Fair Managers and Alberson 1893. Cost in 2017 dollars is estimated from the Consumer Price Index (Measuring Worth 2018).

Table 4.2. Furnishings ordered for the Ohio Building

Item Description	Cost (in 1892 dollars)	Cost (in 2017 dollars)
Blankets	10.00	278.00
Blotters	9.29	258.00
Fire extinguishers (6)	150.00	4,170.00
Furniture (unspecified)	68.04	1,890.00
Furniture (unspecified)	253.40	7,040.00
General decoration	50.00	1,390.00
Letter case	150.00	4,170.00
Pillows, comforters, etc.	25.10	698.00
Rope	5.00	139.00
Rubber mats	30.00	834.00
Rugs	67.05	1,860.00
Settees (20)	120.00	3,330.00
Tables	28.80	800.00
Total Expenses	**$966.68**	**$26,857.00**

Source: Data from Ohio, Board of World's Fair Managers and Alberson 1893. Cost in 2017 dollars is estimated from the Consumer Price Index (Measuring Worth 2018).

fire extinguishers. Overall, the secretary of the Ohio Board of World's Fair Managers lists a total of $31,748.18 (calculated to $882,000 in 2017 dollars) in costs for the Ohio Building and its furnishings (Ohio, Board of World's Fair Managers and Alberson 1893, 12).

Unfortunately, the very members of the Ohio World's Fair Board who ostensibly procured these items for the Ohio Building later faced accusations that cast doubt on the documentary record of their purchases. They were charged with accepting salaries without actually completing any work and with embezzlement. One Ohio fair commissioner, not content to embezzle money, was accused of regularly stealing parts of lunches set aside for other employees of the fair and was reputed to scavenge and then eat "a dozen hard-boiled eggs at a sitting" (*New York Times* 1893, 24). More pertinent to the archaeological record than these gustatory crimes is the charge that exorbitant prices were paid for the furniture in the Ohio Building, with the unstated conclusion that some of these funds went into the pockets of the Ohio Commissioners rather than the coffers of tradesmen. Thus, a definitive inventory of the interior furnishings of the Ohio Building should not be extrapolated from the documentary record created directly by the suspect Ohio Board of World's Fair Commissioners.

The Ohio commissioners were not the only Ohioans who were supposed to procure materials to decorate the interiors of the Ohio Building. Members of the "leading cities" in Ohio took charge of furnishing individual rooms in the Ohio Building: Cincinnati (gentleman's parlor), Cleveland (room), Toledo (room), Columbus (Board of World's Fair Managers room), and Portsmouth (room) (Ohio, Board of World's Fair Managers and Ryan 1892, 30). To honor the theme of the exposition, the room furnished by the city of Columbus was decorated in "1492 style," with a mosaic floor stating "Columbus, Ohio, 1892–1492." This date configuration shows the emphasis on the imagined tie between the 1492 Columbian encounter and the imperial aspirations of the United States. Photographs of theses room show the furniture and small pieces of bric-a-brac like vases and small figurines, akin to the same examples of aspirational Victorian consumerism found in individual households (see Mullins 2004).

Even if the rooms' full contents are not verifiable, we do know the types of rooms and spaces that were built within the Ohio Building from other accounts. The building had facilities including "reception halls, Board of Manager's Room, Executive Commissioner's Room, ladies' public and private parlors, gentlemen's public and private parlors, smoking room, reading room, assembly room, post-office, railroad ticket office, information room, press room, check room with safes, and a room for the Ohio Propaganda Company" (Ohio, Board of World's Fair Managers 1892, 3). The "private" parlors refer to the building's toilet facilities. A version of the approved plan for the Ohio Building was published in the May 1892 issue of *Inland Architect* (figure 4.2), which provides a sense of the interior space of the first floor of the building. Here note the spatial separation and demarcation of rooms by gender, with four male-oriented rooms (Gentlemen's Parlor, Gent's Writing Room, Gent's Toilets, and a Smoking Room) and only two smaller female-oriented rooms (Ladies Parlor and Ladies Toilet). Moreover, the second-floor plans and room listings—the places where female servants surely lived—are not included in this publication

A guide to the fair is mostly in accord with the Ohio commissioners' account but additionally lists the significant rooms found on the second floor of the south wing: a servant's room, bed, and bathrooms. That servants clearly lived within the Ohio Building, within the fairgrounds generally, for the six months of the fair reinforces the quasi-domestic character of these small state buildings. The running and maintenance of an upper-class residence of the scale of the Ohio Building—and even as small

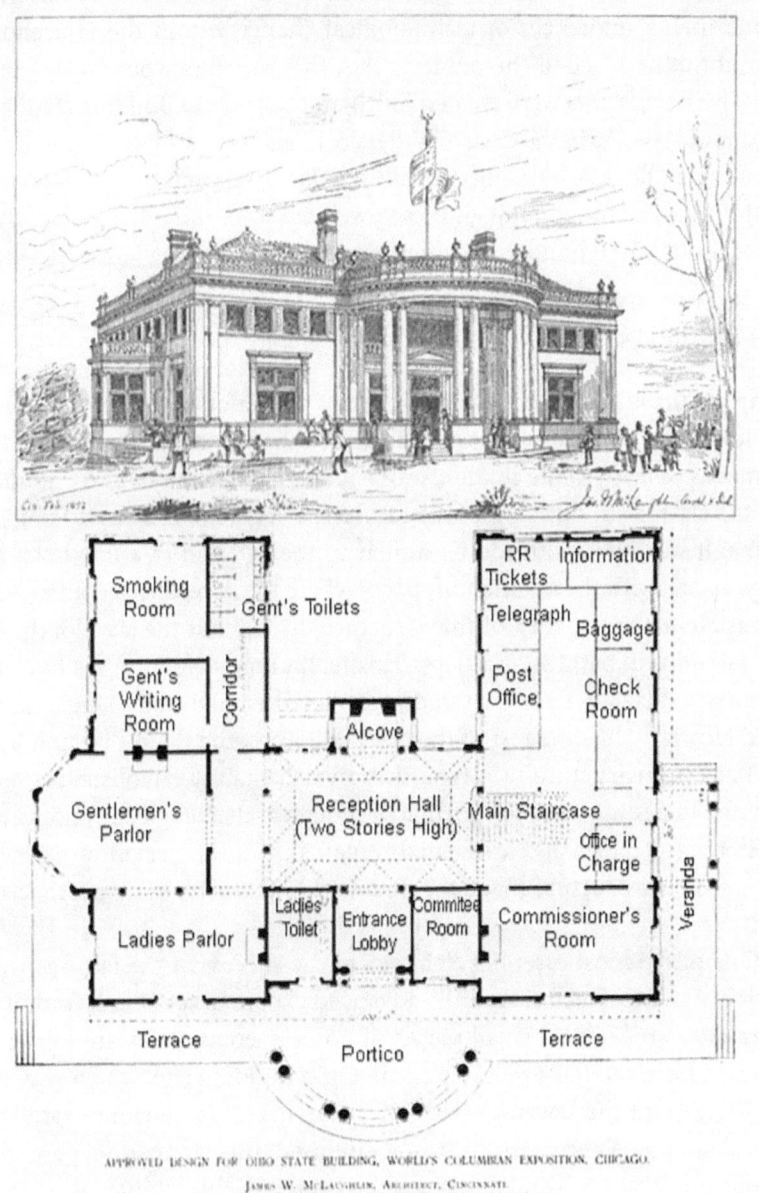

Figure 4.2. Approved design for the Ohio Building, World's Columbian Exposition, Chicago. Note that only the ground-floor rooms are shown. *Inland Architect and New Record*, May 1892. Illustration labeled by author.

as the Charnley House—would have necessitated domestic servants. The modernizing influences of technological change within the household had not quite reached the point in 1893 that servants would "live out;" thus, living quarters were created for them in the Ohio Building (Sutherland 1992, 251). As in the Charnley-Persky House or any of the upper-class homes that the state buildings visually emulated, servants proved essential to the seamless functioning of these dwellings even though notice of this labor is not often found in the documentary record of the fair.

The (White) Porcelain City

With luxurious furnishings and servants to maintain them, the Ohio Building was used in a quasi-domestic manner similar to many elite homes as well as an elite clubhouse or a grand hotel's lobby. Ohio's "home" for the six-month duration of the fair resembled a luxurious yet familiar home. It was filled with rooms similar to those found in a fine hotel or large estate, with the addition of spaces where the domestic servants—responsible for the upkeep of this structure throughout the six months of the fair—lived, bathed, and slept. This temporary structure was built as Burnham dictated: from materials substantial enough for a single summer. However, like the rest of the fair's buildings, the Ohio Building had sanitary infrastructure of a type that rivaled that of established urban centers. In addition to the ephemeral, though archaeologically enduring, plaster architecture and artifactual remains from the period of the fair, the fair's infrastructure made the memorable experiences of fair tourists possible.

One of the most essential elements to the success of the fair—as well as one of its most technologically advanced experiences—was its sanitary infrastructure. Several small pieces of porcelaneous stoneware were recovered from the fair-era levels of the Ohio Building site, which may be evidence from the sewerage and water systems. Also known as sanitary porcelain, porcelaneous stoneware is still used today to manufacture toilets in much of the United States; these vitreous china toilets were first manufactured in the 1890s, replacing the sanitary earthenware fixtures that were made beginning in the 1870s (Stone 1979, 286). Although these small fragments recovered from the excavation may not be from the Ohio Building's toilet facilities, the documentary record of the fair contains information on the extent, type, and spatial patterning of its toilet facilities.

Furthermore, the number of defunct sewer pipes found by our archaeological investigation of Jackson Park—and notably at the Ohio Building site—emphasize the massive infrastructural project that made the individual experience of new technologies possible and must have affected the perceptions of Ohio Building servants and tourists.

During the multiyear construction period of the fair, laborers could use only privies and earth closets while they lived and worked at the site (Burnham et al. 1989, 2:82). In contrast, fair tourists had access to both free and pay toilets throughout the fairgrounds, found within buildings and in freestanding restroom facilities. There were a total of 3,116 "water closets" at the fair: 2,221 installed and operated by the Clow Sanitary Company and the remaining 895 operated by different concessions and offices (Higinbotham 1898, 219–20). Of the Clow Company's 2,221 facilities, which were installed in thirty-two locations throughout the fairgrounds, 1,491 were free and 730 were pay toilets. One needed a five-cent ticket to access the pay toilets, which had, as a guidebook said, "better style and are better provided with toilet convenience" (Flinn 1893, 21) as they were "fitted up with expensive appliances and provided with soaps, towels, clothes brushes, attendants, etc." (Higinbotham 1898, 220). Such facilities were themselves an exhibit of the latest in sanitary services, and the detailed record keeping of the 1893 fair shows that 4,568,428 admission tickets were collected from those who experienced the Clow pay toilet "exhibit" (Burnham et al. 1989, 2:84). In contrast, toilets in the state buildings, like the Ohio Building, were always available free of charge (Flinn 1893, 22), perhaps making them preferred facilities for many fair tourists.

In the utopian White City of 1893, toilets were plentiful, often free to use, and eminently modern—a convenience that often stood in stark contrast to the daily experiences of many fair tourists, even in urban spaces of 1893 America. For example, an archaeological study of privy architecture in Louisville, Kentucky, emphasizes the uneven and slow switch from unplumbed privies to toilet facilities in American cities, with privies being used well into the 1930s (and out of compliance with local sanitation ordinances), in part because of the expense of installing costly plumbing infrastructure (Stottman 2000). This unevenness is also found in the famous sociological study of "Middletown," Indiana, where, in 1925, one in four homes still did not have running water, and their inhabitants would have continued to use privies (Lynd and Lynd 1929, 97). By looking at the trends in American sanitation at the time of the exposition, a toilet in the

Ohio Building reveals itself as part of the transformation of the city into an "arena of modernity" (Joyce 2003, 64).

City sewerage systems were not new to the nineteenth century, although the particular systems and related technologies used at the fair were. Historian Dominique Laporte, in *The History of Shit* (2000), reminds us that Sigmund Freud's three requirements of "civilization" were cleanliness, order, and beauty, which seem similar to the goals of the tenets of the World's Fair planners in creating the White City. Sewers were originally designed to remove storm water rather than human waste, and it was not until the mid-nineteenth century that sewers were developed for waste purposes (Melosi 2000, 22). This came about in part because of the successful implementation of water systems in urban areas. People still used cesspools and privies for their wastes, but the increased amount of water that now filled these areas—generally in the back of houses and apartments—proved too much for the existing "cesspool-privy vault-scavenger system" to mitigate. Another infrastructural technology was needed to eliminate the effluvia (Melosi 2000, 41).

Providing urban sanitary services like sewerage, water, and trash disposal is now considered the duty of a municipality's government, although this is a relatively recent development (Melosi 2000), as evidenced by the Charnley-Persky House's trash midden, discussed at length in chapter 5. This change in service came about through what Laporte calls "the politics of shit" (2000, 43) when, at least in Laporte's case study of the French Edict of 1539, political will came to affect intimate parts of human life. Borrowing from Michel Foucault's concept of a disciplinary society, Patrick Joyce sees the introduction of sewerage and water technologies into urban areas—material changes brought into being through liberal governmental structures or "the rule of freedom"—as the vehicles for social change, including the naturalization of a "sanitary economy" or "civic toilette" of the late nineteenth century (Joyce 2003, 65; see also Corbin 1986). Most strikingly, Joyce argues that personal conduct and social interactions similarly change through the introduction of new forms of sanitation, not in the least the "capacity to defecate in private" (2003, 12). The development of the "civic toilette"—"the cleaning, clearing, paving, draining and ventilating" of the city—becomes a key component of the modern urban experience, something Joyce sees as constitutive of liberal, political infrastructure (2003, 65, 70).

The structures of the White City—from small state buildings like Ohio to the largest building in the world, Manufactures and Liberal Arts—were monumental but ephemeral, constructed from cheap materials that needed to last mere months, yet the underground infrastructure of the White City was built as well as, if not better and more durably than, equivalent public works in American cities. While the much-lauded White City disappeared, the underground city of the Chicago fair never really vanished. It remains materially and archaeologically robust and enduring. Its existence and functioning behind the scenes played a key part in ensuring that the experiences of the fair might permanently transform those who visited it.

The revolution in urban sanitary and related technology experienced intimately within the Ohio Building and other spaces of the fair demonstrated that this robust and extensive "underground city" (Mumford 1961, 478–80; see also Melosi 2000, 8) was in many ways the essential transformative experience of the fair, although it was mediated by its consumption in the familiar quasi-domesticity of the Ohio Building. For the tourists to the 1893 World's Columbian Exposition, even those who already used similar yet very new technologies in urban centers, the experiences of the White City as a mandate for the future was aided by something as simple as the drip of a faucet, the flicker of an electric light, and, of course, the flush of a toilet.

It is not surprising that the tourist recollections of their time in the Ohio Building make no mention of their partaking in the toilet facilities; indeed, it would have been strange, given the social mores of the time, to find any usage so deliberately noted. Like the minimal documentary coverage of the homey social gatherings within the home-like Ohio Building, such documentary absences are met with material and archaeological presences. But the particular documentary record of the Charnley House—contemporaneous though more enduring—affords a different line of evidence with which to question the meanings of domesticity and domestic spaces in 1893 Chicago.

Social Life in an Enduring Home: The Charnley House

James and Helen Charnley lived in their architecturally significant home for only a decade before leaving it, and Chicago, behind. As discussed in chapter 2, James (1844–1905) and Helen (1854–1930) lived in Chicago, including in the Gold Coast, for several decades before they commissioned

Adler and Sullivan to design them a new, modern home on Astor Street. In contrast to the ephemeral Ohio Building, the enduring Charnley House was the domestic heart of its owners, renters, and laborers lives for over one hundred years, continuing through the present day.

In comparing the social life of the Charnleys and those who lived and worked within in the house on Astor Street in subsequent decades, the analytical lens for this domestic space is finer grained than for the Ohio Building. Not only does the Charnley House have a longer temporal duration with which to situate the histories and the material record of the site, the documentary record provides a more vivid accounting of social interactions there, although with some important absences remaining. The opening vignette of this chapter sets up the question: what sorts of social lives did people who lived in the Charnley House have? How, if at all, did these residents' webs of interactions reflect and instantiate preexisting elite connections? Where can we see exceptions or slippages in these moments (e.g., Marion Stephens)? And what does this indicate about changing ideas of the meanings of home and the cult of domesticity? While the next chapter looks more specifically at the *things* that these home dwellers discarded alongside the Charnley House, the people themselves take center stage here, much as the tourists who populated the White City's Ohio Building.

Social Life with the Charnleys

In comparison to many of their social peers, there is little documentation to flesh out the lives of the wealthy and socially prominent Charnley family. As noted in his chapter "The Elusive Charnleys," historian Richard Longstreth writes: "To date, no letters, diaries, or any other family papers have come to light. No clues indicate the Charnleys' intellectual inclinations, their taste in art or their leisure pursuits. Nor have any photographic or written accounts surfaced to suggest how the house was originally furnished or the particulars of its use" (2004, 4). Contrast this with Chicago's Glessner family, whose former home is also a local museum (the Glessner House Museum). In their case, not only a gift of the original contents but also photographs by son George Glessner allowed museum specialists to reconstitute the original décor of the house (Glessner House Museum n.d.). But in the last few years Charnley family photographs as well as correspondence have surfaced, much of the latter due in part to research in Chicago and in Connecticut by Jack Brown, former director of the Ryerson & Burnham Libraries.

There are some mentions of Charnley family social activities available in the society columns of the *Chicago Tribune* that confirm their place within the Chicago elite of the turn of the twentieth century. In 1892 Helen served as adjunct hostess for a seven-hundred-person reception that included the most prominent Chicago citizens (the Potter Palmers, Marshall Fieldses, Carter Harrisons, etc.) as guests (*Chicago Tribune* 1892a, 4). Further society page mentions include Helen giving a tea in December 1895 (*Chicago Tribune* 1895a, 4), a "young people's card party" in December 1896 (*Chicago Tribune* 1896, 9), and a party for son Douglas on December 31, 1896, whose guests included his Charnley cousins from across the street (*Chicago Tribune* 1897f, 7). In 1899 Helen held a reception at the Charnley House to introduce her niece, Nora Neef, to society (*Chicago Tribune* 1899a, 42) and a month later cohosted a New Year's Day "At-Home" reception with her sister, Annie Douglas Neef (later Harley-Brown) (*Chicago Tribune* 1899b, 35). The columns also note James and Helen's travel, such as a trip they took to New York and then on a steamship to Southampton on February 10, 1897 (*Chicago Tribune* 1897c, 3).

While the mentions of these scattered activities are less numerous than those of other elite families whose personal diaries and other effects were saved and willed to local archives, this still establishes that the Charnleys were not quite as silent in the documentary record as previously claimed. But many speculate that the 1897 scandal that rocked the family may be part of the reason for the decrease in documented public happenings and their slow withdrawal from the Chicago social scene.

Charnley Family Scandal (1897)

Charles Meigs Charnley (1845–1931), younger brother and erstwhile business partner of James, lived for a time with his family across the street from the Charnley House at 50 E. Schiller (formerly 309 Schiller). Like James a graduate of Yale University (class of 1865), Charles moved to Chicago and reported himself a lumber merchant in the 1880 U.S. census. In 1870 he married his first wife, Louisa Edelston Averill, in Chicago. The couple had four children—Charles Jr., James Jr., Louis, and Constance. Louisa died in 1893 in Pasadena, California, where the family had relocated in the winter for the warmer climate (*Chicago Tribune* 1893h, 7). In addition to his business responsibilities, Charles served as the Treasurer of the Presbyterian Board of Aid for Colleges and Academies and the Benevolent Fund of the Fourth Presbyterian Church in Chicago. He had served in these positions since the early 1880s and received some small compensation for this work (Brown 2016, 5).

Charles's main business, the American Cooperage Company of Baton Rouge, Louisiana, was destroyed by fire in 1894, which dealt a serious blow to his finances (*Chicago Tribune* 1897h, 5). Shortly thereafter Charles and the rest of his family—including his second wife, Ellen Mills Averill (niece of his first wife), and his son, James Charnley Jr.—moved in with James, Helen, and Douglas at the Charnley House on Astor Street. This move was hastened by their unpaid rent at the Schiller property (*Chicago Tribune* 1897e, 3).

In 1897 Charles embezzled about $115,000 from the Fourth Presbyterian Church, causing an estimated sixty church-supported institutions to suffer or close (*Chicago Tribune* 1897a, 1). After being confronted by the church's board, and even with a detective monitoring him, Charles and Ellen skipped town on September 1 (*Chicago Tribune* 1897g, 9). The American Surety Company hired private detectives to find the couple, but they had no success (*Chicago Tribune* 1897d, 10).

In the midst of the scandal, James Charnley Jr. (1876–1897), Charles's son, went missing; in November he was discovered dead by suicide in Milwaukee, Wisconsin's Pfister Hotel (*Alton Telegraph* 1897, 1). Douglas Charnley brought James's body back to Chicago, and the family interred James Jr. in Graceland Cemetery (*Chicago Tribune* 1897b, 4). The following June, another son, Charles M. Charnley Jr. (1873–1898), committed suicide in Los Angeles (*Chicago Tribune* 1898a, 4). That two of Charles Charnley's four children died so soon after his embezzlement scandal and disappearance suggests the terrible impact of the crime on his family, which may have also impacted James and Helen.

Recent documentary research by historian Jack Brown uncovered the end of Charles Charnley's sordid trail. While still a fugitive, Charles continued to have himself listed in the 1904 edition of the *Directory of the Living Graduates of Yale University*, suggesting that he continued to be in touch with people at his alma mater (1904). Through this collegiate connection, Brown located Charles and Ellen in Canada and then eventually in Gainesville, Georgia, where they had been living under assumed names. Charles died in 1931 and Ellen followed in 1932 (Brown 2016). Still, the effect of the scandal on the Charnley family—James, Helen, and Douglas as well as their direct descendants—is difficult to know but must have been significant within such the tightly surveilled and monitored social sphere of Chicago. SAH comptroller Beth Eifrig located an 1898 real estate ad that lists the Charnley House for sale: "New 2-story brick house/address C.E., 99 Astor-st" (*Chicago Tribune* 1898b, 22). The timing suggests that James and Helen may have put their 99 Astor Street home on the market because of the scandal, although the Charnleys continued to reside on Astor Street for four more years.

The Charnleys after Astor Street

Even though they stayed in Chicago throughout their family's scandal, James and Helen left Astor Street in 1902 for another reason: health. James was diagnosed with Bright's disease in the 1890s, and a standard treatment for it was moving to a warmer climate. In 1902 the family left Chicago and eventually settled (after a brief residency in Santa Barbara, California) in Camden, South Carolina, where James Charnley died on February 11, 1905; almost nothing is known about the Charnley family's time in South Carolina.

Rather than return to Chicago or remain in South Carolina after James's death, Helen and Douglas moved to Europe. Over the years they resided in England, Italy, Switzerland, and France (NARA 1921). While living in Europe, Douglas served in World War I as a member of the Red Cross in Italy and received several medals for his service. Douglas died in Gardone Riviera, Lombardy, Italy, in 1927, the same year he married Renée Canu (b. 1887). He is buried in Montreux-Clarens, Switzerland (Yale Obituary Record 1928, 143–44). According to a report from the American Consular Service, Helen Charnley died from pneumonia at the Hotel Lausanne-Palace in Lausanne, Switzerland, on January 4, 1930. She, too, is buried in Montreux-Clarens, Switzerland. Her sister, Annie Douglas Neef Harley-Brown of Sussex, England, took her effects (NARA 1930). Of what Helen and Douglas did in the almost thirty years after they moved from Astor Street, few records remain. So whether they continued their familial and social connections in Chicago—to their Charnley and Douglas family relatives; to their friend, Louis Sullivan; to their peers with whom they socialized as captured in the society columns—is not known. Instead, the history of the Charnley House picks up with tenants and owners who lived and worked there after 1902.

An Intricate Social Web: Charnley House Tenants and Owners, 1902–1969

The Astor Street home did not stay vacant after the Charnleys left Chicago: it was first rented, then sold. The Charnleys may have been less socially active than their peers, but even with their relatively limited community involvement, some of the people they knew socially became their tenants on Astor Street. The first renters began living in the property while the Charnleys were in South Carolina: Joseph H. and Genevieve Winterbotham and their son and his wife (1903), Ogden and Marion McClurg (1905), and Redmond and Marion Stephens (1906–11 as renters, 1911–18 as owners; see table 4.3).

It is clear that the Charnleys personally knew these early tenants. A 1900 *Chicago Tribune* article describes a "bachelors' dance" hosted by Douglas Charnley, Stewart Patterson, and future tenant and eventual Charnley House owner Redmond Stephens. Future renter Joseph Winterbotham also attended the dance and was obviously a member of their social circle (*Chicago Tribune* 1900a, 7). Those tenants were also part of each other's social circles outside of their Charnley family connection, both before and after their time on Astor Street. For example, Genevieve (Joseph) Winterbotham would work for the war effort in Paris alongside Marion (Redmond) Stephens in 1918 (*Chicago Tribune* 1922b, 21).

The Charnley's intricate Gold Coast social web also included the Waller family, who purchased the Charnley House in 1918. The Charnleys and a possible branch of the same Waller family were socially involved, in part because they had been Gold Coast neighbors in the 1890s and the first years of the twentieth century. Douglas—along with Redmond Stephens—was an usher at the wedding of Nannine Waller (daughter of James Lees Waller and niece of William Waller of 40 East Bank Street) to Stewart Patterson in 1902 (*Chicago Tribune* 1902b, 37). The exact relationship of that branch of the Waller family with the James Breckinridge Waller Jr. family—whose family would live in the Charnley House for the longest duration—is not clear. Still, the Waller family members who

Table 4.3. Charnley House renters and owners

Name	Years	Type
James and Helen Charnley; Douglas Charnley	1892–1902	owner
Joseph H. and Genevieve Winterbotham and family	1902–4	renter
Odgen and Marion McClurg	1904–6	renter
Redmond and Marion Stephens	1906–11	renter
Redmond and Marion Stephens	1911–18	owner
James Breckinridge Waller Jr. and family	1918–20	owner
James Breckinridge Waller III and family	1920–49	owner
Nettie Johnson Waller (Mrs. James Waller III)	1949–69	owner
Hawley L. Smith Jr. and brothers (renters)	1969–79	owner
Lowell Wohlfeil	1979–86	owner
Skidmore, Owings and Merrill Foundation / Chicago Institute for Architecture and Urbanism	1986–94	owner
Seymour H. Persky	1994	renter
Seymour H. Persky	1995	owner
Society of Architectural Historians	1995–present	owner

bought the Charnley House in 1918 also owned the property adjacent to it beginning in 1892, so they were neighbors of a sort, either way (Bluestone 2004, 53–54).

What follows is an overview of the tenants and owners of the property in an effort to clarify the residential timeline of the property and potentially associate the midden materials with a particular resident. Much of this work was accomplished via an exploration of the *Chicago Blue Book*—a social register of the white elite of Chicago and its suburbs published annually by the Chicago Directory Company from 1885 to 1916. The *Lakeside Annual Directory of the City of Chicago* similarly provides information on these families and their businesses. An overview of the tenants was made in 1987 at the behest of Skidmore, Owings and Merrill (Barton 1987), but the purpose was to provide information on the interior and exterior architectural transformations that post-Charnley residents made to the house. As a result, its discussion of the men and women who called 1365 Astor Street home is not detailed.

The Winterbothams

The Winterbotham family arrived in Chicago in 1892 from Joliet, Illinois (Delliquadri 1994). By 1901 Joseph Humphrey (1851–1925) and Genevieve Baldwin (1853–1906) Winterbotham, along with two of their four children, Joseph Jr. (1878–1954) and Rue Winterbotham (later Carpenter, 1876–1931), lived at 15 Walton Place. Joseph Sr. along with his brother, John, ran their father's Joliet cooperage firm, Joseph H. Winterbotham and Sons (*Chicago Tribune* 1894a, 12). The following year, the family—now listed as "the Mr. and Mrs.," "Sr." and "Jr."—moved to the Charnley House. The family kept up their itinerant residential pattern in the same neighborhood. After leaving Astor Street, Joseph Jr. moved to 111 Walton while Joseph Sr. left for the Virginia Hotel at Ohio and Rush Streets. By 1906 both Joseph Winterbothams are residing at the Virginia Hotel, although at some point that year Joseph Jr. and his wife moved to 407 Superior Street (*Chicago Tribune* 1906a, I3.). Although their post-Astor Street lives are well recorded, what the Winterbothams thought of their time on Astor Street, however brief, is not captured in the historical record. The Winterbotham family is, however, known as patrons of the arts beginning in the decade after they left Astor Street. Rue Winterbotham Carpenter founded the Arts Club of Chicago in 1916 (Delliquadri 1994), and in 1921 Joseph Sr. gave fifty thousand dollars to the Art Institute of Chicago for the acquisition of thirty-five European paintings. Joseph Jr. donated paintings by Salvador Dalí and El Greco, and he continued to make financial donations (Delliquadri 1994). It is intriguing but only speculative to wonder if living in the Charnley House for a brief period affected their aesthetic sensibilities in the manner that Sullivan and Wright sought.

The McClurgs

Ogden Trevor McClurg (1878–1926), like James and Douglas Charnley, was a Yale graduate and moved in similar Chicago social circles as his landlords. He married Marion Ewen (1881–1909) in 1903 and worked in his father's publishing house (A. C. McClurg and Company) at the time of his residency of Astor Street (Longstreth 2004, 24; Barton 1987, 17). From publishing, McClurg turned his attention to his expanding real estate empire (he was key in the development of the Streeterville neighborhood), and he and Marion moved from Astor Street to 1444 Lake Shore Drive in 1906 (Barton 1987, 17). In 1908 Marion rented an apartment in

Colorado Springs, Colorado, to spend her winters, most likely for her health (*Chicago Tribune* 1908, 9). An accomplished yachtswoman and pilot who "mingled little in society," Marion died from tuberculosis in 1909 (*Chicago Tribune* 1909, 6). Both Ogden's and Marion's personal experiences while living on Astor Street, like those of the Winterbothams before them, are not documented.

The Stephens

Redmond Davis Stephens (1874–1931) and Marion Buckingham Ream (1877–1963) were married on February 18, 1903. They held their reception at Ream's family home at 1901 Prairie Avenue—interestingly for this overview, in the neighborhood that was Chicago's first "Gold Coast" (*Chicago Tribune* 1903a, 7). The couple moved to Stephens's "bachelor apartment" at 87 Rush Street, not far from the Charnley House (*Chicago Tribune* 1903b, 12). In 1906 the Stephens had moved into the Charnley House as renters, eventually purchasing the home in 1911. They are listed at that address from 1906 to 1916 in the *Chicago Blue Book* and continued to live there until 1918.

Perhaps reflecting their longer residential duration at the site, there is a larger amount of documentary evidence about Redmond and Marion Stephens while on Astor Street. Redmond was characterized as a "wealthy club member, society man, and athlete" (*Chicago Tribune* 1918c, 1). He worked at the law firm Scott, Bancroft, Lord, and Stephens—later Scott, Bancroft, Martin, and Stephens—and also served as president of the Chicago and Oak Park Elevated Railroad Company. Marion appeared quite frequently in the local papers, with her clothes and appearances at various balls and other social events noted and sometimes accompanied by photographs (*Chicago Tribune* 1907, 3; English 1911).

As noted in the opening to this chapter, the Stephens ended their marriage in 1918, with a final society note that Marion served as one of the patronesses at a ball for the Chicago Lying-In Hospital (*Chicago Tribune* 1918b, 11). After their contentious divorce, Marion went on to involve herself with the White Russian Fascist movement and its leader, Anastase Andreivitch Vonsiatsky (Providence College 2008). In 1922 she announced her impending marriage to a "Russian youth with whom she will pursue happiness in a workman's cottage" (*Chicago Tribune* 1922a, 2). That part of the change in her marital relations involved a move from an architecturally significant house in an elite neighborhood to a modest, working-class cottage emphasizes the ideological power of physical spaces of domesticity. Two years later and living in Washington, D.C., Redmond Stephens married Edna Davis Moore but does not seem to have intentionally changed his class status and political affiliation as Marion did (*Chicago Tribune* 1924, 15). In 1931, divorced from Moore, Redmond was killed by a train in French Lick, Indiana (*Chicago Tribune* 1931, 1). Despite the more detailed documentary history of the Stephens, there is an only one suggestion that the house on Astor Street figured profoundly in the Stephenses' lives. The newspaper account of the Stephenses' divorce that opened this chapter reported Redmond's lament that "the house on Astor street could not hold her interest" (*Chicago Tribune* 1918a: 15). Here the idea of the house stood in for Redmond and Marion's marriage, and her departure from it, her rejection of their marriage and her assigned role in the cult of domesticity.

The Wallers

In 1918 Stephens sold the house to real estate agent James Breckinridge Waller Jr. (1856–1920) and his family, whose descendants would live in the house for its longest period and would make the major modifications on the structure. James was born in Lexington, Kentucky but soon moved with his family to Chicago. His brother, Robert A. Waller (ca. 1850–99), was one of the earliest members of the 1893 World's Columbian Expositions governing board (Higinbotham 1898). He and his wife, Elizabeth Wallace Waller (d. 1919), had two children, James Breckinridge Waller III and Ellen Waller Borden (*Chicago Tribune* 1920, 1; Barton 1987, 24). As mentioned in chapter 2 to show the small and interconnected social sphere of these Chicagoans, note that Ellen divorced her first husband in 1924 and married John Alden Carpenter, who had previously been married to another Charnley House occupant, Rue Winterbotham (Barton 1987, 24). The 1920 census lists James Jr. (65) and his son, James III (34), at the Astor Street residence.

When Waller Jr. died in 1920, the Astor Street property went to James III (1888–1949) and his family. James III was a Chicago politician, real estate agent, and publisher. He had studied at Princeton and Harvard, joining the Illinois Bar in 1913 and entering Illinois politics as a Republican that same year, eventually becoming an alderman of the 43rd Ward (*Chicago Tribune* 1949, 1). James III married Sarah J. Given in 1925, and they had two children—James IV (1926–99) and Robert A. (b. 1928). The

1930 U.S. census lists James III, Sarah, and their two sons at the residence. By 1935 James III and Sarah had divorced, and James married Nettie Johnson Griffith Waller (1888–1976). The 1940 census lists James III; Nettie; Nettie's son, Harry P. Griffith (26; her other son, Robert, 21, is not listed) at the Charnley House. After James III's death, Nettie took full ownership of the property and lived there until 1969 (Barton 1987, 25).

The Wallers are notable for their radical architectural transformation of the Charnley House, but their connections with the block started long before their residence on Astor Street. In 1892 James B. Waller Jr. purchased part of the original Charnley lot—a fifty-foot section that the family subdivided soon after their 1890 purchase (see chapter 2; Bluestone 2004, 53–54). In 1897 he also purchased the twenty-five-foot lot immediately to the east of the Charnley House that had been originally sold in 1890 by the Charnleys to Sarah and Ephraim Otis, months after the purchase of the original property. But no one, neither the Otises nor the Wallers, built on that small lot, which currently serves as a driveway for the SAH as well as the site of the Charnley-Persky House Archaeological Project (see chapter 5). James Jr. constructed the Binderton Flats—a very modern, six-story elevator apartment building—to the east of the Otis lot in 1896–97 (Bluestone 2004, 58). Jenney and Mundie, one of five Chicago firms chosen to design the architecture at the 1893 World's Fair, planned the Binderton. Therefore, even before the Wallers moved into the Charnley House, they owned and used the land adjacent to it, including the eventual midden site.

In 1927 the Wallers built an enormous two-story addition at the southern end of the house. They also placed a door and windows on what had been intended as a party wall to the east and remodeled some of the original home's third floor rooms (Longstreth 2004, 25). This arrangement altered the spatial flow of the house. While the southern addition was demolished in the 1980s, some of the Waller alterations (e.g., a door placed into the party wall) persist within the architecture of the house to the present.

Transitions and Threats: Adaptive Reuse of the Charnley House, 1969–Present

After Nettie Waller moved, the Charnley House entered a new phase—one that would culminate in its current commercial use as office space and museum. From time to time, the house would regain tenants but never for very long. This situation, coupled with the fact that the manufacture dates of the items in the archaeological deposits from the Charnley-Persky House midden date into the Waller family's residence but not beyond, makes a detailed enumeration of the post-Waller era less pertinent to the questions of domesticity posed earlier. Nevertheless, what follows is a brief overview of the site into the present, to both acknowledge the totality of the documentary and archaeological record at the site and to emphasize the long temporal existence of the Charnley House as opposed to the ephemeral Ohio Building, which makes its analysis more like a typical domestic structure that endures beyond a six-month duration.

The Speculators, 1969–1986

In 1969 Hawley L. Smith Jr. and his brothers assumed the title to the Charnley House and to properties at 35, 37, 38, and 41 East Schiller Street, although they did not reside there. Smith, president of Pryor Computer Industries, planned to build a high-rise apartment building east of the Charnley House. During this period the Charnley House was not always empty. Some records of tenants are found serendipitously, such as in this *Chicago Tribune* article about the architectural significance of the Charnley House: "Mr. and Mrs. [Barbara] Bruno Pons of Paris have lived in Charnley House for one year while Pons is working as an international accounts executive for the J. Walter Thompson Co. advertising agency" (Bukro 1972, E11). In 1979 developer Lowell Wohlfeil (1937–96) purchased the property from Smith. He may have intended to raze or drastically modify the Charnley House to turn it into more profitable condominiums, as he did with similar properties in the area. However, a 1981 *Chicago Tribune* article describes Wohlfeil as "painstakingly restoring the Charnley House . . . as his eventual residence" (Brenner 1981, J22).

While these transactions surrounding the Charnley House were under way, the area of the Gold Coast was undergoing its own transition. Many of the townhomes and mansions were razed so that high-rise condominiums and apartment buildings could be constructed in the neighborhood. Even before 1950, when the Palmer Castle was demolished, the area transitioned from nineteenth-century mansions to multiunit construction. Still, there remain many landmarked examples of the architecture of the period amid the new. Public outcry (see Gapp 1974) may have helped to save the remaining structures.

Skidmore, Owings and Merrill, 1986–1994

In 1986 the famed architecture firm Skidmore, Owings and Merrill (SOM), designers of such notable structures as the John Hancock Center, bought the Charnley House from Wohlfeil and moved its offices into it. After working to restore the house and demolish the Waller-era additions, the firm used the house for its new Chicago Institute of Architecture and Urbanism (Saliga 2015; Skidmore, Owings and Merrill Foundation 1986). While residents, the firm commissioned an historic overview of the house and its residential history (see Barton 1987), with an emphasis on the way that previous owners modified the structure. During this time, SOM demolished the Waller extension and restored the house to its original footprint. After the SOM Foundation stopped its research program at the site, the house remained vacant from approximately 1992 to 1994 (Storch 1995).

Seymour H. Persky and the Society of Architectural Historians (SAH)

Philanthropist, preservationist, real estate investor, and attorney Seymour H. Persky (1922–2015) rented the Charnley House in 1994, purchasing it in 1995. Shortly thereafter he deeded it to the SAH to serve as its new headquarters, a condition of his purchase (Saliga 2015). Previously headquartered in Philadelphia, the SAH agreed to Persky's conditions and moved to their new location in 1995, adding the "-Persky" to the home's name to recognize his gift. Today the SAH continues to operate its headquarters in the Charnley-Persky House, an adaptive reuse of the space. Most Wednesdays and Saturdays, the home is open for tours, operating as a house museum. The brick-lined driveway to the east of the house, where the midden was located, provides enough parking for four cars and is used by SAH staff.

This enumeration takes us to the present-day social life of the Charnley House—a pattern likely to continue for the years to come as the learned society uses the home as office space. But rather than end things here, with a look at the middle- and upper-class men and women who owned or rented the Charnley House and the corporate groups that used it for offices, the people who labored within the structure deserve note. Unsurprisingly, there is again a glaring lack of attention to the servants of the Charnley House in most of the documentary record. This makes the assessment of both ideologies of domesticity and the material experience of those domestic spaces difficult, though not impossible, to assess.

Social Lives of Servants on Astor Street

Besides the relative paucity of documentary evidence about the lives of the Charnley family while living on Astor Street, there is the more typical lack of documentation about the men and women who worked as servants on Astor Street—even those who lived within the household and could have very well contributed to the large midden. This absence is striking since the 1870 census, which was the first to systematically record women's employment, showed that approximately half of all employed women in the United States were in domestic service (Cowan 1983, 120).

The 1900 census recorded those residing in the Charnley House's "mixed household of family, friends, and servants" (Bluestone 2004, 55). It lists James, Helen, and Douglas along with Helen Charnley's brother, John M. Douglas Jr. (b. 1860), a boarder named Paul Delano Hamlin (1873–1944), and the family's two live-in servants. Hamlin, like Douglas, was a class of 1896 graduate of Yale University. His close and familial relationship to the Charnleys is evident—he went to work for the Garden City Wire and Spring Company, the business owned by the Charnleys (Day 1907, 382), and when Hamlin got married in 1900, Douglas Charnley was his best man (*Chicago Tribune* 1900b, 16). The 1900 census captures a group of five adults served by two live-in servants in a home with only five bedrooms.

Originally from Sweden, the Charnley's servants, Annie Larson (b. 1874) and Hannah Carlson (b. 1870), would have occupied the small servant bedrooms on the third floor of the house (U.S. Census 1900; Barton 1987, 10). While only Larson and Carlson were recorded as living in their workplace, "the Charnleys may have employed additional servants such as a butler, cook, laundress, handyman, or coachman when their needs required it" (Cromley 2004, 122). Critically examining the historical record means understanding what was and was not included in government census documents, but having the basic demographic information on the Charnley's live-in staff allows a glimpse into the social and possibly material life on Astor Street.

In 1910 the census shows that Redmond and Marion Stephens employed three live-in servants: James Crawford (butler and/or servant, thirty-eight years old, from Scotland), Anna Holdfeld (nineteen, from Germany), and Marie Frederick (twenty-three years old, born in Illinois of German parents). A decade later James Jr. and James III Waller likewise employed three live-in servants: Rosina Gross (maid, seventy, from Germany), Wanda Winderman (waitress, thirty-four, from Germany), and Edith Owens (cook, forty-four, from Canada) (U.S. Census 1920). By 1930 James III, Sarah, their two sons employed Else Fleig (nurse, twenty, from Germany), Ezabelle Tulloch (cook, forty, from Scotland), and Ella Roe (maid, thirty). In 1940—the latest census publicly available—James and his second wife, Nettie, and her son employed John G. Hartley (houseman, fifty) and Marie Hartley (cook, thirty-seven).

The demographic data supplied by the census shows a couple of important patterns, although it is far too brief to be anything more than a microhistory without further longitudinal and aggregate analyses (e.g., Perkins 1987; Pooley 2009; see table 4.4). First, the national origin of the Astor Street servants changes across time, although until 1940 the majority of the servants employed in each household were white Northern Europeans, then replaced by white Americans. Second, their ages vary from nineteen to seventy, and only in 1940 were the domestic workers themselves part of their own legal domestic relationship: marriage. These data points do map to the overall trends in the United States during the first decades of the twentieth century, where single, white, immigrant women who lived in as servants gave way to married women (white and black) who worked as day labor in domestic spaces (Cowan 1983, 121–22).

While there are records of social lives of nineteenth-century servants in diaries, autobiographies, contemporary studies (e.g., Salmon 1897), and more recent sources (e.g., Katzman 1978; Strasser 1982; Dudden 1983), it is clear that "social life" as modeled by their employers was not possible for these servants. A 1902 *Chicago Tribune* article followed the efforts of a Wilmette (a wealthy suburb on Chicago's North Shore) women's group to find out why their female domestic workers "did not try to become cultured and educated." A servant, somewhat obviously, replied that they "had no opportunity, were not able to meet cultured people, had no home of their own and no privileges in the homes where they worked" (*Chicago Tribune* 1902a, 1). It would be left to union organizers, the growth of home economics, and flows of labor to and from sites of industrial labor to solve this element of the "servant problem" (Wright 1980, 150–70; Katzman 1978). Still, the ideological force of employing a domestic servant continued to be a source of middle-class identity into the twentieth century (Cowan 1983, 120).

Table 4.4. Employers and employees at the Charnley House 1900–1940, compiled from U.S. census data

Census Year	Family	Family Members and Boarders	Servants	Total people in household
1900	Charnley	James, Helen, and Douglas Charnley; John M. Douglas (Helen's brother); Paul Delano Hamlin (boarder and college friend of Douglas)	Annie Larson (servant, 26, from Sweden) and Hannah Carlson (servant, 30, from Sweden)	7
1910	Stephens	Redmond and Marion Stephens	James Crawford (butler and/or servant, 38, from Scotland), Anna Holdfeld (19, from Germany), and Marie Frederick (23, born in Illinois of German parents)	5
1920	Waller	James Jr. and James III Waller	Rosina Gross (maid, 70, from Germany), Wanda Winderman (waitress, 34, from Germany), and Edith Owens (cook, 44, from Canada)	5
1930	Waller	James III and Sarah Waller; James IV and Robert A. Waller (their sons)	Else Fleig (nurse, 20, from Germany), Ezabelle Tulloch (cook, 40, from Scotland), and Ella Roe (maid, 30, American)	7
1940	Waller	James III and Nettie Waller; Harry P. Griffith (Nettie's son from her first marriage)	John G. Hartley (houseman, 50, American) and Marie Hartley (cook, 37, American)	5

Conclusion

The overview of the men and women who lived and worked in the Charnley House from 1892 to the present shows an interesting parallel to the Ohio Building in several areas. In some ways the current uses of the Charnley-Persky House—as a domestic-appearing structure with a decidedly nondomestic work function as the headquarters for the SAH—is much closer to the 1893 uses of the Ohio Building. There World's Fair tourists could see both the architectural and furnishing achievements of the state of Ohio while socializing with other friends and neighbors, punctuating this by a free visit to modern toilet facilities segregated by gender, like many of the building's other rooms. Likewise, the days that the Charnley House Museum opens to the public for architectural tours means that tourists are allowed to enter the famous structure, look at its striking décor, perhaps avail themselves of the toilet facilities (here not segregated by gender), maybe stop at the gift shop for a souvenir, and think about the transformations of the 1890s and the present day.

Both sites maintain a parallel silence in their documentary records of the servants whose invisible work made it possible for these great houses to function as "homes" in the nineteenth and early twentieth centuries, promoting the ideologies of domesticity still so powerful today. Although I included the census data on the servants that was available for the Charnley House, there is not a comparable record yet found that provides information on the Ohio Building's domestic workers. And even if we had those names, ages, racial designations, and national origins for those women, that would still paint only a perfunctory picture of their identities and nothing of their experiences of working and living in these spaces.

So here the servants are, again, at the end—a note, an afterthought, although undergirding the entire domestic and literary exercise. It was through the results of their daily working lives that fair tourists and Charnley House occupants alike could effortlessly consume the experience of domesticity. And it was their hands that used and washed and ultimately disposed of the objects found within the Ohio Building ruins and the trash midden by the Charnley House. Marion Stephens would leave the house on Astor Street because, even with three live-in domestic laborers to do the dirty work, it was not enough to capture her interest, as would have been expected and proper for a woman of her class background. Within these moments of rupture, though, are spaces to look more closely at the things they left behind.

Fortunately, this parallel silence of the servants in both the Charnley House and the Ohio Building documentary records does not extend to the sites' archaeological records. Like the servants who were not much acknowledged but were nevertheless essential to a household's smooth functioning, the infrastructure of the Ohio Building and the garbage of the Charnley midden were unexamined but central to the successful experience of social life.

5

Consumption and Conspicuous Disposal

The materials recovered from the Charnley-Persky House Archaeological Project consist primarily of mass-produced consumer goods dating from 1880 to 1920. Of the over 150 identified brands found in that midden, many are perfumes and colognes. One of these—Mäurer and Wirtz's No. 4711 cologne—continues to be manufactured today. With an herbal-citrus fragrance consisting of notes of bergamot, neroli, lavender, and rosemary, the blend was already considered an "antique" fragrance at the turn of the twentieth century. With its recipe devised in 1792, No. 4711 cologne represents one of the oldest versions of "aqua mirabilis"—the formula for miraculous water that became what we know as "cologne," also called *wunderwasser* ("wonder waters") and later "Florida water" in the United States. The company initially marketed No. 4711 as a revitalizing drink or broth (1792: Mäurer and Wirtz, n.d.). Twentieth-century Americans developed a new, modern—and topical—use for this product. An advertisement in a 1913 edition of the *Chicago Tribune* suggest that uses of No. 4711 expanded with the new inventions and innovations of the day: "Used in the bath, on the handkerchief, after motoring or traveling, for the relief of headache, after shaving—it is wonderfully invigorating and refreshing" (1913, F13). Rather than being consumed in a warm broth as recommended in the eighteenth century, the advertisement suggests that No. 4711 be used as an aid to help the modern automobile passenger recover from a still new and bracing form of transportation. It is an old perfume but with a new, modern use.

At the height of Veblenian conspicuous consumption and the consumer revolution fomented by world's fairs, department stores, catalogs, and advertising, the residents of Chicago at the turn of the twentieth century had access to a large array of consumer goods from all over the globe, from Germany's aforementioned No. 4711 cologne to Canadian MacLaren's Imperial Cheese Company's cheddar to Chinese export porcelain dinnerware. Many of these items would have been debuted and introduced to national and international markets at the 1893 World's Columbian Exposition or its predecessor fairs. These and other consumer goods unearthed in the Charnley House and the Jackson Park archaeological excavations form an assemblage of material culture that can aid in our understanding of the ideologies and the materiality of the "modern" American, whether at home on Astor Street or at the fair.

However, the discovery of a large midden deposited against the entire rear length of the Charnley House (a total area of approximately 22 m × 3 m) complicates any straightforward identification of modernity and modern life with the experience of dwelling in this very modern home. Those who lived in the Charnley House consumed these goods behind a spare architectural façade and within an open-plan spatial arrangement of the "first modern house," but somehow this refuse (which has not been definitively associated with the Charnleys or later residents) was discarded right against their home. During what was heralded as a new age of rational, scientific, and hygienic urban life, this garbage was disposed of in a seemingly premodern manner. Even though archaeological evidence revealed that some of the refuse was burned, consider how this dump, surrounded by the mansions of Chicago's elite, must have smelled in the summer!

At the turn of the twentieth century, the elite Gold Coast residents did not have a modern system of refuse removal that fulfilled the sanitary future on display at the 1893 World's Fair. The fair's planners enacted a regime of daily removal of "all garbage, sewage sludge, waste, refuse, manure and the bodies of animals" to the far southeast corner of the fairgrounds where it was burned in the Engle Sanitary garbage cremator (Morse 1893, 316). Such an effort to keep the fairgrounds clear of the detritus of 27 million tourists was simultaneously a scientific way of removing trash and an exhibit of what the sanitary city of the future would be. The conditions that created the Charnley House midden seem at odds with the ideologies of modernity—especially modern sanitation—presented at the fair despite the house's proximity and its avowed modernity.

This chapter examines that beloved element of archaeological research: garbage. Its survey of garbage includes a look at the world's fair markets that brought new consumer goods into Chicago homes like the Charnley House; garbage contents and the consumption practices they index; and the spatial distribution and removal of garbage, drawing from both the Charnley House midden and the World's Fair Ohio Building's trench. Most importantly, I turn some focus away from the contents of garbage as a way to gain insight into consumption and consumers. Instead I consider the changing scales of garbage disposal practices—what I term "conspicuous disposal"—as an important hallmark of the turn of the twentieth century and one that we certainly continue to ponder in our urban centers today. Trashmaking (see Strasser 2000, 5)—not merely consuming—is the suitable critical lens for examining consumption in theorizing of modernity and constitution of subject.

World's Fairs as Sites of Consumption

Fairs as Marketplaces

With an audience of thousands, if not millions, from all over the globe, world's fairs were eminently suited for promoting a variety of transformational ideologies via their exhibits, including ones that concerned the necessity for expanding empires and building markets; the proper comportment for the working class; and ways to understand race and to racialize difference. The vehicles for such lessons were also the consumer goods on display. Through consumption of these mass-produced goods, emulative consumers might seek to cross class and status lines (e.g., Fitts 1999), racial boundaries (e.g., Mullins 1999), ethnic categories (e.g., Voss 2005), or all of the above via the "dominant group material culture" on display in and "translated" by fairs (Praetzellis, Praetzellis, and Brown 1988). As scholarship on consumption shows (e.g., Douglas and Isherwood 1979; Miller 1987; Mullins 2011), choosing to purchase one good or another—"shopping"—is "meaningful action" in the sense that it creates, informs, and mediates social relations in addition to or instead of a solely economic or utilitarian motivation (Cook, Yamin, and McCarthy 1996).

The late eighteenth- and early nineteenth-century English and French precursors to modern international fairs were explicitly instituted to develop markets and to sell goods. Beginning in 1760 the British Society for the Encouragement of Arts, Manufactures and Commerce held exhibitions of fine arts and manufactures, all shown to "edify" the society's members as well as "farmers, manufacturers and businessmen" in the general public (Greenhalgh 1988, 8). By 1837 the institution added the Mechanics Institutes, whose goal was to advance industry to those who attended the exhibitions (Greenhalgh 1988). In France the 1798 Exposition publique des produits de l'industrie française provided an immediate market for goods left over from revolutionary stockpiles to demonstrate that the French state was functioning well and to push for the mass acceptance of what was tremendous societal change—a sort of "propagandist ceremony of state" (Greenhalgh 1988; Wesemael 2001, 63). Subsequent French fairs began to incorporate instructive elements in their vast displays, still via the modality of consumption. Still further European countries instituted similar national fairs to those in England and in France, as did the United States, beginning in 1828 with a fair held in New York (Greenhalgh 1988, 9).

London's 1851 Crystal Palace Exhibition—the world's first modern fair—had over seventeen thousand displays that translated into hundreds of thousands of individual objects for people to see. Fairs were collections of consumer goods in the same way that zoos, botanical gardens, libraries, and museums serve to collect, present, and classify the world. At the 1867 Paris Exposition Universelle, fair planners decided that some of these objects should be accompanied by lessons, and thus they introduced a new classificatory scheme of "articles exhibited with the special object of improving the physical and moral condition of the people" (Giberti 2002, 11). Walter Benjamin, writing in the early twentieth century, saw this as a pedagogical injunction, characterizing world's fairs as "training schools" where "the masses, barred from consuming, learned empathy with exchange value. 'Look at everything; touch nothing'" (1999, 201). In effect, fair tourists were supposed to leave the fairs as transformed people, having feasted on the lessons on display at the fair in addition to Cracker Jack or Vienna Beef sausages. Fair visitors as well as those who did not visit the physical fair itself found themselves, shortly afterward, consuming, if not the ideologies on display, the very wares that the fair debuted, including new foods, household appliances, and hygienic products.

World's fairs were planned and financed by the business elite of a society, and it was this elite class who promoted consumerist ideologies at world's fairs. As in previous fairs, the 1893 Chicago fair relied on local businesspeople—particularly Potter and Bertha Palmer and other Gold Coast dwellers—to provide the additional capital and the organizational scaffolding, shaping a new course for American consumer experiences through their plans. Sometimes these individuals had very direct connections to the commodities at the fair. For example, John Alfred Lomax, president of the Chicago Consolidated Bottling Company, unsuccessfully ran for a seat on the World's Fair board of directors in 1890 (*Chicago Tribune* 1890, 2). His company bottled mineral water and soda as well as beer for local breweries (*Chicago Tribune* 1891a, 3). Although Lomax did not win the seat on the board that he desired, he gained some measure of financial success from the increased market of the fair, as indicated by the Chicago Consolidated Bottling Company bottles recovered from both the Charnley-Persky House and the Jackson Park archaeological projects. With so much of the fair marketplace created by elite business owners and merchants, how can we consider the messages consumers encountered therein?

Conspicuous Consumption and Fairs

It is not a coincidence that economist and social scientist Thorstein Veblen (1857–1929) produced his most famous work, *The Theory of the Leisure Class* (1899), while he lived in Chicago and taught steps away from the fair's Midway Plaisance. While a faculty member at the University of Chicago from 1892 to 1906, Veblen developed his socioeconomic theory by studying wealthy Chicagoans in their "everyday life, by direct observation or through common notoriety" (1899, vi), most notably, their consumer and leisure practices. Members of an elite nonlaboring class, the "leisure class," emerged as separate from the working class in his cultural evolutionary schema. The leisure class is so named because the act of abstaining from productive labor "is the conventional evidence of wealth and is therefore the conventional mark of social standing and this insistence on the meritoriousness of wealth leads to a more strenuous insistence on leisure" (1899, 41). Veblen's concept of "leisure" is not laziness but the "non-productive consumption of time," which is made possible by their capital accumulation, whether inherited or newly made (1899, 42). This is opposed to those classes who must engage in labor-intensive economic activities, such as industrial factory work, with little time for leisure. While some forms of leisure are more performative, such as "quasi-scholarly or quasi-artistic accomplishments" like knowing ancient Greek or having expertise in "domestic music and other household art" or "dress, furniture, and equipage," many are materially signaled and presented (1899, 45).

As members of the leisure class, elites engage in "conspicuous consumption," or the materially evident use of expensive goods. Veblen argued that, "since the consumption of these more excellent goods is an evidence of wealth, it becomes honorific; and conversely, the failure to consume in due quantity and quality becomes a mark of inferiority and demerit" (1899, 74). This performative consumption signaled the social status of the leisure class by providing the spectacle and material basis for one's prestige and reputation. Because this formulation of personal reputation is based on material forms, members of all social classes—even the "most abjectly poor"—can engage in conspicuous consumption to emulate the leisure class, to pursue their attendant status, and to gain their own reputability (1899, 85). Following Veblen, some scholars see nineteenth-century material consumption as an imitative, aspirational process: the upper class sets the dominant tastes, the middle class emulates them, and the working class consumes the visions of the middle class (e.g., Praetzellis et al. 1988).

World's fairs were the venues where the dominant tastes of the elite, as filtered by the middle class, could be "translated" for a larger public. The Philadelphia Centennial Exposition—the major American fair prior to the 1893 Chicago fair—contained exhibits displaying "material correlates of middle-class domesticity for review by groups as yet unassimilated and thus served as a model for such groups" (Praetzellis et al. 1988, 198). In this way the world's fair is "the cultural image of an elite" (Cawelti 1968, 319), but its envisioned consumers were middle- and working-class people. And with the dawn of modern advertising aided by refinements in print technologies, even after the actual fair concluded, the circulation of world's fairs catalogs forced assimilative "homogenizing processes" on racial, ethnic, and class identity via the consumption of advertised goods by the middle class (Praetzellis et al. 1988; Hardesty 1981). At the 1893 Chicago fair, the American Cereal Company created a large display of their new product, Quaker Oats. They also provided tourists with decorative souvenir booklets containing scenes of "modern grain farming, processing, and distribution," a new, more scientific way to consume one's breakfast than past practices (Strasser 1989, 163). In his study of San Francisco's 1915 Panama-Pacific Exposition, anthropologist Burton Benedict argued that in these moments, fairs could transform middle-class tastes: "people were to be educated about what to buy" via fair exhibits (Benedict 1983, 2).

Certainly, while some aspirational consumers may have viewed the exhibits at the Chicago fair with an eye to establishing or changing their class status, a unidirectional and simplistic interpretation of this process masks the real social relations of class within a capitalist system. The ideological claim that the purchase of a good or class of goods had the potential to transform an individual's socioeconomic status was clear in the exhibits at the fair. But more nuanced interpretations of these messages via archaeology show that the "mechanical invocations of artifact value and social standing now appear contrived" (Mullins 2011, 177). LouAnn Wurst (1999, 8) cautions that these class relations are internal although they "define concrete entities" and are lived dialectically within the capitalist system. Therefore, unproblematic identification of material "correlates" for class—such as the consumer goods at the fair—reifies what are really shifting levels in the lived experience of class, including the scales of the individual, family, and community. Still, it remains important to note that there was a coherent ideological message framed by the elite for nonelite consumers. The elites may not have determined how people were affected by the consumption of these goods, but they were trying to be the drivers of social change nevertheless.

Even without a clear tie between class status and the consumption of a product, we know that many of the products recovered and identified from the Charnley-Persky House midden and from the Jackson Park excavations were first debuted at those perfect ideological marketplaces: world's fairs and expositions, including the Chicago fair. If they received medals at these events, future iterations of the products would include mention of these achievements on their containers or labels, pointing to the market value of these designations. Alexander Ferguson MacLaren, whose tiny milk glass containers of MacLaren's Imperial Cheese Company brand cheddar and Roquefort cheese were recovered from Charnley-Persky House, not only showed his products at the Chicago fair but also served as a judge of the fair's dairy products (Roberts and Tunnell

Table 5.1. World's fair products from the Charnley-Persky House Archaeological Project

Product	Received Award and/or Debuted
James Keiller & Son Marmalade	London 1862, Vienna 1873
Hannis Distilling Co.'s Mount Vernon Pure Rye Whiskey	Philadelphia 1876
Hires Root Beer	Philadelphia 1876
J. E. Jeffords & Co. (pottery)	Philadelphia 1876
Burroughs & Mountford Co. (pottery)	Chicago 1893
Tarrant & Co.'s Johann Hoff Malt Extract	Chicago 1893
MacLaren's Imperial Cheese Co. (various cheeses)	Chicago 1893
A. M. Foster & Co. (glass)	Paris 1900
Abilena Sales Co.'s AbilenA Natural Cathartic Water	St. Louis 1904

1910, 143). Perhaps unsurprisingly, MacLaren's cheese received a perfect score at the Chicago fair, which it then touted on post-1893 product labels (MacLaren's Imperial Cheese Co. 1904). Some products recovered from the Charnley-Persky excavation debuted and won awards at fairs prior to 1893: Hannis Distilling Company's Mount Vernon Pure Rye Whiskey won an award at Philadelphia's Centennial Exposition in 1876 (Pennsylvania Historical Review 1886, 171); J. E. Jeffords and Company presented its yellow, Rockingham, majolica, and lava wares at the 1876 Philadelphia Exhibition (Barber 1904, 32). Other Charnley-Persky House products connect to post-1893 fairs. At the 1900 Paris Exposition Universelle, glass manufacturers A. M. Foster and Co. debuted their "Paris" bottle (Bethman 1991, 76), and, thanks to exhibits at the 1904 St. Louis fair, Abilena Sales Company's AbilenA Natural Cathartic Water became a "well-known brand" (Kansas Board of World's Fair Commissioners 1905, 126; see table 5.1).

Although the focus in this chapter is on the consumption and eventual deposition of goods at world's fairs, it remains important to note that the category of "consumable" also extended to people in 1893 Chicago. In a fairscape that was simultaneously a marketplace, so too was there what Curtis Hinsley calls the "commodification of the exotic" beyond the commodification of award-winning cheese or bottles or dishes (1991). World's fairs were both reflective and constitutive of a society's view of itself, and there is no clearer way to see this than in the manner in which racial and ethnic minorities were exhibited at the 1893 Chicago fair (see chapter 3 for a discussion of the Midway's native villages). This sense of racialized difference and the resultant commodification of that difference are evident in a passage from Clara Burnham's novel of the fair, *Sweet Clover*. After viewing the members of the Midway's Javanese Village, the white heroine exclaims, "I want one of those brown girls to take home as bricabrac. . . . Aren't they the roundest, prettiest little creatures!" (Burnham 1894, 305). Thus the racialized Other is not only different from us; she is a collectible—a tourist souvenir. If the Javanese woman seemed collectible to the heroine of *Sweet Clover*, it is only because one of the most pervasive didactic object lessons found at world's fairs concerned the modern self's orientation toward and engagement with the world by way of consumption.

Department Stores as Fairs

The connection between consumption and world's fairs also has another linkage: department stores. As part of his unfinished *Arcades Project* (1999), Walter Benjamin focused his attention on the phenomena of world exhibitions in the section of his documentary synopsis *Paris, Capital of the Nineteenth Century* titled "Grandeville, or the World Exhibitions" (Benjamin 1986). Benjamin characterized world's fairs as "sites of pilgrimages to the commodity fetish" as well as a sort of "phantasmagoria that people enter to be amused" (1986, 151; 152). Constructed in the early nineteenth century, Parisian arcades—covered passages between elegant shops that allowed customers (and flâneurs) a place to stroll and consume, unimpeded by urban distractions—still remain in some parts of the city as well as in other European countries. They are, in some respects, "ur-shopping malls" (Buck-Morss 1989, 3) and resemble an elongated Crystal Palace—yet another connection to world's fairs—with iron and glass roofs. Arcades, according to Benjamin, were a dialectical image, ambivalently exciting their viewers with scenes of utopian plenty while at the same time holding them captive by the ideology of consumption (Rollason 2002). Likewise, world's expositions, with their inordinate amounts of goods on display and for sale, reflected "the discord between [their] utopian and cynical elements" (Benjamin 1986, 152).

Functioning as a "pedagogy of modernity" (Trachtenberg 1982, 131) in

Figure 5.1. Cruet or decanter tops from the 2008 Jackson Park Archaeological Project, EU 3/5, ctx 61 (interface between stratum C and E). Photograph by author.

their own right, department stores taught many Americans how to be a specific sort of middle-class consumer in part by making the "world of goods" available to the consumer under one roof. Starting in Paris in 1852 with creation of Le Bon Marché, department stores made enormous strides in capturing public interest. Similarly, in the United States the great department chains, many of them still part of the American landscape today, were founded at this time: A. T. Stewart; Lord & Taylor; Arnold Constable & Company; R. H. Macy's; John Wanamaker; Jordan Marsh; Field, Leiter and Co. (which became Marshall Field and Co.); and the Fair Store in Chicago whose motto read "everything for everybody under one roof" (Wilson 2005). Initially located in the city center, department stores offered a wide range of goods for sale—clothing, household wares, dry goods, and furnishings—and allowed customers to browse their available choices in person rather than through a salesperson intermediary (Boorstin and National Portrait Gallery 1975), resulting in the "intensification of desire" (Schlereth 1991, 148) as endless rows of possible purchases whetted appetites that shoppers may not have even known they had before encountering the world of goods in this way.

Fairs visually resemble department stores, and department stores look like fairs. They have, it seems, an almost symbiotic relationship. At the 1855 Paris Exposition Universelle, goods on display were marked with visible price tags, making clear the path from observer to consumer. Tourists to the 1893 Chicago exposition received information about the fair at the department stores in Chicago's Loop, and guidebooks to the fair were full of advertisements from area department stores (Lewis 1983, 41; see Heckel 1893). Department stores, like expositions, shaped tastes, created consumers, and generated urban markets through entertaining and spectacular display (Lewis 1983). The symbolic universe of world's fairs itself could be found in department stores. A small copy of Daniel Chester French's *Statue of the Republic*—the "golden lady" who became the symbol of the 1893 Chicago fair—became a focal point in New York's Siegel-Cooper Department Store. Even more tangibly linking American world's fairs and department stores is a bronze eagle statue from the St. Louis 1904 Louisiana Purchase Exposition that found a new roost in Philadelphia's Wanamaker department store. The eagle is still there today, although it is now is in the Center City Macy's rather than the defunct Wanamaker's. Once these world's fairs had been removed from both their associated fairgrounds and perhaps diminished in public memory, department stores became a key site for enshrining these relics of the ephemeral cities. By creating tastes that could result in future profits for companies and stores, the goods on display and for consumption at world's fairs and at department stores hinted at transformation in the daily lives of fair tourists and nontourists alike.

Consumption and Disposal in the Fair's Ohio Building

While there is ample documentary description and scholarly discussion of the world of goods on display at the 1893 Chicago fair in the "frontstage" spaces of its exhibits, there is far less information about the "backstage" workings of the fair, including the processing of foods in its central mass-production kitchens and the particular ways the fair buildings were maintained via the domestic servants who worked and lived within them (see Graff and Edwards 2018; see also chapter 4 for a discussion of the Ohio Building servants). In this case, the specific artifactual array recovered from 2008 excavations in Jackson Park provides a glimpse into the backstage consumption within the fairgrounds itself.

Artifacts found in and around the contexts with the Ohio Building's plaster architectural remnants hint at the social activities that took place in the Ohio Building. Two glass cruet stoppers (ctx 61) and a Wedgwood plate fragment with cut marks (ctx 136) demonstrate particularly clearly that people dined in the Ohio Building (figure 5.1). This becomes more important in the sense that the Ohio Building was not listed as a site with a restaurant, café, or other concession, so the fact that one can interpret these moments of dining via the archaeological records highlights the disposal side of these consumptive practices as well as what is and is not included in the fair's narratives of those who work backstage.

The Ohio Building's glass cruets might seem to index an upper-class form of conspicuous consumption and affluent behavior for 1890s Americans. However, an increasingly large array of mass-produced goods meant than many more items could be consumed at far cheaper prices than had previously been available, making the dining practices that relied on such material open to people from a wider range of socioeconomic classes. The 1897 Sears, Roebuck and Company catalog advertised similar glass stoppers as part of a silver-plated castor set (ranging from 90 cents to $2.20) and as individual glass cruets (for $1.55 or $2.85) (Sears, Roebuck and Company 1993, 447, 686). Sears, Roebuck and Company claimed to make such items affordable to the masses—they called themselves the "Cheapest Supply House on Earth, Chicago" in their 1897 catalog. The use of such specific tableware, regardless of price point, implies correspondingly elaborated dining practices and concomitant ideologies of domesticity (see chapter 4).

To take the cruet example further, it is clear that a wide range of specialized dining accoutrements became fashionable at the end of the nineteenth century in order to conspicuously serve "new foods"—such as canned items like deviled crab or condensed milk—at dinner parties and social events. As a result, an entirely new category of specialized serving dishes was created to show off these novelties to best effect. For example, having a glass or silver celery "vase" became a necessary part of any respectable middle-class dining service to present that labor-intensive and expensive vegetable (Williams 1996, 110). These distinct utensils and dishes—among them lemon forks, asparagus tongs, and ice cream knives—were used within a strict and codified system of proper upper- and middle-class dining behavior.

When considering the phenomenon of world's fairs in terms of the whetting of consumer appetites that their exhibits-cum-marketplaces presented, it is not surprising that even the people who dined backstage in the Ohio Building also consumed these messages. And this would likewise be true for those who dined in any of the other fair structures, temporary or permanent, that created the logistical scaffolding for the successful tourist experience. While we do not have documentary access to the experiences of the servants who lived in the Ohio Building, or even the Ohio state representatives who may have consumed private repasts within the small hushed rooms of their state structure, the assemblage of materials from the Charnley-Persky House Archaeological Project provides a valuable site of comparison.

The Charnley House as a Site of Consumption

The Charnley House's Missing Piece: The Party Wall, the Driveway, and the Midden

The twenty-eight thousand artifacts recovered from the Society of Architectural Historians' small 3-meter by 22-meter driveway—officially recorded with an area of 958 square feet (89 square meters, Cook County Property Tax Portal 2018)—provide a tantalizing and plentiful counterpoint to the smaller-scale artifactual array of nonarchitectural materials recovered from the 1893 fair's Ohio Building. That the SAH currently owns the driveway, tying it back to the original Charnley property, is a recent development, and one that itself must be centrally interpreted within the disposal-side narrative of the consumptive activities represented in its contents. It was the discovery of the midden via a 2003 construction project that began this archaeological endeavor, so understanding the significance of its contents as well as the social trends that made such a disposal possible occupies the second part of this chapter. After all, if the consumption and disposal practices of the 1893 Chicago fair were supposed to model future American urban experiences, how else can one assess the ways that these ideologies were brought home than to delve right into the muck?

In the midst of this modern home and modernizing domestic space in a newly desirable Gold Coast neighborhood of Chicago, was there a similarly modern array of new products and technologies in the daily life of those who lived and worked there? How do these changing experiences of mass consumption and modern architecture intersect with what appear to be premodern sanitary and disposal practices? And finally, whose garbage was this anyway?

James Charnley sold the small piece of property directly to the east of his house to Sarah K. Otis in 1891. The Charnleys and Otises intended to build another structure alongside their home, constructing the eastern side of the Charnley House as a "party wall" and recording a formal party wall agreement on November 5, 1891 (Bluestone 2004, 53–34). Party walls were designed to abut another structure and therefore lacked the ornate stone facing and decoration of the other elevations of the house. But the Otises never built their intended home at the site, selling the property to James Breckinridge Waller Jr.—the future owner of the Charnley House—in 1897. One final note about Ephraim Otis, Sarah's husband: he was appointed as a member of the citizen's committee for the World's Columbian Exposition, once again connecting the Gold Coast to Jackson Park (World's Columbian Commission 1893, 103).

By 1892 Waller already owned the two lots east of the Otis lot, also originally part of the Charnley purchase. Currently 39 East Schiller Street, the site was home to the Binderton Apartments (1892), and today a multiunit condominium sits on the original Binderton site. Considering Waller's eventual ownership of the four lots on Schiller Street to Astor Street, it may be possible to tie the Charnley House midden to him, his family, or his tenants. Still, connecting the items in this midden to known individuals or households, even after archaeological excavation and analysis, may not ultimately be possible. Instead a look at broad trends in consumption, trashmaking, and trash disposal sets this question within its larger sociocultural context, showing just how the creation of the midden within the confines of the elite Gold Coast neighborhood may not be that unusual after all.

Dating and Situating the Midden Artifacts: Consumer Goods, Conspicuously Consumed

With the discovery of the rich midden east of the Charnley House in 2003 during construction on the home came the hope, and even the assumption, that the materials found beneath the driveway were somehow attached to James and Helen Charnley. Because the lot on which the Charnleys built their home was on the same block as the earlier Potter and Bertha Palmer property, there had also been an initial hope that the materials from the driveway midden related to the Palmers. Excavation in 2010 and 2015 failed to yield definitive tie to an individual or individual household. As noted in chapter 4, in contrast to their social contemporaries—say, the Palmers or other socially prominent families of Chicago—we know little about the Charnley family. Until quite recently, Helen Charnley's date of death was incorrectly thought to be 1927 rather than 1930. We know that Helen, James, and Douglas Charnley left this house in 1902 and moved to Camden, South Carolina, where James Charnley died in 1905. Helen and Douglas spent the remainder of their lives living in Europe. There were no descendants, and, as a result, no original photographs of the interior or other family information on the house has ever been found. To find a material record of their lives via the objects they threw away was a compelling and desirable possibility.

That the current driveway lot was never used as a building site further complicates an attribution of the midden to a known household. Recall, though, that the Charnleys did not own the driveway area after 1891. Waller bought it in 1897, but never built on it, even after he purchased the Charnley House itself. Identifying the possible individuals with ties to that garbage, or even why there was garbage there in the first place, necessitates a look at Chicago and urban U.S. refuse and waste disposal practices in the nineteenth and early twentieth centuries.

Happily, the very contents of the midden, regardless of attribution to individual households, provide a fascinating look into consumer trends from approximately 1880–1920. What follows, to aid in interrogating the spatial location of the midden site, is a look at several themes and patterns drawn from the site report that tie to the consumer promises of the World's Columbian Exposition.

The bulk of the Charnley-Persky House artifacts date from the 1890s to the 1910s, although these dates come from known manufacture or introduction dates rather than from a stratigraphic analysis (e.g., Miller et al. 2000). The excavation units from the 2010 field season consisted solely of redeposited soils that had been moved after a 1999 construction project at the site—something we became aware of toward the end of the field season. We placed the 2015 excavation units at the eastern edge of the property, both to circumvent the known construction project and to see if

Table 5.2. Identified pottery companies from the Charnley-Persky House Archaeological Project

Pottery Company	Place of Manufacture	Date Range
Belleek (first black maker's mark)	Ireland	1863–91
Bourne & Leigh	England	1892–1920
Burley & Co.	Chicago	1871–1907
Burley & Tyrrell Co.	Chicago	1884–1923
Burroughs & Mountford Co.	New Jersey	1879–82
C. H. Pillivuyt et Cie	France	1818–present
Charles Allerton & Sons	England	1903–12
Charles Field Haviland	France	1882
Coalport Porcelain Works	England	pre-1891
Edwin M. Knowles	Ohio	1901–9
Empire Porcelain Company	England	1896–1912
Greenwood Pottery	New Jersey	post-1886
Haviland & Co.	France	1888–96
Henry Alcock	England	post-1891
J. E. Jeffords & Co.	Pennsylvania	1868–1920s
Johnson Brothers	England	1883–1913
Meissen (Blue Onion pattern)	Germany	1825–1924
Mercer Warranted China	New Jersey	1868–ca. 1937
Minton Ltd. (Kitten plate)	England	1891
New Wharf Pottery Co.	England	1878–94
Pitkin & Brooks	Chicago	1900–14
Royal Doulton (Rosamond pattern)	England	1891–1902
Silver & Co. N.Y.	New York	1900s
Theodore Haviland	France	1903–25
Union Potteries (Corinne pattern)	Ohio	1900–1905
Utzschneider/Sarreguemines	France/Germany	1894–1918
W. A. Pickard	Wisconsin	ca. 1898–ca. 1903
W. H. Grindley	England	1880–91
W. T. Copeland	England	1867–90
Wedgewood & Sons (tile)	England	n.d.
Zeh, Scherzer & Co.	Germany	1880–1910

Note: Dates were derived from maker's marks, patterns, and known dates of incorporation and/or dissolution.

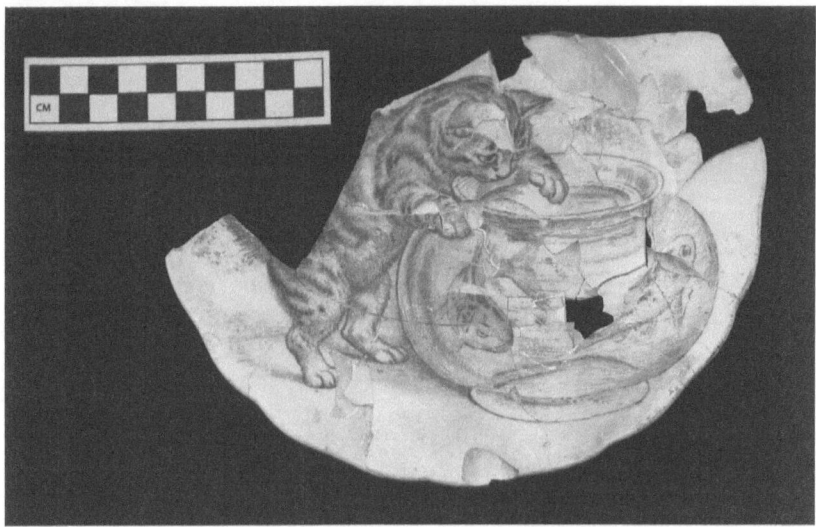

Figure 5.2. Minton cat plate, ca. 1873–1891, from the 2015 Charnley-Persky House Archaeological Project. Photograph by Ryan J. Cook.

an edge to the deposit could be seen. Yet even with additional excavation, we could not discern any features or edges of features. Confoundingly, the entire site seemed one immense garbage deposit with no meaningful stratigraphy or features.

Still, the manufacture dates of the artifacts begin to contextualize their consumption, at least temporally, with several manufacture dates suggesting a TPQ (*terminus post quem*) of 1903 (Charles Allerton & Sons, Theodore Haviland, and W. A. Pickard), the year after James and Helen Charnley vacated the building. For example, a look at the identified maker's marks from the ceramic assemblage provides the following sites and dates of manufacture (table 5.2).

Note the diversity of ceramics recovered from the one site: the global spread of these pottery companies epitomizes the assemblage from the site. Locations of manufacture include France, England, Ireland, Germany, and the United States, represented by Illinois, New Jersey, Ohio, Pennsylvania, and Wisconsin. One especially nice example of the work of England's Staffordshire Potteries, of which products from eight different companies were recovered from the Charnley-Persky House excavations, is a Minton dinner plate depicting a kitten attempting to grab a fish from a bowl. The plate was one of a series of cat plates manufactured between 1873 and 1891 (National Trust Collections n.d.; figure 5.2). Not listed in

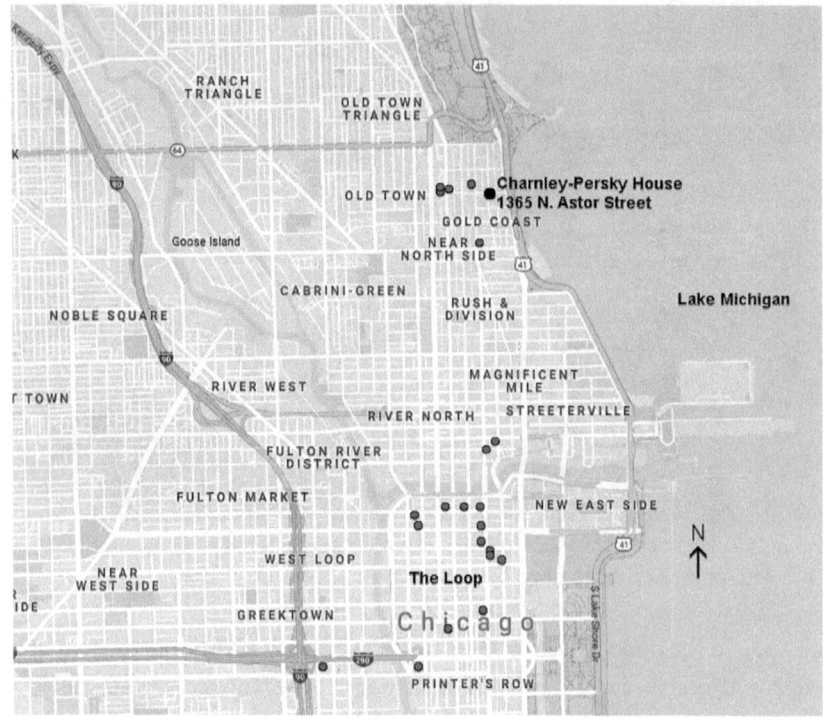

Figure 5.3. Chicago Artifact Map, Charnley-Persky House Archaeological Project, from Graff 2016. The circles indicate sites of manufacture or points of sale, and dark circle indicates the location of the Charnley-Persky House. Map by author.

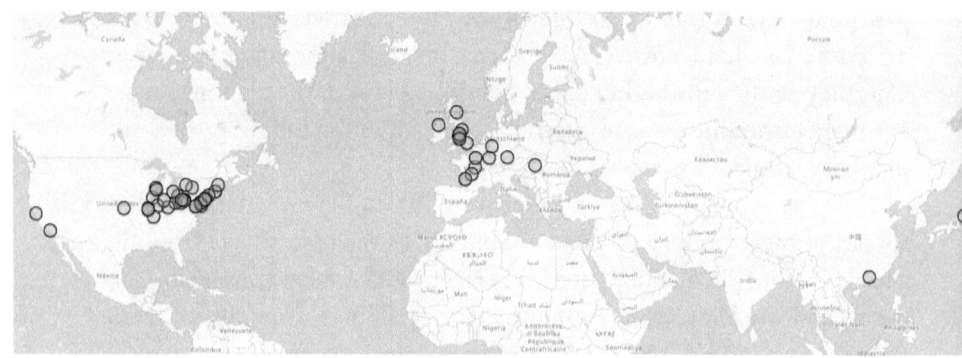

Figure 5.4. World Artifact Map, Charnley-Persky House Archaeological Project, from Graff 2016. The circles indicate sites of manufacture or points of sale. Map by author.

this table but found on our digital map of manufacture sites (see Graff 2016) are ceramics from China (Canton porcelain) and Japan ("Geisha Girl" porcelain and "sharkskin" glazed porcelain).

A digital project completed in 2016 mapped additional examples of the global scale of the assemblage, extrapolated from the known points of sale or manufacture of the Charnley-Persky House Archaeological Project materials via their identified brands or maker's marks (Graff 2016; figures 5.3 and 5.4). What is striking in this collection is the clear tripartite pattern: goods were sold or manufactured only blocks away from the Charnley House (e.g., the bottle from the Scherer Pharmacy at State and Division Streets or bottles from three pharmacies on Schiller Street), from major U.S. cities (e.g., Philadelphia, New York, Boston), or from major European and Asian cities or manufacture districts (e.g., Stoke-on-Trent, Paris, Guangzhou). In this sense, the assemblage echoes the consumer promises of the 1893 World's Columbian Exposition, where "all the world" (Reed 2000) was there for the taking.

Coupled with this global spread, a look at the functional categories of the identified products provides a sense of the ways the Gold Coast consumers sought to maintain themselves via new forms of goods (table 5.3). Of this array, the items that were used on the "modern" body—such as the cologne in opening of this chapter—and the "modern" stomach provide another look at the ways that ideologies and messages of the fair were consumed through products within this domestic site.

The Modern Body

Many of the artifacts recovered from the Charnley-Persky House midden were products designed for use on the body: perfumes and colognes, hair "invigorators," manicure lotions, and even partial dentures. Like the bottle of No. 4711, another identified perfume flacon has a relation to what is "modern": a bottle of Le Trèfle Incarnat perfume, manufactured by L. T. Piver of Paris. This perfume house was founded in 1774, but Le Trèfle Incarnat was invented in 1898. "Invented" rather than "formulated" is the signifier in its description, as the chemical amyl salicylate was first used in this perfume to provide the synthetic smell of clover, a practice that resulted in Le Trèfle Incarnat being touted as "the first synthetic perfume to produce a totally new odor" (Delbourg-Delphis in Stamelman 2006, 96–97). The late nineteenth century saw the creation of many synthetic

Table 5.3. Identified brands and products from the Charnley-Persky House Archaeological Project by functional category

HEALTH

MEDICINES (INCLUDING PATENT)
Abilena Sales Co. (AbilenA Natural Cathartic Water)
Andreas Saxlehner Mineral Spring Water Co. (Hunyadi Janos Bitterquelle)
Anglo American Drug Co. (Mrs. Winslow's Soothing Syrup)*
Dr. A. Gude & Co. (Pepto-Mangan)*
Dr. Harter's Wild Cherry Bitters*
E. E. Sutherland Medicine Co.
Emerson Drug Co. (Bromo-Seltzer)
Fairchild Brothers & Foster (Digestive Ferments)
Hamlin's Wizard Oil
John Wyeth & Brother
Katharmon Chemical Co.
Keasbey & Mattion Co.
McClintock Drug
Phillips' Milk of Magnesia
Scott & Bowne, Manufacturing Chemists (Scott's Emulsion Cod Liver Oil)
Sharp & Dohme
Tarrant & Co. (Johann Hoff Malt Extract)
Yergin Oil

DRUGGISTS AND PHARMACIES (ALL IN CHICAGO)
Andrew Scherer
Colbert Drug Co.*
D. R. Dyche Drug Co.
Dinet & Delfosse
Economical Drug Co.
Emil A. Dorner, Pharmacist
Gale & Blocki Druggists
John J. Schmitt Pharmacy
Morrison, Plummer & Co.
O. W. Tanke
Schiller Pharmacy

TOILETRIES/GROOMING
A. S. Hinds (lotion)
Chesebrough Manufacturing Co. (Vaseline)
Daccett & Ramsdell's Perfect Cold Cream*
Docteur Pierre (Eau Dentifrice, mouthwash)*
Dr. E. L. Graves Unequaled Tooth Powder

Dr. J. Parker Pray's Manicure Solution*
E. W. Hoyt & Co. (Hoyt's German Cologne)*
Ed. Pinaud (cologne and hair dressing)
Espey's Fragrant Cream*
James C. Crane (Creme Elcaya, face cream)*
Kress & Owen Co. (Glyco-Thymoline, mouthwash)
L. T. Piver (Le Trèfle Incarnat Cologne)*
Lambert Pharmacal Co. (Listerine)
Mäurer & Wirtz (No. 4711 Cologne)
Mum Manufacturing Co. (deodorant)
Palisade Manufacturing Co. (Borolyptol, mouthwash)
Ponds Extract (cold cream)*
R. E. Rhode Pharmaceutical Chemist (toothpaste)*
Richard Hudnot (Marvelous Cold Cream)*
Sanitol (tooth powder)*
Trichobio (hair tonic)
Van Buskirk's Fragrant Sozodont for the Teeth and Breath (mouthwash)

FOOD

Alexis Godillot Jeune (olive oil)
Armour & Co. (beef bouillon)
Borden Eagle Brand Condensed Milk
Bowman Dairy Co. (milk)
Charles Hires Co. (Hires Root Beer)
Charles Teyssonneau Jeunes (conserves)
Dr. Price's Delicious Flavoring Extracts
Eskay's Albumenized Food (baby food)
Gulden's Mustard
H. J. Heinz Co. (pickles)
Horlicks Malted Milk
James Keiller & Son Marmalade
James P. Smith & Co.*
Joseph Burnett Co. (Burnett's Flavoring Extracts)
Kee & Chapell Dairy Co. (milk)
Kehoe & Co. (confectionary)
Lea & Perrins (Worcestershire sauce)
MacLaren's Imperial Cheese Co.
Palisade Manufacturing Co. (Tournade's Kitchen Bouquet)*
Puhl-Webb Co.
Seville Packing Co. (Pim-Olas olives)
T. A. Snider Preserve Co.*
Yacht Club (salad dressing)

(continued)

Table 5.3—*Continued*

DRINK

Alcohol

Duffy Whiskey
Gordon's Dry Gin
Hannis Distilling Co. (Mount Vernon Pure Rye Whiskey)
Klein Brothers Harvard Rye
P. Dawson/Dufftown Glenlivet (scotch)*
Roxbury Distilling Co. (whiskey)

Beer

Chicago Brewing Co.
Chicago Consolidated Bottling Co./George Lomax
Lemp Beer
Schlitz Beer
Schoenhofen Brewing Co. (Edelweiss beer)

Non-alcoholic

A. Carpenter (soda)*
Consumers' Company (Hydrox Water)
H. W. Tessendorff (soda)*

HOUSEHOLD

Ayling Brothers (stove polish)
Carters Ink
Higgins' Ink
Laundry Blue Co. (laundry bluing)
L. H. Thomas Co. (ink)*
Master Lock Co. (keys)
S. M. Bixby & Co. (ink)
Sanford's Manufacturing Co. (ink)
Sperm Sewing Machine Oil

PERSONAL ADORNMENT

Boston Garters
Waterbury Button Co.

OTHER

Dunkley Canning Co. (canning)
E. H. Sargent & Co. (chemists)
Karl Kiefer Machine Co. (bottling machinery)
The Graduated Nursing Bottle (nursing bottle)*

Note: Items with * indicates that they were recovered from the 2003 construction project rather than the 2010 or 2015 excavations.

chemicals for perfumes: benzaldehyde (the scent of peach kernels and bitter almonds, 1837), coumarin (hay, 1868), vanillin (vanilla, 1874), ionone (violet, 1893), and synthetic versions of rose (1877) and musk (1888–1891) (Stamelman 2006:96–97).

Some suggest that it took a while for consumers to accept mass-marketed synthetic fragrances like Le Trèfle Incarnat over natural perfume oils, citing advertising and pricing as key in drawing these wary consumers to market. Such marketing is akin to what has been described for mass-produced meat during this same time period (Cronon 1991). Perfume historian Richard Howard Stamelman writes that "until World War I only a sophisticated elite was ready to accept synthetic scents" (Stamelman 2006, 97). A short story by Haitian writer Carl Brouard titled *Trèfle Incarnat* suggests that this scent was favored by working-class women as well as by prostitutes and thus carried negative connotations for people of higher socioeconomic class (Kaussen 2008, 52). Advertising and novel experiences at the world's fairs may have also helped create future consumers for these modern perfume formulations. For instance, the Rimmel Company created a perfume fountain at London's 1851 Crystal Palace Exhibition; tourists might dip their handkerchiefs into the fragrant waters and perhaps in so doing be moved to purchase a Rimmel scent—such as "Great Exhibition Bouquet"—in the future (Groom 1997, 285; Maxwell 2017, 22).

Turning from the whole body to the hands and nails, the next illustrative item from the Charnley House assemblage is a bottle that contained Dr. J. Parker Pray Manicure Lotion. An 1891 advertisement heralds Dr. Pray's invention of "the manicure arts and goods in America" in 1876 and 1878 (*Chicago Tribune* 1891b, 15). The lotion found in this bottle, along with emery boards, diamond nail enamel, and other Dr. Pray products, made Dr. Pray the originator of the manicure, or at least, the husband of Mary E. Cobb, the woman who actually invented the products that allowed people to file, cleanse, tint, and enamel their nails in the late nineteenth century (*New York Times* 1898, 7). Dr. and Mrs. Pray's professional titles were "manicures" before the term took its present use as the act of shaping and dressing nails (*New York Times* 1884, 3), and they opened a manicure shop in New York while also nationally distributing their products.

Mary Cobb Pray's manicure invention was indeed new and modern, at least according to an 1889 article that describes her demonstrations of

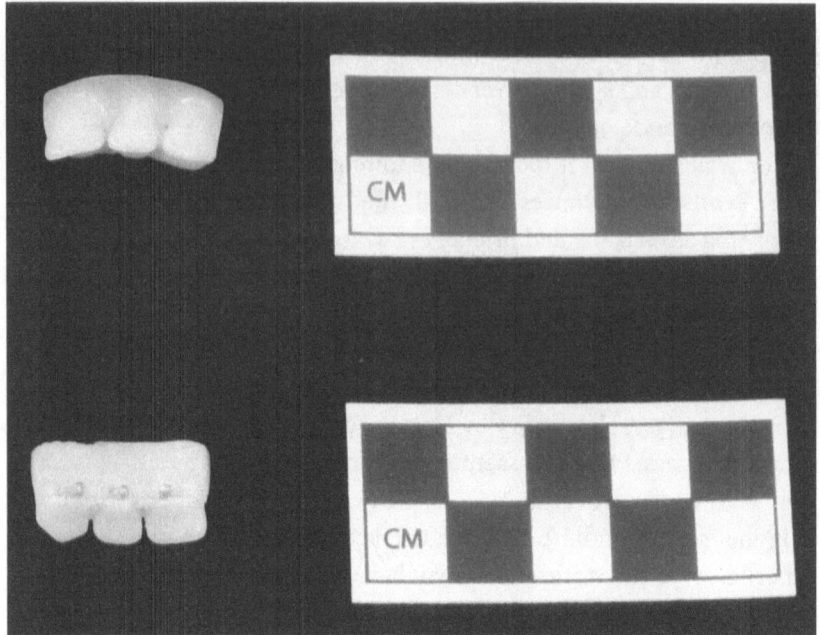

Figure 5.5. Partial dentures recovered from the 2010 Charnley-Persky House Archaeological Project, EU 2, wall cleaning. Photograph by Ryan J. Cook.

manicuring arts in Britain: "Whether or not manicure will ever become the rage in London remains a problem of the future" (*Nursing Record* 1889, 241). Some element of social class is embodied in these products since the ability to maintain soft, clean, and groomed hands might prove difficult for people in certain industries or professions, even if the price of grooming products was not an issue. Indeed, the condition of a person's hands has long been used as an indicator of class as understood through the "physical effects of diet, work, and environment" (Goffman 1951, 301). Aspirational consumers may have had their desires for these products whetted by advertisements like a 1914 piece in *Good Housekeeping*. It shows a young woman in three-quarter profile touching her face with one beautiful hand, with a list of Dr. Pray products including "Gloria Lily Lotion, an emulsion which softens and whitens the hands," appearing below (Dr. J. Parker Pray's Toilet Preparations 1914, 74).

Finally, the set of partial dentures from EU 2 is one of the most intimate artifacts from the assemblage (figure 5.5). Made of vulcanite, porcelain, and metal screws, the extremely realistic dentures helped the wearer maintain an illusion and function of a full set of healthy teeth. These dentures are a modern version of an ancient tradition, found archaeologically at 700 BC Etruscan sites (Corrado 1990) and known in its colonial form to any American school-aged child who learned about that famous denture-wearer, George Washington. What makes these modern is, first, the way they were produced. Unlike Washington's handcrafted, spring-loaded wood and ivory appliance, modern dentures featured porcelain teeth set in industrially molded vulcanite (1855), celluloid (1869), Bakelite (1920), or acrylic resin (1934) (Peyton 1975). A second modern aspect of these partial dentures was the way products of this type were marketed. Colorful chromolithograph advertising cards, a vehicle that peaked with the 1893 fair, promised pain-free and aesthetically pleasing (i.e., hidden, natural looking) appliances from any number of competing dentists (Croll and Swanson 2006).

The Modern Stomach

Just as Chicagoans at the fair and in the Charnley's Gold Coast neighborhood had access to new preparations for topical use on their bodies, so too were there new forms of food and drink available to sate them from within. By the 1870s Chicago was a center for salad dressing manufacture, a new product that had not previously been commercially bottled and sold (Smith 2007, 513). Tildesley and Company's Yacht Club salad dressing was one of the best-selling products (figure 5.6). A 1912 advertisement in an Evanston, Illinois, church cookbook provides fascinating copy, linking domesticity, class, and modernity with condiments. It reads:

> Socially speaking, good breeding and good salads are almost synonymous terms. One of the brightest club-women in America happily expressed this idea when she wittily said: "In good society a woman is known, not by the company she keeps, but by the salads she serves." . . . In "Yacht Club" you have the "perfect dressing." A combination of the finest ingredients scientifically blended. (First Presbyterian Church 1912, n.p.)

Thus class aspirations can be made material through salads, with the aid of scientific production techniques. In another Yacht Club advertisement from a 1914 *Yacht Club Manual of Salads*, a young woman dressed in what appears to be a maid's uniform is shown dolloping Yacht Club salad

Figure 5.6. Yacht Club salad dressing recovered from the 2010 Charnley-Persky House Archaeological Project, EU 1, ctx 34. Photograph by Ryan J. Cook.

dressing into a tomato (figure 5.7). This image again signals class status—here it couples the ability to employ domestic laborers in one's home (see chapter 4) with the salad dressing product being advertised (Hayward 1914). Of course, it is debatable that consumers of this and similar advertisements truly believed in a full class transformation via mayonnaise-based salad dressing, but the fact that this ad copy could read as such suggests some consumer resonance.

Another local product recovered from the Charnley House midden was a milk bottle from the Kee & Chapell Dairy Company (1913–20), a small Roselle, Illinois, firm that was subsumed into a vast Bowman Dairy Company monopoly. It is unusual to find many milk bottles other than ones from Bowman in Chicago, a company and eventual monopoly that opened in 1885. Bowman supplied milk and other dairy products to many of the World's Columbian Exposition's restaurants and concessions, an action that helped to further advance its reputation (Reitzel 1949, 15). At this same time, Bowman aggressively acquired most of the smaller dairy firms

Figure 5.7. Cover of *Yacht Club Manual of Salads*. From Hayward 1914.

Figure 5.8. MacLaren's Imperial Cheese Company Roquefort cheese recovered from the 2015 Charnley-Persky House Archaeological Project, EU 4, ctx 22. Photograph by Ryan J. Cook.

in the area, eventually including Kee & Chapell (Reitzel 1949). Bowman controlled most of Chicago's dairy industry until 1966, when the Dean Milk Company purchased it (Boles, Janzen, and Popp 2004). The scale of this aggressive consolidation of smaller, rival firms was itself a modern, capitalist practice.

In contrast to these two Illinois products, a large number of foodstuffs recovered from the Charnley-Persky House came from much farther afield, reflecting the widespread flows of goods available to consumers at the turn of the twentieth century. These products include Alexis Godillot Jeune olive oil and Charles Teyssonneau Jeunes conserves (France); Andreas Saxlehner Mineral Spring Water Company's Hunyadi Janos Bitterquelle mineral water (Hungary, although this was also used for medicinal purposes); Lea & Perrins Worcestershire sauce, Gordon's dry gin, and James Keiller & Son marmalade (United Kingdom). Products from American cities were also represented, including H. J. Heinz Co. pickles (Pennsylvania), Joseph Burnett Company flavoring extracts (Massachusetts), and Hannis Distilling Company's Mount Vernon Pure Rye Whiskey (Philadelphia and Baltimore). Add to that the MacLaren's cheese (figure 5.8)—from a Toronto company—and the idea arises that consumer choice may not have been motivated by price or convenience (there was certainly ample cheese available from nearby Wisconsin) but from successful advertising and brand awareness.

One final product recovered from the Charnley-Persky midden presents both a look at modern foodways as well as a mystery. Several glass bottles of Eskay's Albumenized Food were recovered from the excavation. Frank Baum developed an infant formula for babies needing to gain weight, something of great concern at a time with high infant mortality. In 1890 he was commissioned by the pharmaceutical firm Smith, Kline & French to manufacture it for a larger public, and he renamed the product Eskay's Albumenized Food (Apple 1987). Here the name "Eskay" is the sounding out of "S" and "K" of Smith and Kline, today part of the pharmaceutical giant GlaxoSmithKline. What is unexpected about this find is not that it was a product promoting the scientific feeding of infants but that there were no known infants ever living within the Charnley House (see chapter 4). While it is not impossible that someone was visiting the Charnley House residents and brought along an infant and the formula—in fact, there were also glass nursing bottles recovered from the midden during the initial 2003 construction product—such an item complicates the assignment of the midden to any of the people who lived at 1365 N. Astor Street.

Finally, there was a sizable amount (3,885 specimens) of identifiable animal bones recovered from the site, representing remains of meals that deserve mention alongside processed food products. Analyzed by Grace A. Krause in 2017, the highly fragmented and burnt remains included those from eight identified food species: cattle (*Bos taurus*), sheep or goat (*Ovis aries* or *Capra augagrus hircus*), chicken (*Gallus gallus domesticus*), turkey (*Meleagris gallopavo*), eastern oysters (*Crassostrea virginica*), pig (*Sus scrofa domesticus*), clam (*Mercenaria mercenaria*), and scallop (*Argopecten irradians*), with chicken (19.2 percent) and cattle (4.3 percent) making up the highest percentages of identifiable remains (Krause 2017). Krause also identified mice (*Mus sp.*), rats (*Rattus sp.*), and domestic cats (*Felis silvestris catus*) in the assemblage, although not likely used as livestock. Furthermore, 93.8 percent of the animal bones exhibited evidence of burning, with the largest portion of calcined specimens falling under the 420–500° C temperature range (Krause 2017, 8). Such burning would have reduced the total volume of material for disposal as well as rendering some of it less pungent.

The interpretation of the Charnley-Persky House artifacts as indicative of modern, progressive trends in consumption is one that is only partly correct. An alternate interpretation must also recognize that in using these modern products, people were able to simultaneously maintain familiar ties to older consumer habits. These products for modern bodies and modern stomachs, like the quasi-domestic spaces of the Ohio Building, had familiar echoes despite their novelty. At the same time, like the distinctly "modern" architectural style of the Charnley House, many of these products were geared to very new experiences—driving in automobiles, wearing scents created not from nature but the laboratory, eating scientifically produced foods—that were as yet unfamiliar to the vast majority of Americans at the turn of the twentieth century.

Conspicuous Disposal: Modern Trashmaking Practices

To city dwellers in the twenty-first century, it defies easy explanation why the extensive midden excavated at the Charnley-Persky House exists in the first place. Chicago residents, especially in that wealthy neighborhood, would have had access to various garbage disposal options, from hiring private scavengers or using public contractors, both of whom would remove these foul-smelling materials from alongside a home. The proximity and extent of this dumpsite seems confusing and even repellent to many twenty-first-century urbanites whose own trash is removed from garbage cans or dumpsters at mandated intervals by municipal employees. But norms of what is or is not "healthy," "gross," or "offensive," may differ within these different time periods, although the familiar location of the site in an elegant historic district obscures the formidable temporal breach between nineteenth- and twenty-first-century waste disposal practices. It was common and acceptable in the nineteenth century to "use the borders of the house for disposal" (Strasser 2000, 7). To find a midden adjacent to a home, even one like the Charnley House, reflects this set of traditional practices that has also been verified by archaeological research.

Anthropologist Mary Douglas famously wrote that trash was only "matter out of place" (Douglas 1966, 35), suggesting that the work of deciding what is or is not refuse is culturally specific and constituted in practice. In her work on the social history of American trash disposal practices, Susan Strasser follows Douglas by emphasizing the process of "trashmaking": the sorting and categorization that makes something "trash" or "not trash." This process is aligned with, but qualitatively different from, trash disposal (Strasser 2000, 5). Once something has been categorized as trash, it is often moved outside the house for disposal, and this disposal "takes place in the intersection between the private and the public, the borderland where the household meets the city, the threshold between the male and female 'spheres' of the nineteenth century" (Strasser 2000, 6).

At the beginning of the twentieth century, Americans were still not producing very much trash. The familiarity of some of the products found at the Charnley House midden—particularly those that continue to be manufactured today such as Gordon's dry gin or James Keiller & Son marmalade—obscure the tremendous change in commercial packaging and wider socioeconomic distribution that began in the 1870s. This packaging changes with the development of "new processes for making and filling cardboard cartons and tin cans, and new materials such as cellophane and aluminum foil" (Strasser 2000, 13–14). The mass manufacturing of the "packaging revolution" made a greater diversity of potential "trash" available to a wider array of consumers. Now goods could be sold in individual containers, replacing what had previously been available only in bulk (Licence 2015, 15). Rather than reusing hard-to-come-by containers of goods that were themselves rarified and price prohibitive, all sorts of provisions and goods could be consumed and their containers then discarded.

The Veblenian "conspicuous consumption" of the nineteenth century becomes, at the turn of the twentieth century, what I term "conspicuous disposal." Although he is best known for his formulation of conspicuous consumption, Veblen notes a process of "conspicuous waste" as a related process in creating a leisure class, although in specifically economic rather than material terms. Veblen writes that he does not use the term "waste" derogatorily. Instead,

> It is here used for want of a better term that will adequately describe the same range of motives and of phenomena, and it is not to be taken in an odious sense, as implying an illegitimate expenditure of human products or of human life. In the view of economic theory the expenditure in question is no more and no less legitimate than any other expenditure. It is here called "waste" because this

expenditure does not serve human life or human well-being on the whole, not because it is waste or misdirection of effort or expenditure as viewed from the standpoint of the individual consumer who chooses it. (1899, 97–98)

Indeed, for Veblen, to conspicuously consume in a manner that signals one's wealth, status, and reputation is to be wasteful—it wastes time, it wastes goods (1899, 8).

My term "conspicuous disposal" highlights the materiality and sense of place of the discard and final deposition of consumer goods rather than equating this with Veblen's concept of conspicuous waste. This disposal is the material manifestation of many of the emulative status processes Veblen and others have studied. And in this case, it is literally "waste"—garbage, refuse, trash—the stuff of archaeology and the end cycle in the life of a good.

World's fairs, then, are doubly places for conspicuous consumption and the zenith of conspicuous disposal. While the former practices may be clear and have been covered in previous scholarship, the latter concept demands consideration. Huge investments of capital are fed into world's fairs, notably including the construction of immense structures and durable, underground infrastructure, all of which were intentionally created to be disposed of and transformed into waste, often after only months of use. What is more a reflection efforts of Chicago's leisure class who planned the fair than to build an entire city only to purposefully to destroy it? And this is even more evident when considering the Ohio Building's defunct infrastructure, which, having been left in the ground at the fair's conclusion, essentially itself became "waste," conspicuously disposed. In this way the Chicago elites who rallied for the chance to host the World's Columbian Exposition ultimately used the conspicuous disposal of the fair to signal their leisure-class status to the world.

It is not surprising that class can be interpreted via conspicuous disposal and trashmaking, as it underscores and creates social differences based on economic status (Strasser 2000, 9). Performance of class status could be derived from the extensive waste that a household produced, with new fashions in dinnerware, bric-a-brac, and furnishings driving affluent households to replace their possessions with newer ones and thus create items for conspicuous disposal. Prefiguring the planned obsolescence of the mid-twentieth century—where goods were designed to have short use-lives in order to sustain a market (Burdick 2012)—the creation of larger amounts of urban waste forms the other side of increases in individual household consumption. The ramping up of manufacture and consumption of these mass-produced goods "made the scale and the magnitude of the waste problem much greater" than that of premodern urban centers (Melosi 2005, 8). What "matter" would be able to be understood as "out of place" to even become appropriate to discard and for whom "matter" was in fact disposable rather than reusable were new concerns in turn-of-the-twentieth-century trashmaking and new ways to signal status.

Archaeology and Conspicuous Disposal Practices

Archaeological research, and urban archaeology in particular, has long focused on household middens like the one at the Charnley-Persky House. What people throw away provides a compelling look at their values, tastes, and concepts of health. These insights are especially key for those whose lives were not considered important enough to be captured in the documentary record—often women, people of color, and working classes. Even those whose diaries and journals line the shelves of historical societies or the ether of digital archives may not have captured the minutiae of their consumption practices in their official recollections. Middens, then, "can be linked to households whose names are recorded, but whose stories emerge only through their rubbish" (Licence 2015, 2).

As garbage disposal practices change over time with an increasing public sanitary infrastructure and municipal ordinances, so too will these changes appear in the archaeological, documentary, and even oral historical records (cf. Crane 2000, 20). In her work on the archaeology of two nineteenth-century privy vaults in New York City, Joan Geismar (1993) looked at municipal laws and directives to see the relationship between the official waste disposal regulations and household implementation. Privy vaults were sites for human waste to be deposited, although both archaeologists and bottle hunters know that such places are also used as garbage dumps during the end of their uses. Similar archaeological attention to changing urban waste disposal repertoires has been documented in Washington, D.C., and many, if not all, other urban U.S. locations where archaeological research has taken place (Crane 2000). William Rathje's groundbreaking research on disposal habits in 1970s Tucson, Arizona ("Le

Projet du Garbàge"), brought garbology from the literal underground of archaeological excavation, where we dig up "other people's garbage," to an anthropological and ethnographic turn with lasting policy implications (Rathje 1974). Reflecting on the decisions made as the debris from the Twin Towers was removed and material sorted after 9/11, Michael Shanks, David Platt, and Rathje remind us that "putting aside choice of what to keep: this is the real stuff of archaeology and history—what gets thrown away—garbage" (2004, 64).

Garbage in the nineteenth and early twentieth centuries is multivalent, most particularly in industrializing urban centers like Chicago. Changing standards and understandings of sanitation, hygiene, public health, and disease imbricate the concept of "garbage." The movement from a consumer culture of reuse to one of immediate disposal is itself a transformation of use that was aided by technological innovations that increased marketing of mass-produced goods. To understand the social and historical conditions that led to the creation and location of the Charnley-Persky House midden, the next section provides an overview of garbage and sanitation practices.

Sanitation and Garbage Disposal in the Urban United States

The English "sanitary idea" of the mid-nineteenth century, championed by reformer Edwin Chadwick, linked filth to disease: this idea held that "the physical environment exercised a profound influence over the well-being of the individual, that health depended upon sanitation" (Melosi 2000, 43). In England, legislating this belief into practice resulted in improvements in public sanitary systems and made Britain a world leader in sanitary technology. An increased concern with public health as it related to theories of disease also changed sanitation practices. The ancient miasma theory of disease, still dominant by the 1850s, gave way, by the 1880s, to germ theory, which helped push through further sanitation efforts.

Historian Martin Melosi cheekily notes that the increasingly industrialized society of the nineteenth-century Western urban centers was the original "effluent society" (Lampard 1973, 43, in Melosi 2005, 8), a punning nod to mid-twentieth-century social-scientific debates over which was the original affluent society (viz. Sahlins 1972). Like other rapidly urbanizing centers in the late nineteenth century, a barrage of infectious diseases—cholera, typhoid, diphtheria, and scarlet fever—hit Chicago, many of which were exacerbated by poor sanitary conditions (Nugent 2005). New immigrants, often with different cultural practices than native Chicagoans, were easy scapegoats for increased mortality rates. In the Chicago Department of Health's report on the years 1881 and 1882, Commissioner of Health Dr. Oscar C. DeWolf writes, "The immigration of 1881 was the largest ever received in this country to that time, and it brought the anticipated pestilence" (1883, 6).

Municipal sanitation and refuse disposal evolved alongside notions of the miasma theory of disease versus germ theory and other concepts of health. Sanitation and sanitation reform covers the emptying and maintenance of cesspools and privy vaults; the removal of garbage; the eradication of swamps or other disease vectors, often by the use of fill; and the creation of sanitary infrastructure, including pipes for sewerage and water systems. To discuss waste removal, then, is also to discuss efforts in sanitation reform.

The U.S. Sanitary Commission was founded during the Civil War in 1861 to improve and maintain the sanitary conditions of Union troops and support personnel (Thompson 1956). Sanitary fairs—in many ways predecessors of the 1893 World's Columbian Exposition—were held to earn revenue to support the goals of the U.S. Sanitary Commission. Chicago hosted its first sanitary fair in November 1863 and another in the summer of 1865. Frederick Law Olmsted, landscape architect of the 1893 Chicago fair, was the executive secretary of the Sanitary Commission during the Civil War (Oberly 1987). Despite Chicago's history as a mid-nineteenth-century venue for fairs to support increased sanitation, it took quite a long time to institute personal and municipal practices that would make the city sanitary.

The History of Garbage Disposal in Chicago

Potter Palmer's 1882 move to fill in the so-called plague spots along Lake Shore Drive (*Chicago Tribune* 1882b, 9) was a local manifestation of a city-wide and nationwide movement to improve health by using garbage as fill, at the same time creating new land. In his overview of Chicago's waste disposal practices and its related urban expansion, geographer Craig Colten (1994) characterizes the practice of using refuse to expand shorelines—or urban reclamation—as the first period of disposal regimes (1840–1900). A second, overlapping suite of practices began in 1871 after post-fire rebuilding projects created clay and limestone borrow pits that were then used to dump refuse. This continued until the 1950s in the related practice of using waste as grading material to build up low-lying areas and raise city streets for the new sewerage system. Finally, although filling in quarry sites continued in what Colten characterizes as the third generation of waste disposal practices, much of Chicago's garbage began to be moved to rural dumps.

During the time that the Charnleys lived in Chicago, municipal garbage collection was still haphazard and dependent on contracted labor, and not all districts were equally served. Lake Michigan was still used as a dumping ground for barges full of municipal trash through 1882, and garbage continued to be used to build up Chicago's lakefront Grant Park into 1900 (Colten 1994, 128, 129). A 1906 *Chicago Tribune* article, "Picturesque Stretch of the 'Streeterville' Dump," follows one Sanitary Inspector Doherty, who, after a complaint from the Imperial German Counsel posted in Chicago, notes "decaying refuse from the stores and peddlars' [sic] supplies" and "two large and unsightly holes with green and brown colored water" (1906b, 3). The owners of the site—who included Adrian Honoré, brother of Bertha Honoré Palmer—were ordered under threat of suit to clean it up.

Although the city of Chicago was invested in removing garbage for public health, the first moves toward citywide waste removal relied on independent contractors rather than instituting full municipal services. A law adopted on November 5, 1867, revoked private licenses of "day scavengers"—or garbage collectors—and mandated that only licensed subcontractors were allowed to remove refuse from the city (Tuley 1873, 181). The system depended upon large numbers of these licensed and contracted scavengers, employed as needed by the Board of Health (Tuley 1873, 114). With whatever conveyances they had—carts, horses, and so on—the scavengers removed "offal, garbage, swill" and sometimes ash only after the city left printed notices for Chicagoans to have their garbage ready in "suitable vessels" (Tuley 1873, 114). "Night scavengers" were licensed to pick up human waste after paying the city a $500 bond and a $17 fee for access (Tuley 1873, 114). In 1881 alone, Chicago issued 6,484 night scavenger permits that allowed for a recorded 12,758 tons of material removed, while a total expense of $46,507.24 was noted for "day scavenger work" by

•

sixty-five teams per day that same year (Chicago Department of Health 1883, 161–62).

The mechanism that forced Chicagoans to pay for private removal of their trash and human waste in the absence of municipal service was simple: fines. In 1873 the city ordinances clearly stated that no one should dispose of "any filth, offal, dung, dead animal, vegetables, oyster shells, or any unsound or offensive matter whatever" on "their premises, or in any outhouse, stable, privy . . . or in any alley or street" (Tuley 1873, 50). Fines were levied against "offensive privy vaults" by the Department of Health, although these fines were coupled with city ordinances preventing unlicensed people from cleaning their own privy vaults without written permission from the city health officer (Tuley 1873, 115–116). A decade later, scavenger ordinances continued to control the removal of trash, with more lawsuits and fines to force Chicagoans to obey sanitary regulations. In 1882, 393 suits were made by the Department of Health against citizens for violations including "filthy premises," "insufficient privy accommodation," and "stagnant water" (Chicago Department of Health 1883, 166).

Still, the contractor-based garbage removal system as such was not sufficient for the population, due in part to its overly complex and inefficient bureaucracy. Chicago split the work of waste removal between at least two departments. In describing the sanitation work of 1884, the inspector writes that "the custom of assigning the cleaning of streets to the care of the Department of Public Works, and the cleaning of alleys and removal of house garbage from alleys and streets to the Department of Health, has resulted in the usual confusion and extravagance of expenditure, which have, heretofore, more or less, characterized the work" (Chicago Department of Health 1885, 5). By 1890 this labor continued to be divided between various agencies and agents, although the Department of Public Health was newly in charge of some sanitation in alleys too.

By 1892 Chicago reached a garbage "crisis" after the addition of annexed lands into the city proper taxed the already insufficient trash disposal system. Although the 1889 annexation increased Chicago's size by 125 square miles and population by 225,000 (Cain 2004), there was no concomitant expansion of city trash collection. The only dump for all this refuse was located at 35th Street and Western Avenue (Knight 2006, 12). By the 1890s city officials across the United States were realizing that "the complexities of urban life in the late nineteenth century made collection and disposal of refuse by private citizens impractical" (Melosi 2005, 23).

In 1892—the year the Charnley House was completed—citizen groups largely made of middle- and upper-class women launched a "garbage campaign" in Chicago (Knight 2006) to address the sanitation crisis.

The impetus for local sanitary reform groups to solve this sanitation problem coincided with work to prepare the city of Chicago for the 1893 World's Columbian Exposition. How could Chicago host the world if all around it was putrid, stinking, disease-laden garbage? Those citizen groups who came together to tackle the garbage crisis groups included the Chicago Woman's Club and the Illinois Woman's Alliance, eventually joining to form the Municipal Order League (Knight 2006), which distributed twenty thousand printed cards containing "suggestions for the disposal of wastes" and noting local ordinances on refuse (Melosi 2005, 29).

Chicago's sanitation problems were not fixed at the conclusion of the fair in November 1893. Concerned citizens then founded the Civic Federation of Chicago and formed a sanitary committee. Reformer Jane Addams was a founding member and, eventually, the volunteer garbage inspector for the nineteenth ward (Knight 2006, 19–20). The campaigns of the reformers encouraged an ideology of cleanliness where the state of one's house-adjacent alleys—where much of the garbage was placed—was linked to one's own household's virtue (Knight 2006, 23–24).

In 1894 garbage disposal was much the same as it had been before the World's Columbian Exposition, with the Department of Public Works overseeing cleaning of streets and alleys and continuing to employ contractor scavengers to do this work (Binmore 1894, 4). Although an 1893 ordinance (5134) mandated that garbage from hotels, restaurants, and cafes be privately removed, private residences were still not included in the directive (Binmore 1894, 128–29). An 1894 ordinance established garbage crematories "for the purpose of consuming by fire the garbage in the city of Chicago"—something that would be on display and instrumental in the upkeep of the White City during the 1893 fair (see Morse 1893). But these crematories were not placed systematically and evenly through the city; they were instead placed wherever the commissioner decided to erect them, as long as they were on public property (Binmore 1894, 128). However, this ordinance was followed by one that allowed the commission to instead contract out for the use of private crematories as needed, thereby continuing to keep work within the private realm. Faced with inadequate municipal waste disposal for private residences, wealthy

Chicagoans continued to hire private scavengers well into the first years of the twentieth century (Colten 1994, 321).

But some of the efforts of the citizen-led sanitation commissions did work to change Chicago's waste practices. In 1897 the state of Illinois mandated that cities with a population over one hundred thousand had to make contracts for removing garbage. By 1898 "the city had abandoned the use of the wooden garbage boxes for metal cans and, although the contracting system was still in use, a new plan was implemented that year to enter into five-year contracts for garbage removal and disposal in order to reduce the opportunities for patronage" (Knight 2006, 24). Chicago's 1911 Sanitary Code was supposed to end disorganized and inadequate waste removal. It legally parsed the term "garbage" with the intent of separating the containment, removal, and, imposition of fines for each class. Garbage was "taken to include any and all rejected or waste household food, offal, swill and carrion," while ashes included "all ashes of wood, coal, coke and the residue from the combustion on any material or substance, and soot, cinders, slag and charcoal." Finally, a category of "miscellaneous waste" included "dust ... and all refuse, except excrement, and dead animals and parts thereof" or anything under the categories of garbage and ashes as well as "manure" (Chicago City Council and John Siman 1916, 84). A household's waste then would need to be separated into vessels that matched these descriptions, with the specific dimensions and materials for building the vessels likewise mapped out in the code. Once built and filled with waste, the household was required to place the containers "upon the edge of the sidewalk adjoining said premises, or on the rear of the lots," although when this would take place would be directed by the commission of public works (Chicago City Council and John Siman 1916, 85). Alleys, though, were expressly not a permitted location for waste bins, in contrast with twenty-first-century Chicago practices. Scavengers, still licensed by the city, were the only people allowed to remove the contents. Household ashes were collected by the city, but ashes from buildings of more than five flats had to be removed at the expense of the owner (Chicago City Council and John Siman 1916, 86).

The 1914 addition of yet another piece of legislation from the City Council, in a section called "Unfinished Business," seems to indicate that the 1911 Sanitary Code was not a success. Old disposal habits died hard, and in 1914 the City Council ordained that "no person, firm or corporation shall empty, dump or deposit any ashes, soot, sand, dust, refuse, offal, rubbish, cinders, dirt, manure, street sweepings . . . upon any private property or upon any vacant lot or grounds within the limits of the City of Chicago" unless "the written consent of the owner or owners or their duly authorized agent shall first be obtained and filed with the commissioner of health," who would then issue a permit (Chicago City Council 1914, 1391).

It took until 1916 for Chicago to create a Bureau of Waste Disposal (Chicago City Council and John Siman 1916, 87). This did not mean that the municipality was in total control of waste disposal—contracted, private scavengers were still vital to the removal of the city's waste (Chicago City Council and John Siman 1916, 91). One of the businesses, the Chicago Reduction Company, became a leading contractor when the city made it illegal to dump garbage within the city limits, instead pushing for incineration (Citizens' Association of Chicago 1912). Regardless of the work of this contractor, at the time of the Charnley House midden's probable creation, it was illegal to dump trash within the city limits unless the public health commissioner gave consent to the individual petitioner (Colten 1994, 133).

Why, then, was such a large amount of household garbage, with materials dating from 1880 to 1920, dumped next to the Charnley House? There is no record of anyone using the legal loophole of obtaining permission to dump on site. Was it opportunistic and surreptitious dumping? Was it a practice that, having been the norm for decades, continued into the twentieth century despite the location within a wealthy district with greater access to hiring scavengers? Were concepts of what was and was not offensive to both smell and to concerns of health so different from today that the question of whether you had garbage next to your home—especially highly burnt material—was not a cause for concern?

Conclusion

Archaeologists Shanks, Platt, and Rathje categorize the association of archaeology and garbage as essential to understanding "the heart of the composition and decomposition of modernity and modernism" (2004, 64). Garbage is the "perfume of modernity" from which wafts the scents of meanings lost and found, of structures ruined or erased, and of objects decaying or preserved. With that powerful sensory image, Shanks and colleagues force us to reckon with the fundamental relationship between garbage and modernity.

By the 1920s—the end date of most of the Charnley midden items and a quarter-century after the Chicago fair—American households approached a more modern relationship with the material world via their waste disposal habits: "People made fewer things and bought more than their parents and grandparents had. They saved and fixed less and threw out more, for the habits of reuse had always been intertwined with the skills of household production" (Strasser 2000, 199). In this "empire of the ephemeral," a new, faster-paced consumption and disposal regimen, "Americans got rid of things sooner" than previous generations (Strasser 2000, 200). The conspicuous consumption that was said to characterize a certain socioeconomic class of Chicagoans had been fully met with a regime of conspicuous disposal that spanned far more groups of people. And this conspicuous disposal included all those who partook of world's fairs, those exemplars of modernity's conspicuous disposal.

On Astor Street, what was truly ephemeral were not the goods that were consumed and discarded there and that populate the archaeological record of the site. Instead, the lives of the James and Helen Charnley family, whose desire and connection led them to commission this spectacular modern home, are what was fleeting, transient, and not captured in a record of any sort. The waste uncovered in 2003 and through archaeological excavations in 2010 and 2015 may not shed particular light on their lives, or even on the McClurgs, the Winterbothams, the Stephenses, the Wallers, and their household staff, but it does connect the changes in the built environment with changing consumer habits that institutions like world's fairs made possible.

6

Conclusion

At the Center of the World, Again

Beginning from the archaeological results from excavating the World's Columbian Exposition's quasi-domestic Ohio Building and the unquestionably domestic Louis Sullivan and Frank Lloyd Wright–designed Charnley-Persky House, I looked at the way concepts of temporality, domesticity, consumption, and a related set of conspicuous disposal practices formed an interpenetrating network of meaning for Americans at the turn of the twentieth century. I explored several currents in turn-of-the-twentieth-century American urban life to understand the Ohio Building as a familiar-seeming refuge from the panoply of ideological messages about past, present, and future American ways of life on display at the fair. Within the vast fairgrounds, the Ohio Building, although a Beaux-Arts confection of little architectural renown, was nonetheless appreciated by fair tourists for its sheltered spaces that could be used for moments of intimate social life, relaxation, and even bodily relief. By contrast, whether or not Frank Lloyd Wright really did pronounce the Charnley House "modern," it was a startlingly different domestic space than the dark, ornamented homes that predominated since the Victorian period. And, like the bottle of No. 4711 cologne recovered from the Charnley-Persky House Archaeological Project—a product from the eighteenth century still available for purchase in the twenty-first—the Ohio Building and the Charnley House combined familiar and unfamiliar elements, used in both old and new ways.

The current battles about the future of Jackson Park and, to some extent, the current challenges for the preservation of the Charnley-Persky House, provide echoes of themes covered in this book. The imbricating networks of white elites in Chicago's Gold Coast and at the 1893 fair; the unsettled and twisted temporalities as made material through architecture and aesthetics; the powerful messaging of domesticity as translated through modernity's technological and societal changes; the "perfume of garbage" and, literally, garbage made from perfume—all impact the present to various degrees. In this final chapter, I turn to a brief consideration of three moments in the lifecycle of Jackson Park to lay the groundwork for my final points.

First, in the immediate post-fair period the intentional erasure of the monumental Chicago fairscape only heightened the ideological messages found in the exhibits, amusements, and consumables found there. Author Robert Herrick included the emotional reactions and sense of loss from the July 1894 fires that swept through Jackson Park in his novel *The Web of Life* (1900). Distressed by the blaze surrounding Daniel Chester French's Statue of the Republic (see figure 2.4), Herrick's protagonist, Dr. Sommers, looked at the ruins and voiced its effect upon himself to a friend:

> The colossal figure rising from the lagoon in front of the Peristyle [the Statue of the Republic] was still illuminated,—the light falling upon the gilded ball borne aloft,—solemnly presiding even in the ruins of the dream. . . . "It dies," Sommers replied. "Burnt out!" "No," she protested eagerly; "it remains in the heart, warming it in dull, cold times, and its great work comes after. It is not well to live without fierceness and passion." (Herrick 1900, 174, 175)

This exchange again contains the trope of the lasting ideological messages of the fair as a source of comfort to those who lamented its material loss. And this soothing message is found almost without question or alternative in newspaper accounts, memoirs, and even fiction about the fair (see the excerpt from Burnett 1895 in chapter 3). Remarkably, given the evocative power that the Statue of the Republic seemed to have for Herrick and others as the rest of the fair was gradually destroyed, there remains a way to commune with it today. Although the original sixty-five-foot tall Statue of the Republic was destroyed by another fire in 1896, a one-third-size replica, dedicated in 1918, now sits in Jackson Park in a traffic circle on Hayes Drive. Commemorating the twenty-fifth anniversary of the fair, the replica statue was funded from the last remaining monies of the World's Columbian Exposition Company, which ultimately dissolved in 1915 (Gregerson 1996, 279). The "Golden Lady" as she is widely known, is an important marker in the current landscape of Jackson Park though many do not know its origin.

The second stage to consider in Jackson Park's use history was the postfire reclamation of the site back into usable parkland, something Herrick, a professor at the nearby University of Chicago, likely witnessed firsthand. Work began to convert both fantasy and ruins back to urban park, and planners claimed that, "in preparing these attractions and conveniences, the primary purpose of the park has never been lost sight of. The landscape is the essence of the park. The green pastures and still waters, the outlook over the great inland sea, all the commanding charm of the place has been preserved and heightened for the refreshment of city-wearied senses" (*New York Times* 1896, 16). While there were no longer exhibits, architectural marvels, or exotic fair restaurants to visit, Frederick Law Olmsted's landscape design firm of Olmsted, Olmsted and Eliot revised Jackson Park with a beach and promenade, playing fields, and lush plantings (Chicago South Park Commissioners and Olmsted, Olmsted and Eliot 1895). Thorstein Veblen, also teaching at the nearby University of Chicago, characterized this transformation of the fairgrounds back to parkland as a form of conspicuous consumption, that expensive and performative way of signaling social status. Veblen understood the installation of topiaries as indexes of pecuniary rather than aesthetic taste of the Chicago Park Commissioners; thus, their choice of topiaries in Jackson Park was a costly rather than a beautiful one (Veblen 1899, 38).

This takes us to the current place of Jackson Park in the public imagination. In 2016 President Barack Obama and First Lady Michelle Obama announced that the Obama Presidential Center would be built in Jackson Park in partnership with the University of Chicago (Skiba 2016). This choice captures Jackson Park's continued prominence in the public imagination. Although lawsuits against the $500 million project continue to thread back and forth through the courts, the Obama Foundation has proclaimed the transformative possibilities of their new dream for Jackson Park: "The [Obama Presidential] Center will be a new landmark for the South Side and an economic engine for the city of Chicago. It will draw hundreds of thousands of visitors every year, creating thousands of new jobs on the South Side, while giving new life to Frederick Law Olmsted's vision of a cohesive, walkable, and iconic Jackson Park" (Obama Foundation 2018). Like Herrick and Veblen, Obama was also a former University of Chicago professor. The Law School building where he taught is located on the former Midway Plaisance of the 1893 fair. One wonders how much this personal proximity to the former fairscape affected this choice of site.

In attempting to gather the threads of the past, present, and future connections between the World's Fair and the Charnley House as understood through archaeological and historical research, I keep noticing how familiar these experiences seem to us living in the twenty-first century. So, too, is the other side of this the case: experiences in the present day, especially heightened emotional appeals to civic pride as in the Obama Presidential Center, are pervaded with reference to, or nostalgia for, these pivotal experiences of the last hundred years. Whether these are experiences of time, domesticity, consumption, or disposal, or are experiences and concerns regarding ruins, landscape erasure, or reconfiguration, this is the "strangely familiar" part of the recent past that we grapple with today. With knowledge hard-won from media reaction to our excavations in Jackson Park, where the archaeology of this recent past was dismissed by National Public Radio with a news story titled "Hunt for World's Fair Artifacts Turns Up Junk" (Graff 2011a, 230), what has become clear is that this time period and these actions linger profoundly into the present day. In fact, to arbitrarily separate this period from contemporary life is ontologically inaccurate: it is a type ideology disguised as temporality like those I discuss in chapter 3. In this final chapter, I look more closely at the historical period(s) of the fair and Charnley House, making interventions, or better, reframing of the results through contemporary archaeology, just as Jackson Park prepares to return to the word stage yet again.

The "Modern" World of the Fair and the House

Dubbed the "Gilded Age" by Mark Twain (Twain and Warner 1873), and also known as the Brown Decades (Mumford 1955), the Mauve Decades (Beer 1926), or simply the Victorian period (Blodgett and Howe 1976, although this period begins in 1837 with Queen Victoria's ascension to the throne), the span from the end of Reconstruction to the beginning of World War I (1877–1915) is commonly bound off and characterized as a complicated milieu of monumental social and cultural change, especially within urban centers. This period also overlaps with the third and final period of Eric Hobsbawm's "long nineteenth century," his "Age of Empire," 1875–1914 (Hobsbawm 1987). Lewis Mumford described postbellum America at the beginning of this time period as a nation trying to find its footing. Yet, for Mumford, this historical period was not altogether dark and dismal; he pointed out that the era was also the "source of some of the most important elements in our contemporary culture" (1955, 21–22). Mumford found these changes in the preponderance of modern architecture, while others saw them in technological innovations that promised easier and more comfortable lifestyles for Americans.

Also attending to this historical period, Robert Rydell characterizes an American "search for order" from 1877 to 1920, as originally formulated by Robert Wiebe (1967), which was distinctly manifest in the creation of the rational, planned world of fairscapes (Rydell 1984). Wiebe argues that this time period coincided with a fundamental shift in American values, seen in movements from small towns to cities; from traditional family-based values to middle-class individualism; and from living as "a nation of loosely connected islands, similar in kind" where self was defined in relation to community, to participating in the bureaucratic modernity of cities where one's job and socioeconomic position carried far more weight than did customary bonds of kin or community (1967, 4). These binaries are akin to Ferdinand Tönnies's categories of Gemeinschaft (natural will, oriented to the collectivity and community) and Gesellschaft (rational will and individualism), further developed by Max Weber (1968) as well as to Émile Durkheim's (1984) distinction between mechanical and organic solidarity. Wiebe contends that the emerging middle class developed "new values of continuity and regularity, functionality and rationality, administration and management" to effectively deal with these challenges of modernity (1967, viii), a process characterized elsewhere as the "incorporation of America" (Trachtenberg 1982). Rydell claims that fairs constituted a way to "alleviate the intense and widespread anxiety that pervaded the United States" as a result of these and other social changes by providing "an opportunity to reaffirm [Americans'] collective national identity in an updated synthesis of progress and white supremacy that suffused the blueprints of future perfection offered by the fairs" (Rydell 1984, 4).

In opposition to much of this scholarship, I take the historical period that encompasses the creation of both the Chicago fair and the Charnley House as neither a break with earlier practices nor a telos for any foregoing socioeconomic processes. In his reading of the events surrounding the

French Revolution of 1848, David Harvey calls the concept of modernity "a myth because the notion of a radical break has a certain persuasive and pervasive power in the face of abundant evidence that it does not, and cannot, possibly occur" (2003, 1; see also Appadurai 1996). Dawdy's (2010) characterization (after Trouillot 1995) of "Modernity 1" (the content of modernity) and "Modernity 2" (the "stories told about the present") shows that historical as well as archaeological practice has too often been invested in telling these stories by reifying modernity's temporal rupture and creating a distinct periodization within which to slot human experience. More recent archaeological research on this time period refutes Wiebe's and others' simplistic binaries as well as their seeming inevitability. This scholarship points instead to the intersectionality of racial, ethnic, gender, and class identity in lived experience (see, e.g., Wall 1999; Mullins 1999; Wurst 1999; Voss 2008). Accepting the analytic weight of intersectionality—the idea that these categories of difference are entangled, covalent, and mutually constitutive (see Crenshaw 1989; Casella and Fowler 2005; Battle-Baptiste 2011; Collins and Bilge 2016; Ruíz 2017)—is only one example of how human experience cannot be simply parsed. A reliance on only one interpretative lens for the 1893 fair and the Charnley House would obscure what we seek to understand. It is all too tempting to look for and find a narrative with a smooth, straight path to the present about the changes set in motion from the 1893 fair and architectural spectacle of the modern Charnley House.

Since the 2000s, and building from the "archaeology of us" genre of material culture studies (Gould and Schiffer 1981; see Rathje 1979; and chapter 5), scholars interested in "contemporary archaeology" (also called "archaeology of the contemporary," "archaeology of the recent past," and "later historical archaeology") have willfully broken down such a periodization, "implicitly considering how the past intrudes into the present" (McAtackney and Penrose 2016, 148; see also, e.g., Graves-Brown 2000; Buchli and Lucas 2001; González-Ruibal 2008; Holtorf and Piccini 2009; Harrison and Schofield 2010). This notion of "intrusion" fits readily into urban archaeological research, where palimpsests, traces, erasures, and the like profoundly and obviously constitute a global assemblage created out of years of dense, dynamic human occupation (see McAtackney and Ryzewski 2017). Alfredo González-Ruibal notes that with this "extension of the boundaries of the contemporary past beyond what is strictly contemporary," we move to a periodization where "we can say that we are contemporaries of First World War soldiers, even if no one is alive anymore, because we live in the same historical phase" (2014, 1684). Perhaps this work's effort to defamiliarize the familiar components of the World's Columbian Exposition and the Charnley House—the racist ideologies of white supremacy, the taste of a Vienna Beef hot dog, the flush of a toilet—is difficult precisely because we are still of this era.

Chicago, Familiar and Strange

Embracing more fully the framing concepts of contemporary archaeology allows for the examination of processes that may have begun in the nineteenth century but still operate much in the same manner today. These include the way that the material changes of the nineteenth-century landscape played out in urban centers. Anthropologist Nancy Munn (2004) argues that the "spatio-temporalizing" processes in antebellum New York, such as the sudden removal of a decaying mansion or the widening of a street, left many New Yorkers with the sense that their memories of the city were obliterated by modern construction projects. This sense of loss was furthered heightened by the rapid pace of change that decentered their understanding of their self and their city. In Chicago, Chief Simon Pokagon of the Pokagon Band of Potawatomi had his *Red Man's Rebuke* to the 1893 World's Columbian Exposition printed on white birch bark rather than paper. He included within the book an illustration of a rural and unpeopled "Chicago in my grandfather's days." The small booklet, through both its physical material and its content, was intended to forcefully demonstrate the cultural continuities of the Pokagon Band in Chicago and to remind the reader that the fair was held on "our land" (Pokagon 1893, n.p., 2; see also Low 2016). Yet in the face of modernity's "creative destruction" (Schumpeter 1942), in the loss of recognition of familiar places that Munn terms the "becoming-past" of places, and in the ethnographic accounts of indigenous leaders, we perceive the material continuities and palimpsests that remain in the archaeological record.

It should be clear now that the purposeful vanishing of the White City—the planned destruction and removal of the 1893 World's Columbian Exposition—would have been both familiar to its tourists as well as somewhat unfamiliar or strange due to its enormous scale (see Tarlow and West 1999; Tarlow 1999). So too would the novel appearance of the Sullivan-and-Wright-designed Charnley House be something unfamiliar yet also not entirely strange in a city that was rewriting its narrative and rebuilding its streetscape as it transformed from a small, swampy outpost to "nature's metropolis" (Cronon 1991). These transformative processes, like those unleashed in Haussmann's Paris (Harvey 1989, 2003), were already part of global urban experiences. Perhaps the commonsensical inference of a vast difference of experience that the Charnley family felt as they moved from their ornate Victorian mansion to their modest, modern home was likewise not homogeneous but simultaneously familiar *and* strange. So too could the Ohio Building itself be framed as familiar/strange: Tourists' encounters with the fair's futuristic infrastructure and future-oriented urban planning (both permanent and also transformative) were almost always mediated by familiar and impermanent architectural forms. Classical architecture and quasi-domestic spaces provided the backward-looking, familiar-seeming context for those harbingers of modernity, toilets and electric lights.

Another example of the interpenetration of the past and present and the coterminous experiences of familiar and strange comes from another Jackson Park–related venture. I was in New Orleans working at an archaeological site in the French Quarter when I heard the news that Chicago had lost its bid to host the 2016 Olympic Games, an event that also centered on Jackson Park and the evocative power of the fair. The 2016 Chicago Olympic Bid Committee touted "This will be our World's Columbian Exposition" and accompanied their advertising with Daniel Burnham's renowned quote, "Make no little plans; they have no magic to stir men's blood" (Chicago 2016 Applicant City 2008). Hoping to convince the members of the International Olympic Committee that Chicago was the superlative site for the 2016 Summer Games, the Chicago organizers created a plan placing the main Olympic stadium in Washington Park and locating additional stadia and playing fields in Jackson Park. But on that fall day in 2009 the International Olympic Committee decided that Rio de Janeiro, rather than Chicago, would be the future home of the XXXI Olympiad. Having attended contentious meetings in Jackson Park the previous year about the possible impact such an event would bring to the park and the neighborhood, I was relieved to find that site would not be changed beyond recall, or destroyed, as it became center of twenty-first-century Olympic tourism. Like many others, I was particularly concerned about potential damage to what I found personally meaningful in Jackson Park: the natural space, the Olmsted landscape, and the archaeology.

Having found the remnants of the Ohio Building, I was deeply troubled by thoughts of the damage that would come to Jackson Park's archaeological resources—resources that would most likely never be mitigated before construction commenced.

So when the Obama Foundation announced that the new Obama Presidential Center would not be in Washington Park—a site many of us supposedly in the know had guessed—but in Jackson, I was surprised. Colleagues working with the Illinois State Archaeological Survey conducted Phase III excavations at the site (Tolmie and Porubcan Branster 2018), and I was fortunate to meet with them to discuss their findings. I have no doubt there remains incredible material from the 1893 World's Fair still underground in Jackson Park. Removing (or conspicuously disposing of) an entire city, even if it is just designed for a single summer, leaves discernable and not easily eradicated traces.

When writing this chapter, I learned that a 1958 Frank Lloyd Wright–designed commercial structure was demolished in the middle of the night and against great public outcry in Whitefish, Montana (Kamin 2018). It was on the National Register of Historic Places, but when negotiations failed, the developer could legally do what he wished with the structure. Back in Chicago, the Charnley-Persky House Foundation and the Society of Architectural Historians were raising funds to fix ongoing structural problems with the 127-year-old building. While the site is not at risk for demolition thanks to the foresight of Seymour Persky and the hard work of those at SAH, it will, like other structures, need regular influxes of revenue and technology to prevent its physical erasure.

Leonard Schoch's letter, which opened the second chapter and started me thinking about how ordinary people experienced the ephemerality of world's fairs and widespread urban landscape change, again provides insight into the ways that people process their experiences of both loss and change. Schoch wrote, in this letter to his friend Anna, about his touristic experiences of the fair: "Yet I think any one who had had an opportunity to but imperfectly see what was to be seen may truly be thankful. . . . Chicago in this has won the civic crown. Her fame is now secure" (1893, 5). The White City—like the ephemeral sister cities of world's fairs and enduring homes like the Charnleys'—concealed and revealed a transformational ideology in every spigot and valve of its infrastructure, in every show of electrical lighting or flush of a toilet, even after it materially "vanished." The fair's 125th anniversary year, 2018, was also the 126th anniversary of the Charnley House. Reaching such commemorative milestones further emphasizes how the past always intrudes into the present—or the present into the past—and how this is itself all too familiar.

Disposing of Modernity

The cover of a small volume of fiction set at the 1893 Exposition shows a family of four observing the gleaming structures of the fair (figure 6.1). They are close to, but not within, the White City and the Midway Plaisance, although they can see the Ferris wheel and the dome of the Administration Building from where they stand. Positioned as they are, one can ask: did they just arrive at the fair and are ready to enter the fairgrounds, or, instead, did they finish their tour of the Dream City and are contemplating what comes next? Had they passed any time in their particular state building, and what did it mean to them in the context of the fair? Did they know how their experience of the fair would transform them, whether as its makers intended or not? What did they do, and how did they live their lives, once back home from their visit to the Vanishing City?

The documentary and archaeological records show that the 1893 World's Columbian Exposition was indeed a transformative event for the many people who experienced it as well as those who saw it only from afar. In creating new consumer tastes, articulating a national identity, teaching how to see "race," debuting technologies that remain constitutive of our modern lives, and creating a tourist experience that echoes in Disneyland or the Olympic Games, the fair did cause broad structural change. In addition to those tourists who visited to the fair in person were those people—perhaps even the Charnleys themselves—who would, shortly afterward, be able to consume the very wares that the fair debuted, all within the ideology of modernity's progression as insurmountable and indisputably beneficial. But this change was not met without reservation, and, even within Jackson Park at the peak of the fair, visitors took the opportunities to sit back in a chair in the quiet comfort of the Ohio Building and perhaps ask where things were going. And such a journey, in the pluritemporal imaginary of the 1893 fair, could take place in a single summer and within a single park.

The 1893 Chicago fair had to disappear to further this transformation. As a symbol lacking a material correlate beyond scattered souvenirs, it could be called upon to promote almost unlimited ideas, tastes, and

Figure 6.1. Cover of *The Adventures of Uncle Jeremiah and Family at the Great Fair*. From Stevens 1893.

trends. If it had been left as ivy-covered ruins, as the editorial in the introduction to this volume proposed, the show of age and deterioration might have diminished the evocative power of this ephemeral city. Although impermanent in this sense, the ideologies became permanent, while one of these, materialized in sanitary infrastructure, still remains part of the underground city of 1893.

Scholarship here and elsewhere confirms the idea that the Vanishing City of the fair has indeed not vanished and is found in the ideologies of temporality, domesticity, consumption, and conspicuous disposal addressed here. What we determine to have happened in the 1890s—"before"—is materially and ideologically part of "now." The material traces of the fair and the Charnley House, the ideas of the fair's planners and tourists, the social and consumer practices of the Charnleys and the other Chicago elites who lived on Astor Street, even when perhaps unfamiliar, all persist and permeate the present. To think otherwise would be a negation of our own twenty-first-century familiarities.

REFERENCES

Adams, Henry. 1907. *The Education of Henry Adams*. Washington, D.C.
Allen, Thomas M. 2008. *A Republic in Time: Temporality and Social Imagination in Nineteenth-Century America*. Chapel Hill: University of North Carolina Press.
Alton Telegraph. 1897. "Suicide Is Identified." November 25, 1897, p. 1.
Appadurai, Arjun. 1996. *Modernity at Large: Cultural Dimensions of Globalization*. Minneapolis: University of Minnesota Press.
Appelbaum, Stanley. 1980. *The Chicago World's Fair of 1893: A Photographic Record*. New York: Dover.
Apple, Rima D. 1987. *Mothers and Medicine: A Social History of Infant Feeding, 1890–1950*. Madison: University of Wisconsin Press.
Arnold, Charles Dudley, and Harlow N. Higinbotham. 1893. *Official Views of the World's Columbian Exposition*. Chicago: Chicago Photo-gravure Company.
Austin, Lynn. 2007. *A Proper Pursuit*. Minneapolis: Bethany House.
Badger, R. Reid. 1979. *The Great American Fair: The World's Columbia Exposition and American Culture*. Chicago: N. Hall.
———. 2008. Chicago 1893. In *Encyclopedia of World's Fairs and Expositions*, ed. J. E. Findling and K. D. Pelle, 116–25. Jefferson, N.C.: McFarland.
Balesi, Charles J. 1996. *The Time of the French in the Heart of North America, 1673–1818*. Chicago: Alliance Française.
Ballard, Everett Guy. 1914. *Captain Streeter, Pioneer*. Chicago: Emery Publishing Service.
Bancroft, Hubert Howe. 1893. *The Book of the Fair: An Historical and Descriptive Presentation of the World's Science, Art, and Industry, as Viewed through the Columbian Exposition at Chicago in 1893*. Chicago: Bancroft Company.
Barber, Edwin Atlee. 1904. *Marks of American Potters*. Philadelphia: Patterson and White Company.
Barker, David, and Teresita Majewski. 2006. "Ceramic Studies in Historical Archaeology." In *Cambridge Companion to Historical Archaeology*, ed. D. Hicks and M. Beaudry, 205–34. Cambridge: Cambridge University Press.
Barton, Timothy V. 1987. *Charnley House Historical Research Report*. Chicago: Skidmore, Owings and Merrill.
Battle-Baptiste, Whitney. 2011. *Black Feminist Archaeology*. Walnut Creek, Calif.: Left Coast Press.

Beaudry, Mary C. 2004. "Doing the Housework: New Approaches to the Archaeology of Households." In *Household Chores and Household Choices: Theorizing the Domestic Sphere in Historical Archaeology*, ed. K. S. Barile and J. C. Brandon, 254–62. Tuscaloosa: University of Alabama Press.

Beecher, Catharine E., Harriet Beecher Stowe, and Nicole Tonkovich. (1869) 2002. *The American Woman's Home*. Hartford, Conn.: Harriet Beecher Stowe Center.

Beer, Thomas. 1926. *The Mauve Decade: American Life at the End of the 19th Century*. New York: A. A. Knopf.

Beeton, Isabella 1861. *Mrs. Beeton's Book of Household Management . . . Also, Sanitary, Medical, & Legal Memoranda; with a History of the Origin, Properties, and Uses of All Things Connected with Home Life and Comfort*. London: S. O. Beeton.

Bemis, John Claude. 2011. *The White City*. New York: Random House.

Benedict, Burton. 1983. *The Anthropology of World's Fairs: San Francisco's Panama Pacific International Exposition of 1915*. Berkeley, Calif.: Lowie Museum of Anthropology.

Benjamin, Walter. 1986. *Illuminations*. Edited by H. Arendt. New York: Schocken.

———. 1999. *The Arcades Project*. Cambridge, Mass.: Belknap.

Bertuca, David J., Donald K. Hartman, and Susan M. Neumeister. 1996. *The World's Columbian Exposition: A Centennial Bibliographic Guide*. Westport, Conn.: Greenwood.

Bethman, David. 1991. *The Pioneer Drug Store: A History of Washington State Drug Stores and Their Artifacts*. Ferndale, Wash.: D. Bethman.

Binmore, Henry. 1894. *Laws and Ordinances Governing the City of Chicago: From April 2, 1890, to July 10, 1894*. Chicago: E. B. Myers and Company.

Blaske, Mary Steffek. 1982. World's Columbian Exposition: Eating Your Way Down Memory Lane. *World's Fair* 2, no.3: 10–13.

Blodgett, Geoffrey, and Daniel Walker Howe. 1976. *Victorian America*. Philadelphia: University of Pennsylvania Press.

Bluestone, Daniel. 1991. *Constructing Chicago*. New Haven, Conn.: Yale University Press.

———. 2004. "Charnleys by the Lake: Houses, Apartments, and Fashion on Chicago's Gold Coast." In *The Charnley House: Louis Sullivan, Frank Lloyd Wright, and the Making of Chicago's Gold Coast*, ed. R. Longstreth, 37–69. Chicago: University of Chicago Press.

Boas, Franz. 1928. *Anthropology and Modern Life*. New York: Norton.

Boles, Frank, Mary Janzen, and Richard Popp. 2004. *Bowman Dairy Company Records, 1870–1972: Descriptive Inventory for the Collection at the Chicago Historical Society*. Chicago: Chicago Historical Society.

Bolotin, Norman, and Christine Laing. 2002. *The World's Columbian Exposition: The Chicago World's Fair of 1893*. Urbana: University of Illinois Press.

Boorstin, Daniel J., and National Portrait Gallery (Smithsonian Institution). 1975. *Portraits from the Americans: The Democratic Experience: An Exhibition at the National Portrait Gallery based on Daniel J. Boorstin's Pulitzer Prize Winning Book*. New York: Random House.

Brain, Robert. 1993. *Going to the Fair: Readings in the Culture of Nineteenth-century Exhibitions*. Cambridge: Whipple Museum of the History of Science.

Brenner, Elizabeth. 1981. "Millionaires: Riding the Crest of the DePaul-Area Boom." *Chicago Tribune*. Chicago: J22. April 19.
Briggs, Asa. 2003. *Victorian Things*. London: Sutton.
Brown, Jack. 2016. "On an Elder's Trail: The Later Life of Charles Meigs Charnley, Yale College '65." Lecture delivered at the Newberry Library, Chicago, Illinois.
Brown, Julie K. 1994. *Contesting Images: Photography and the World's Columbian Exposition*. Tucson: University of Arizona Press.
Buchli, Victor, and Gavin Lucas, eds. 2001. *Archaeologies of the Contemporary Past*. London: Routledge.
Buck-Morss, Susan. 1989. *The Dialectics of Seeing: Walter Benjamin and the Arcades Project*. Cambridge, Mass.: MIT Press.
Buel, James W. 1894. *The Magic City: A Massive Portfolio of Original Photographic Views of the Great World's Fair and Its Treasures of Art, Including a Vivid Representation of the Famous Midway Plaisance*. St. Louis: Historical Publishing Company.
Bukro, Casey. 1972. "Throwing Charnley House into the Landmark Arena." *Chicago Tribune*. Chicago: E11, May 21.
Bulatao, Jaime. 1964. "The Society Page and Its Value System." *Philippine Sociological Review* 12, no.3/4: 139–51.
Burdick, Alan. 2012. Making Degrade. *Onearth* 34, no. 4: 24.
Burg, David F. 1976. *Chicago's White City of 1893*. Lexington: University Press of Kentucky.
Burnett, Frances Hodgson. 1886. *Little Lord Fauntleroy*. New York: Charles Scribner's Sons.
———. 1895. *Two Little Pilgrims' Progress: A Story of the City Beautiful*. London: Frederick Warne and Co.
———. 1905. *A Little Princess: Being the Whole Story of Sara Crewe, Now Told for the First Time*. New York: Charles Scribner's Sons.
———. 1911. *The Secret Garden*. New York: F. A. Stokes.
Burnham, Clara Louise. 1894. *Sweet Clover: A Romance of the White City*. Boston: Houghton, Mifflin.
Burnham, Daniel Hudson, Joan E. Draper, and Thomas S. Hines. 1989. *The Final Official Report of the Director of Works of the World's Columbian Exposition*. 3 vols. New York: Garland.
Burnham, Daniel Hudson, and Francis Davis Millet. 1894. *World's Columbian Exposition: The Book of the Builders, Being the Chronicle of the Origin and Plan of the World's Fair, of the Architecture of the Buildings and Landscape, of the Work of Construction, of the Decorations and Embellishments, and of the Operation*. Chicago: Columbian Memorial Publication Society.
Butterworth, Hezekiah. 1894. *Zigzag Journeys in the White City: With Visits to the Neighboring Metropolis*. Boston: Estes and Lauriat.
Cain, Louis P. 2004. Annexation. In *The Encyclopedia of Chicago*, ed. J. R. Grossman, A. D. Keating, and J. L. Reiff, 21–23. Chicago: University of Chicago Press.
Casella, Eleanor, and Chris Fowler. 2005. Beyond Identification: An Introduction. *In*

The Archaeology of Plural and Changing Identities, ed. E. Casella and C. Fowler, 1–10. Boston: Kluwer Academic/Plenum.

Cassell, Frank A., and Marguerite E. Cassell. 1984. "Wisconsin at the World's Columbian Exposition of 1893." *The Wisconsin Magazine of History* 67, no. 4: 242–62.

Catholic World. 1893. "A City of Realized Dreams." 57 (340): 566–69.

Cawelti, John G. 1968. "America on Display: The World's Fairs of 1876, 1893, 1933." In *The Age of Industrialism in America*, ed. F. C. Jaher, 317–63. New York: Free Press.

Centennial Exposition. 1876. *The Centennial Exposition Guide: Fairmont Park, with Map and Complete Description of All the Buildings, What to See, Where to Go*. Philadelphia: Hamlin and Lawrence.

Chapman, Tony, and Jenny Hockey. 1999. Preface. In *Ideal Homes? Social Change and Domestic Life*, ed. T. Chapman and J. Hockey, xi–xii. London: Routledge.

Chicago South Park Commissioners and Olmsted, Olmsted and Eliot. 1895. *Revised General Plan for Jackson Park*. Brookline, Mass.: Olmsted, Olmsted and Eliot.

Chicago 2016 Applicant City. 2008. *Response to the Applicant City Questionnaire by the Chicago Bid for the Olympic and Paralympic Games of the XXXI Olympiad in 2016*. Chicago: Chicago 2016).

Chicago City Council. 1914. "Unfinished Business." *Journal of the Proceedings of the City Council of the City of Chicago*, Regular Meeting, Thursday, July 2, 1914: 1292–1391.

Chicago City Council and John Siman. 1916. *Sanitary Code, 1911: With Amendments and Additions Up to and Including July 10, 1916*. Chicago: Chicago City Council.

Chicago Department of Health. 1883. *Report of the Department of Health of the City of Chicago for the years 1881 and 1882*. Chicago: Geo. K. Hazlitt & Co., Printers.

———. 1885. *Report of the Department of Health of the City of Chicago for the Years 1883 and 1884*. Chicago: Geo. K. Hazlitt & Co., Printers.

Chicago Tribune. 1861. "The Tremont House Improvements." January 22, p. 1.

———. 1873. "The City in Brief." June 2, 1.

———. 1882a. "Potter Palmer: His Grand House on the North Side." February 22, p. 8.

———. 1882b. "Real Estate: Contracts Made for Filling Up the Plague-Spots along the Lake-Shore Drive." March 26, p. 9.

———. 1885. "Display Ad 1." January 18, p. 1.

———. 1890. "World's Fair Directors." April 9, p. 2.

———. 1891a. "Damaged by a Lively Blaze." November 12, p. 3.

———. 1891b. "Dr. J. Parker Pray Co.'s Toilet Requisites." October 18, p. 15.

———. 1892a. "In Honor of Miss Mabury." December 18, p. 4.

———. 1892b. "Terracotta, White: The Tribune's Suggestion for 'Municipal Colors.'" October 1, p. 1.

———. 1893a. "After the Fair." October 30, p. 16.

———. 1893b. "Among the State Buildings." October 5, p. 33.

———. 1893c. "Covered with Ivy." September 9, p. 13.

———. 1893d. "Hyde Park Aroused." November 12, p. 2.

———. 1893e. "In State Buildings." May 14, p. 26.

———. 1893f. "Meets Chicago Folks." June 10, p. 1.

———. 1893g. "Saw the Midway." June 25, p. 10.

———. 1893h. "Those Who Have Passed Away." July 13, p. 7.
———. 1893i. "Vermont's Unique Building." January 1, p. 10.
———. 1894a. "Fund for the Chicago Press League." February 27, p. 12.
———. 1894b. "Tramps at the Fair." February 12, p. 1.
———. 1894c. "Tramps Set Fires." February 8, p. 1.
———. 1894d. "Vandals at the Fair." January 8, p. 11.
———. 1894e. "White City Burned." July 6, p. 7.
———. 1895a. "Gay Times in Society." December 29, p. 4.
———. 1895b. "Seen in the Dim Dawn." May 26, p. 42.
———. 1895c. "Statues Most in Favor." November 10, p. 32.
———. 1896. "Ball for Her Daughter." December 31, p. 9.
———. 1897a. "Big Fund Gone." September 4, p. 1.
———. 1897b. "Bring Charnley's Body Home." November 24, p. 4.
———. 1897c. "Dr. Hall Indorsed for Presidency." February 10, p. 3.
———. 1897d. "False Clew to C. M. Charnley." November 8, p. 10.
———. 1897e. "On an Elder's Trail." September 5, p. 3.
———. 1897f. "Other Notable Social Events." January 1, p. 7.
———. 1897g. "Says Charnley Was Sly." October 5, p. 9.
———. 1897h. "Will Try to Find Charnley." September 9, p. 5.
———. 1898a. "Charnley's Son Dies." June 6, p. 4.
———. 1898b. "Classified Ad 16." April 3, p. 22.
———. 1899a. "In the Society World." November 26, p. 42.
———. 1899b. "New Year's Day Receptions." December 31, p. 35.
———. 1900a. "Events in Chicago Society." February 27, p. 7.
———. 1900b. "In Society World." October 31, p. 16.
———. 1902a. "Cooks Invited to Teas by Women of Wilmette." February 17, p. 1.
———. 1902b. "News of the Society World." June 8, p. 37.
———. 1903a. "Events in Society: Arrangements Completed for Marriage of Miss Marion Ream to Mr. Redmond Stephens on Feb. 18." February 3, p. 7.
———. 1903b. "Events in Society: Wedding of Miss Marion Ream to Mr. Redmond Stephens in Second Presbyterian Church." February 19, p. 12.
———. 1906a. "News of the Society World." May 20, p. 13.
———. 1906b. "'Picturesque' Stretch of the 'Streeterville' Dump to which German Consul Wever Strenuously Objects." September 11, p. 3.
———. 1907. "Paintings Posed Like Old Masters: First Dress Rehearsal for Pageant Vivant at Orchestra Hall." December 10, p. 3.
———. 1908. "News of the Society World." October 14, p. 9.
———. 1909. "Mrs. Ogden T. M'Clurg Dead." April 3, p. 6.
———. 1911. "Society Women Sail in Airship." August 25, p. 1.
———. 1913. "Display Ad 50." October 12, p. F13.
———. 1918a. "Divorce Given R. D. Stephens; Wife Is in East." April 5, p. 15.
———. 1918b. "Lying-In Hospital Benefit Ball at the La Salle Tonight." February 14, p. 11.
———. 1918c. "R. D. Stephens Seeks Divorce; Suit Is Secret." February 28, p. 1.
———. 1920. "James B. Waller Dies Suddenly; Heart Disease." August 4, p. 1.

———. 1922a. "In a Cottage." January 31, p. 2.
———. 1922b. "Ream Heiress Has Rival for New Husband." April 26, p. 21.
———. 1924. "Redmond D. Stephens Is Married in West." May 24, p. 15.
———. 1931. "Tragic Death of Attorney Ends Romance." February 19, p. 1.
———. 1949. "J. B. Waller Dies; Leader in 43d Ward." September 14, p. 1.
Citizens' Association of Chicago, ed. 1912. *Bulletin No. 28*. Chicago: Citizens' Association of Chicago.
City of Chicago. 2018. *Astor Street District*. https://webapps.cityofchicago.org/landmarksweb/web/districtdetails.htm?disId=4. Accessed June 21, 2018.
Collins, Patricia Hill, and Sirma Bilge. 2016. *Intersectionality*. Cambridge, UK: Polity Press.
Colten, Craig E. 1994. "Chicago's Waste Lands: Refuse Disposal and Urban Growth, 1840–1990." *Journal of Historical Geography* 20, no. 2: 124–42.
Commercial Club of Chicago, Daniel Hudson Burnham, Edward H. Bennett, and Charles Moore. 1909. *Plan of Chicago Prepared Under the Direction of the Commercial Club during the Years MCMVI, MCMVII, and MCMVIII*. Chicago: Commercial Club.
Commission on Chicago Historical and Architectural Landmarks. 1973. *Prairie Avenue Heritage District*.
Condit, Carl W. 1964. *The Chicago School of Architecture: A History of Commercial and Public Building in the Chicago Area, 1875–1925*. Chicago: University of Chicago Press.
Conkey, W. B. 1894. *The Photographic World's Fair and Midway Plaisance*. Chicago: W. B. Conkey Company.
Connerton, Paul. 1989. *How Societies Remember*. Cambridge: Cambridge University Press.
Conzen, Michael P., and Kay J. Carr. 1988. *The Illinois & Michigan Canal National Heritage Corridor: A Guide to Its History and Sources*. DeKalb: Northern Illinois University Press.
Cook County Property Tax Portal. 2018. Find Your Property. http://www.cookcountypropertyinfo.com/. Accessed December 1, 2018.
Cook, Lauren L., Rebecca Yamin, and John P. McCarthy. 1996. "Shopping as Meaningful Action: Toward a Redefinition of Consumption in Historical Archaeology." *Historical Archaeology* 30, no. 4: 50–65.
Corbin, Alain. 1986. *The Foul and the Fragrant: Odour and the French Social Imagination*. Leamington Spa: Berg.
Corn, Wanda M. 2011. *Women Building History: Public Art at the 1893 Columbian Exposition*. Berkeley: University of California Press.
Corrado, Oliver J. 1990. "Dentures." *British Medical Journal* 301, no. 6763: 1265–68.
Cowan, Ruth Schwartz. 1983. *More Work for Mother: The Ironies of Household Technology from the Open Hearth to the Microwave*. New York: Basic Books.
Crane, Brian D. 2000. "Filth, Garbage, and Rubbish: Refuse Disposal, Sanitary Reform, and Nineteenth-Century Yard Deposits in Washington, D.C." *Historical Archaeology* 34, no. 1: 20–38.
Crenshaw, Kimberle. 1989. "Demarginalizing the Intersection of Race and Sex: A Black

Feminist Critique of Antidiscrimination Doctrine, Feminist Theory and Antiracist Politics." *University of Chicago Legal Forum* 1, no. 8: 139–67.

Croft, Barbara. 2003. *Moon's Crossing*. Boston: Houghton Mifflin.

Croll, Theodore P., and Ben Z. Swanson Jr. 2006. "Victorian Era Esthetic and Restorative Dentistry: An Advertising Trade Card Gallery." *Journal of Esthetic and Restorative Dentistry* 18: 235–55.

Cromley, Elizabeth Collins. 2004. "At Home on Astor Street: Uses of Interior Space at the Charnley House." In *The Charnley House: Louis Sullivan, Frank Lloyd Wright, and the Making of Chicago's Gold Coast*, ed. R. Longstreth, 101–27. Chicago: University of Chicago Press.

———. 2012. "Frank Lloyd Wright in the Kitchen." *Buildings & Landscapes: Journal of the Vernacular Architecture Forum* 19, no. 1: 18–42.

Cronon, William. 1991. *Nature's Metropolis: Chicago and the Great West*. New York: W. W. Norton.

Dawdy, Shannon Lee. 2010. "Clockpunk Anthropology and the Ruins of Modernity." *Current Anthropology* 51, no. 6: 761–93.

Davis, John R. 2008. "London 1851." In *Encyclopedia of World's Fairs and Expositions*, ed. J. E. Findling and K. D. Pelle, 9–15. Jefferson, N.C.: McFarland.

Day, Clarence S., Jr. 1907. *Decennial Record of the Class of 1896, Yale College*. New York: De Vinne Press.

de Wit, Wim. 1993. Building an Illusion: The Design of the World's Columbian Exposition. In *Grand Illusions: Chicago's World's Fair of 1893*, ed. Neil Harris, Wim de Wit, James Burkhardt Gilbert, and Robert W. Rydell, 41–98. Chicago: Chicago Historical Society.

Delliquadri, Lyn. 1994. "A Living Tradition: The Winterbothams and Their Legacy." *Art Institute of Chicago Museum Studies* 20, no. 2: 102–10.

Department of Publicity and Promotion, World's Columbian Exposition. 1892. *Official Guide to the Grounds and Buildings of the World's Columbian Exposition during Construction*. Chicago: Rand, McNally.

Donald, James. 1999. *Imagining the Modern City*. Minneapolis: University of Minnesota Press.

Douglas, Mary. 1966. *Purity and Danger: An Analysis of Concepts of Pollution and Taboo*. New York: Routledge.

Douglas, Mary, and Baron C. Isherwood. 1979. *The World of Goods: Towards an Anthropology of Consumption*. New York: Basic Books.

Dr. J. Parker Pray's Toilet Preparations. 1914. Advertisement. *Good Housekeeping* 58 (June):74.

Dudden, Faye E. 1983. *Serving Women: Household Service in Nineteenth Century America*. Middleton, Conn.: Wesleyan University Press.

Durkheim, Émile. 1984. *The Division of Labor in Society*. New York: Free Press.

Dybwad, G. L., and Joy V. Bliss. 1992. *Annotated Bibliography: World's Columbian Exposition, Chicago 1893*. Albuquerque, N.M.: Book Stops Here.

Eco, Umberto. 1986. "A Theory of Expositions." In *Travels in Hyperreality: Essays*, 289–307. San Diego: Harcourt Brace Jovanovich.

Eisinger, Peter. 2000. "The Politics of Breads and Circuses: Building the City for the Visitor Class." *Urban Affairs Review* 35, no. 3: 316–33.

English, Jane. 1911. "What Chicago Women Wear; Some Handsome Evening Gowns." *Chicago Tribune*, January 22, p. F2.

Fabian, Johannes. 1983. *Time and the Other: How Anthropology Makes its Object*. New York: Columbia University Press.

Findling, John E., and Kimberly D. Pelle. 2008. *Encyclopedia of World's Fairs and Expositions*. Jefferson, N.C.: McFarland.

Finley, Martha. 1894. *Elsie at the World's Fair*. New York: Dodd, Mead, and Company.

First Presbyterian Church (Evanston, Ill.). 1912. *Christopher House Guild Cook Book*. Evanston, Ill.: First Presbyterian Church.

Fischer, Alphonse L. 1893. *A Journal of My Trip to the World's Columbian Exposition at Chicago, August 7th 1893 to August 16th 1893*. Cincinnati, Ohio: Boston Public Library.

Fitts, Robert K. 1999. "The Archaeology of Middle-Class Domesticity and Gentility in Victorian Brooklyn. *Historical Archaeology* 33, no. 1: 39–62.

Fjellman, Stephen M. 1992. *Vinyl Leaves: Walt Disney World and America*. Boulder, Colo.: Westview.

Flinn, John Joseph. 1893. *Official Guide to the World's Columbian Exposition*. Chicago: Columbian Guide Company.

Fogelson, Raymond D. 1991. "The Red Man in the White City." In *Columbian Consequences*. Vol. 3: *The Spanish Borderlands in Pan-American Perspective*, ed. D. H. Thomas, 73–90. Washington, D.C.: Smithsonian Institution Press.

Gapp, Paul. 1974. "A High-Rise Boom Dims the Gold Coast's Luster." *Chicago Tribune*, August 25: E6–E11.

Garland, Hamlin. 1920. *A Son of the Middle Border*. New York: Macmillan.

Geismar, Joan H. 1993. Where Is Night Soil? Thoughts on an Urban Privy. *Historical Archaeology* 27, no. 2: 57–70.

Giberti, Bruno. 2002. *Designing the Centennial: A History of the 1876 International Exhibition in Philadelphia*. Lexington: University Press of Kentucky.

Gilbert, James Burkhart. 1991. *Perfect Cities: Chicago's Utopias of 1893*. Chicago: University of Chicago Press.

———. 1993. "Fixing the Image: Photography at the World's Columbian Exposition." In *Grand Illusions: Chicago's World's Fair of 1893*, ed. Neil Harris, Wim de Wit, James Burkhardt Gilbert, and Robert W. Rydell, 99–140. Chicago: Chicago Historical Society.

Gill, Brendan. 1987. *Many Masks: A Life of Frank Lloyd Wright*. New York. G. P. Putnam's Sons.

Gilmore, Charles M. 1876. *The Herald Guide Book and Directory to the Centennial International Exhibition at Philadelphia*. Philadelphia: Charles M. Gilmore.

Gist, Deeanne. 2013. *It Happened at the Fair*. Nashville: Howards Books.

———. 2014. *Fair Play*. New York: Howard Books.

Glessner House Museum. n.d. *The People*. https://www.glessnerhouse.org/the-people/. Accessed February 17, 2018.

Goffman, Erving. 1951. Symbols of Class Status. *The British Journal of Sociology* 2, no. 4: 294–304.
González-Ruibal, Alfredo. 2008. "Time to Destroy: An Archaeology of Supermodernity." *Current Anthropology* 49, no. 2:247–79.
———. 2014. "Archaeology of the Contemporary Past." In *Encyclopedia of Global Archaeology*, ed. C. Smith, 1683–94. New York: Springer.
Gould, Richard, and Michael Schiffer, eds. 1981. *Modern Material Culture: The Archaeology of Us*. New York: Academic Press.
Graff, Rebecca S. 2005. "Chicago's First Citizen: Jean Baptiste Pointe du Sable as a Black Indian." In *Race, Roots and Relationships: Native and African Americans*, ed. Terry Straus, 384–94. Chicago: Albatross.
———. 2011a. "Being Toured while Digging Tourism: Excavating the Familiar at Chicago's 1893 World's Columbian Exposition." *International Journal of Historical Archaeology* 15, no. 2: 222–35.
———. 2011b. "The Vanishing City: Time, Tourism, and the Archaeology of Event at Chicago's 1893 World's Columbian Exposition." PhD dissertation, University of Chicago.
———. 2012. "Dream City, Plaster City: World's Fairs and the Gilding of American Material Culture." *International Journal of Historical Archaeology* 16, no. 4: 696–716.
———. 2016. "Charnley-Persky House Archaeological Project." *Digital Chicago*. http://digitalchicagohistory.org/exhibits/show/charnley-persky-house/intro.
———. 2017. "Embers from the House of Blazes: Fragments, Relics, Ruins in Chicago." In *Contemporary Archaeology and the City: Creativity, Ruination, and Political Action*, ed. K. Ryzewski and L. McAtackney, 91–110. Oxford: Oxford University Press.
Graff, Rebecca S., and Megan E. Edwards. 2018. "Fair-as-Foodway: Culinary Worlds and Modernizing Tastes at Chicago's 1893 World's Columbian Exposition." *Historical Archaeology* 52, no. 2: 420–37.
Graves-Brown, Paul, ed. 2000. *Matter, Materiality and Modern Culture*. London: Routledge.
Gray, Shelley Shepard. 2014. *Secrets of Sloane House*. Grand Rapids, Mich.: Zondervan.
Greenhalgh, Paul. 1988. *Ephemeral Vistas: The Expositions Universelles, Great Exhibitions, and World's Fairs, 1851–1939*. Manchester, U.K.: Manchester University Press.
Gregerson, Charles E. 1996. The Principle Remnants of the World's Columbian Exposition. In *The World's Columbian Exposition: A Centennial Bibliographic Guide*, ed. D. J. Bertuca, 273–88. Westport, Conn.: Greenwood.
Grier, Katherine C. 1992. "The Decline of the Memory Palace: The Parlor after 1890." In *American Home Life, 1880–1930: A Social History of Spaces and Services*, ed. J. H. Foy and T. J. Schlereth, 49–74. Knoxville: University of Tennessee Press.
Groom, Nigel. 1997. *The New Perfume Handbook*, 2nd ed. London: Blackie Academic and Professional.
Halbwachs, Maurice, and Lewis A. Coser. 1992. *On Collective Memory*. Chicago: University of Chicago Press.
Hales, Peter B. 2005. *Silver Cities: Photographing American Urbanization, 1839–1939*. Albuquerque: University of New Mexico Press.
Handy, Moses P. 1893. *The Official Directory of the World's Columbian Exposition, May*

1st to October 30th, 1893: A Reference Book of Exhibitors and Exhibits; of the Officers and Members of the World's Columbian Commission, the World's Columbian Exposition and the Board of Lady Managers; a Complete History of the Exposition. Together with Accurate Descriptions of All State, Territorial, Foreign, Departmental and Other Buildings and Exhibits, and General Information Concerning the Fair. Chicago: W. B. Conkey Company.

Hardesty, Donald L. 1981. "Historic Sites Archaeology on the Western American Frontier: Theoretical Perspectives and Research Problems." *North American Archaeologist* 2, no. 1: 67–82.

Harris, Neil. 1993. "Memory and the White City." In *Grand Illusions: Chicago's World's Fair of 1893*, ed. Neil Harris, Wim de Wit, James Burkhardt Gilbert, and Robert W. Rydell, 1–40. Chicago: Chicago Historical Society.

Harris, Neil, Wim de Wit, James Burkhardt Gilbert, and Robert W. Rydell, eds. 1993. *Grand Illusions: Chicago's World's Fair of 1893*. Chicago: Chicago Historical Society.

Harrison, Edith Ogden. 1949. *"Strange to Say—": Recollections of Persons and Events in New Orleans and Chicago*. Chicago: A. Kroch.

Harrison, Rodney, and John Schofield. 2010. *After Modernity: Archaeological Approaches to the Contemporary Past*. Oxford: Oxford University Press.

Harvey, David. 1989. *The Condition of Postmodernity: An Enquiry into the Origins of Cultural Change*. Oxford: Blackwell.

———. 2003. *Paris, Capital of Modernity*. New York: Routledge.

———. 2012. *Rebel Cities: From the Right to the City to the Urban Revolution*. London: Verso.

Hayward, Agnes Carroll. 1914. *Yacht Club Manual of Salads*. Chicago: Tildesley and Company.

Heckel, George B. 1893. *A Week in Chicago*. Chicago: Rand, McNally.

Herrick, Robert. 1900. *The Web of Life*. New York: MacMillan.

Higinbotham, Harlow N. 1898. *Report of the President to the Board of Directors of the World's Columbian Exposition. Chicago, 1892–1893*. Chicago: Rand, McNally.

Hinsley, Curtis. 1991. The World as Marketplace: Commodification of the Exotic at the World's Columbian Exposition, Chicago, 1893. In *Exhibiting Cultures: The Poetics and Politics of Museum Display*, ed. I. Karp and S. Lavine, 344–65. Washington, D.C.: Smithsonian Institution Press.

Hinsley, Curtis M., and David R. Wilcox, eds. 2016. *Coming of Age in Chicago: The 1893 World's Fair and the Coalescence of American Anthropology*. Lincoln: University of Nebraska Press.

Hobhouse, Hermione. 2002. *The Crystal Palace and the Great Exhibition: Art, Science and Productive Industry: A History of the Royal Commission for the Exhibition of 1851*. London: Athlone Press.

Hobsbawm, Eric. 1987. *The Age of Empire, 1875–1914*. New York: Pantheon.

Hockensmith, Steve. 2011. *World's Greatest Sleuth!* New York: Minotaur.

Holley, Marietta. 1893. *Samantha at the World's Fair*. New York: Funk and Wagnalls.

Holtorf, Cornelius, and Angela Piccini, eds. 2009. *Contemporary Archaeologies: Excavating Now*. Frankfurt: Peter Lang.

Hoobler, Dorothy, and Thomas Hoobler. 1993. *The Summer of Dreams: The Story of a World's Fair Girl*. Morristown, N.J.: Silver Burdett.

Hotchkiss, George W. 1894. *Industrial Chicago: The Lumber Interests*, Vol. 6. Chicago: Goodspeed Publishing.

Howells, William Dean. 1893. "Letters of an Altrurian Traveller." *The Cosmopolitan* 16: 218–31.

Illinois State Board of Health. 1884. *Sixth Annual Report of the Illinois State Board of Health*. Springfield: H. W. Rokker, State Printer and Binder.

The Inland Architect and News Record. 1891. Residence for Mr. James Charnley, Chicago. Adler and Sullivan, Architects. *Inland Architect and News Record* 18, no. 1: 13.

———. 1892. World's Fair State Buildings. *Inland Architect and News Record* 19, no. 2: 25, plate (n.p.)

Inman, Willis. 1968. The Semantics of Social Status on the Society Page. *Clearing House* 42, no. 9: 560–62.

Israel, Fred L., ed. 1993. *1897 Sears, Roebuck Catalogue*. New York: Chelsea House.

Ives, Halsey Cooley. 1893. *The Dream City: A Portfolio of Photographic Views of the World's Columbian Exposition*. St. Louis: N. D. Thompson Publishing.

Jacknis, Ira. 1985. "Franz Boas and Exhibits: On the Limitations of the Museum Method of Anthropology." In *Objects and Others: Essays on Museums and Material Culture*, ed. G. W. Stocking Jr., 75–111. Madison: University of Wisconsin Press.

Jenks, Tudor. 1893. *The Century World's Fair Book for Boys and Girls: Being the Adventures of Harry and Philip with Their Tutor, Mr. Douglass, at the World's Columbian Exposition*. New York: Century Company.

Johnson, George H. 1893. "The World's Congress Auxiliary of the Columbian Exposition." *Science* 22, no. 552: 116–17.

Johnson, Matthew. 2010. *English Houses 1300–1800: Vernacular Architecture, Social Life*. London: Routledge.

Johnson, Rossiter. 1897. *A History of the World's Columbian Exposition Held in Chicago in 1893*, 4 vols. New York: D. Appleton and Company.

Joyce, Patrick. 2003. *The Rule of Freedom: Liberalism and the Modern City*. London: Verso.

Kamin, Blair. 2015. "Seymour H. Persky: 1922–2015." *Chicago Tribune*, March 24, p. 6.

———. 2018. "Frank Lloyd Wright building in Montana Demolished." *Chicago Tribune*, January 12.

Kansas Board of World's Fair Commissioners. 1905. *Report of the Kansas Commissioners to the Louisiana Purchase Centennial Exposition Commission*. Topeka, Kan.: Crane and Company.

Katzman, David. 1978. *Seven Days a Week: Women and Domestic Service in Industrializing America*. New York: Oxford University Press.

Kaussen, Valerie. 2008. *Migrant Revolutions: Haitian Literature, Revolution, and U.S. Imperialism*. New York: Rowman and Littlefield.

Kenny, Daniel J. 1893. *Illustrated Guide to Cincinnati and the World's Columbian Exposition*. Cincinnati: Robert Clarke and Company.

Kitzmiller, Erika M. 2013. "Imperial Fantasies: Children's Literature in the White City." *Clio* 43, no. 1: 33–53.

Knight, Louise W. 2006. "Garbage and Democracy: The Chicago Community Organizing Campaign of the 1890s." *Journal of Community Practice* 14, no. 3: 7–27.

Koselleck, Reinhart. 2004. *Futures Past: On the Semantics of Historical Time*, trans. K. Tribe. New York: Columbia University Press.

Krause, Grace A. 2017. "Charnley-Persky House Faunal Analysis." Unpublished report. Copy held by Rebecca S. Graff.

Kruty, Paul, Daniel. 2004. "The Charnley House in Its Architectural Context." In *The Charnley House: Louis Sullivan, Frank Lloyd Wright, and the Making of Chicago's Gold Coast*, ed. R. Longstreth, 71–99. Chicago: University of Chicago Press.

Lace, Ed. 2002. "Native Americans in the Chicago Area." In *Native Chicago*, 2nd ed., ed. T. Straus, 23–27. Chicago: Albatross.

Lampard, Eric E. 1973. The Urbanizing World. In *The Victorian City: Images and Realities*, ed. H. J. Dyos and M. Wolff, 3–57. London: Routledge.

Landes, David S. 1983. *Revolution in Time: Clocks and the Making of the Modern World*. Cambridge, Mass.: Harvard University Press.

Lang, Marjory. 1990. "Women about Town: Chroniclers of the Canadian Social Scene at the Turn of the Century." *Journal of Newspaper and Periodical History* 6, no. 2: 3–14.

Langlois, Lisa Kaye. 2004. "Exhibiting Japan: Gender and National identity at the World's Columbian Exposition of 1893." PhD dissertation, Department of Art History, University of Michigan.

Laporte, Dominique. 2000. "History of Shit." Cambridge, Mass.: MIT Press.

Larson, Erik. 2003. *The Devil in the White City: Murder, Magic, and Madness at the Fair That Changed America*. New York: Crown.

Lawlor, Laurie. 2001. *Exploring the Chicago World's Fair*. New York: Pocket Books.

Lawson, Robert. 1957. *The Great Wheel*. New York: Viking.

Lears, T. J. Jackson. 1981. *No Place of Grace: Antimodernism and the Transformation of American Culture, 1880–1920*. New York: Pantheon.

Lewis, Russell. 1983. "Everything under One Roof: World's Fairs and Department Stores in Paris and Chicago." *Chicago History* 12, no. 3: 28–47.

Licence, Tom. 2015. *What Victorians Threw Away*. Oxford: Oxbow.

London, Bernard. 1932. *Ending the Depression through Planned Obsolescence*. New York: Bernard London.

Longstreth, Richard. 2004. "The Elusive Charnley House." In *Charnley House: Louis Sullivan, Frank Lloyd Wright, and the Making of Chicago's Gold Coast*, ed. R. Longstreth, 1–35. Chicago: University of Chicago Press.

Low, John. 2016. *Imprints: The Pokagon Band of Potawatomi Indians and the City of Chicago*. East Lansing: Michigan State University Press.

Lowenthal, David. 1985. *The Past Is a Foreign Country*. Cambridge: Cambridge University Press.

Luckhurst, Kenneth W. 1951. *The Story of Exhibitions*. London: Studio Publications.

Lurie, Nancy O. 1988. "In Search of Chaetar: New Findings on Black Hawk's Surrender." *Wisconsin Magazine of History* 71, no. 3: 163–83.

Lynd, Robert S., and Helen Merrell Lynd. (1929) 1956. *Middletown: A Study in American Culture*. New York: Harcourt, Brace.
MacLaren's Imperial Cheese Co. 1904. *Cheese Relishes: MacLaren's Imperial Cheese*. Toronto, Canada: MacLaren's Imperial Cheese Co.
Mason, Otis T. 1894. *Women's Share in Primitive Culture*. New York: D. Appleton and Company.
Mark, Grace. 1992. *The Dream Seekers*. New York: Morrow.
Martin, Lisa, and Valerie Martin. 2016. *Anton and Cecil: Cats Aloft*. Chapel Hill, N.C.: Algonquin Young Readers.
Mattie, Erik. 1998. *World's Fairs*. New York: Princeton Architectural Press.
Mäurer and Wirtz. n.d. "1792: How Legends Are Born." Accessed October 26, 2012, http://www.4711.com. Published in German: "1792: Geburtsstunde einer Legend." Available at https://web.archive.org/web/20120113225513/http://www.4711.com/historie0.html.
Maxwell, Catherine. 2017. *Scents and Sensibility: Perfume in Victorian Literary Culture*. Oxford: Oxford University Press.
Mayer, Harold M., and Richard C. Wade. 1969. *Chicago: Growth of a Metropolis*. Chicago: University of Chicago Press.
Mazzola, Sandy R. 1986. "Bands and Orchestras at the World's Columbian Exposition." *American Music* 4, no. 4: 407–24.
McAtackney, Laura, and Sefryn Penrose. 2016. "The Contemporary in Post-Medieval Archaeology." *Post-Medieval Archaeology* 50, no. 1: 148–58.
McAtackney, Laura, and Krysta Ryzewski. 2017. Introduction to *Contemporary Archaeology and the City: Creativity, Ruination, and Political Action*, ed. L. McAtackney and K. Ryzewski, 1–28. Oxford: Oxford University Press.
McClendon, Douglas. 2005. "Chicago's Lakefront Landfill" (Map). In *The Electronic Encyclopedia of Chicago*. http://www.encyclopedia.chicagohistory.org/pages/3713.html.
McCrossen, Alexis. 2013. *Marking Modern Times: A History of Clocks, Watches, and Other Timekeepers in American Life*. Chicago: University of Chicago Press.
Measuring Worth. 2018. Relative Value of US Dollars. http://www.measuringworth.com/uscompare/#. Accessed March 15, 2017.
Medill, Joseph. 1871. "Cheer Up." *Chicago Tribune*. October 11, p. 2.
Melosi, Martin V. 2000. *The Sanitary City: Urban Infrastructure in America from Colonial Times to the Present*. Baltimore: Johns Hopkins University Press.
———. 2005. *Garbage in the Cities: Refuse, Reform, and the Environment*. Pittsburgh: University of Pittsburgh.
Michod, Alec. 2004. *The White City*. New York: St. Martin's Press.
Miller, Anita. 1981. Introduction to *The Fair Women*, ed. J. M. Weimann, vii–ix. Chicago: Academy.
Miller, Daniel. 1987. *Material Culture and Mass Consumption*. New York: Basil Blackwell.
Miller, Donald L. 1996. *City of the Century: The Epic of Chicago and the Making of America*. New York: Simon and Schuster.
Miller, George, Patricia Samford, Ellen Shlasko, and Andrew Madsen. 2000. "Telling Time for Archaeologists." *Northeast Historical Archaeology* 29:1–22.

Mitchell, J. A. 1893. "Types and People at the Fair." *Scribner's* 14, no. 2: 186–94.

Moffett, Nancy. 2000. "First Ferris Wheel Foundation Found; Construction Crew Unearths Giant Caissons." *Chicago Sun-Times*, September 15.

Morrison, Hugh. 1935. *Louis Sullivan: Prophet of Modern Architecture*. New York: Museum of Modern Art and W. W. Norton.

Morse, W. F. 1893. "Disposal of Waste at the World's Columbian Exposition." *Science* 22, no. 566: 316–17.

Motz, Marilyn Ferris. 1988. Introduction to *Making the American Home: Middle-Class Women and Domestic Material Culture, 1840–1940*, ed. M. F. Motz and P. Browne, 1–10. Bowling Green, Ohio: Bowling Green State University.

Mullins, Paul R. 1999. *Race and Affluence: An Archaeology of African America and Consumer Culture*. New York: Kluwer Academic / Plenum Publishers.

———. 2004. "Consuming Aspirations: Bric-a-Brac and the Politics of Victorian Materialism in West Oakland." In *Putting the "There" There: Historical Archaeologies of West Oakland*, ed. M. Praetzellis and A. Praetzellis, 85–115. Rohnert Park, Calif.: Anthropological Studies Center, Sonoma State University.

———. 2011. *The Archaeology of Consumer Culture*. Gainesville: University Press of Florida.

Mumford, Lewis. 1955. *The Brown Decades: A Study of the Arts in America, 1865–1895*. New York: Dover.

———. 1961. *The City in History: Its Origins, Its Transformations, and Its Prospects*. New York: Harcourt, Brace and World.

Munn, Nancy D. 1992. "The Cultural Anthropology of Time." *Annual Review of Anthropology* 21:93–123.

———. 2004. "The 'Becoming-Past' of Places: Spacetime and Memory in 19th Century, Pre-Civil War New York." The Edward Westermarck Lecture, 2003. *Suomen Antropolgi / Journal of the Finnish Anthropological Society* 29, no. 1: 2–19.

National Archives and Records Administration (NARA). 1921. *Selected Passports*. Roll 1710—Certificates: 72750–73125, 8 Aug 1921. NARA, Washington, D.C.

———. 1930. *Death Reports of U.S. Citizens Abroad, 1920–1962*, Publication A1 205, NAI: 302021. General Records of the Department of State, Record Group 59. NARA, College Park, Maryland.

National Trust Collections. n.d. Minton's Ltd. Dinner Service Part. http://www.nationaltrustcollections.org.uk/object/1250796. Accessed July 30, 2019.

Neville, Edith. 1893. *Alice Ashland: A Romance of the World's Fair*. New York: Peter Fenelon Collier.

New York Times. 1884. "The Manicures Divorced." May 24, p. 3.

———. 1893. "Ohio Fair Commissioners." November 19, p. 24.

———. 1896. "Jackson Park's Future." May 24, p. 16.

———. 1898. "Dr. Parker Pray, The Manicure, Dead." January 20, p. 7.

New-York Historical Society. 2011. *Guide to the Records of the American Institute of the City of New York for the Encouragement of Science and Invention 1808–1983 (bulk 1828–1940)*, Vol. 2018. New York: New-York Historical Society.

Newport, Olivia. 2013. *The Dilemma of Charlotte Farrow*. Grand Rapids, Mich.: Revell.

Nugent, Walter. 2005. "Epidemics." In *The Electronic Encyclopedia of Chicago*. http://www.encyclopedia.chicagohistory.org/pages/432.html. Accessed September 9, 2017.

Nursing Record. 1889. "Women and Their Work: The Manicure." *Nursing Record*. October 24, p. 271.

Obama Foundation. 2018. "The Obama Presidential Center." https://www.obama.org/the-center/. Accessed December 12, 2018.

Oberly, James W. 1987. "Review: *The Papers of Frederick Law Olmsted*, vol. 4: *Defending the Union: The Civil War and the U.S. Sanitary Commission, 1861–1863*." *Civil War History* 33, no. 2: 182–84.

Ohio, Board of World's Fair Managers. 1877. *Final Report of the Ohio State Board of Centennial Managers to the General Assembly of the State of Ohio*. Columbus, Ohio: Nevins and Meyers, State Printers.

———. 1891. *Ohio in the Columbian Exposition. Regulations of Board of Managers of Ohio. Ohio State law. National Law. National Regulations as to States. Directory of Ohio Board of Managers*. Ashland, Ohio. [publisher not identified].

———. 1892. *Annual Report of the Board of Managers of Ohio*.

Ohio, Board of World's Fair Managers, and W. T. Alberson. 1893. *Detailed Exhibit of the Receipts and Expenses of the Board of World's Fair Managers to January 1, 1893*. Columbus, Ohio: Hann and Adair.

Ohio, Board of World's Fair Managers, and Daniel J. Ryan. 1892. *First Quarterly Report of the Executive Commissioner to the Board of World's Fair Managers of Ohio*. Columbus, Ohio: Journal-Gazette Printing House.

Oliver, Ned. 2011. "First Agricultural Fair Revisited." *Berkshire Eagle*, November 3.

O'Malley, Michael. 1990. *Keeping Watch: A History of American Time*. New York: Viking Penguin.

Ortner, Sherry B. 1972. Is Female to Male as Nature Is to Culture? *Feminist Studies* 1, no. 2: 5–31.

Palmer, Thomas W. 1893. Introduction to *The World's Fair: Being a Pictorial History of the Columbian Exposition*, ed. W. E. Cameron, 5–13. Grand Rapids, Mich.: P. D. Farrell and Co.

Pearson, Arthur Meville. 2009. "Utopia Derailed." *Archaeology* 62, no. 1: 46–49.

Peck, Richard. 2001. *Fair Weather: A Novel*. New York: Dial.

Pennsylvania Historical Review. 1886. *Pennsylvania Historical Review, Gazetteer, Post-office, Express, and Telegraph Guide, City of Philadelphia. Leading Merchants and Manufacturers*. New York: Historical Publishing Company.

Perkins, Elizabeth A. 1987. "The Forgotten Victorians: Louisville's Domestic Servants, 1880–1920." *Register of the Kentucky Historical Society* 85, no. 2: 111–37.

Peterson, Jacqueline. 2002. "The Founding Fathers: The Absorption of French-Indian Chicago, 1816–1837." In *Native Chicago*, ed. T. Straus, 31–66. Chicago: Albatross.

Pettit, Henry. 1874. "Appendix D: Report of Mr. Henry Pettit, Civil Engineer, Special Agent to the Vienna Exhibition." In *National Centennial*, ed. U. S. C. Senate, 279–320. Washington, D.C.: Government Printing Office.

Peyton, F. A. 1975. "History of Resins in Dentistry." *Dental Clinics of North America* 19, no. 2: 211–22.

Pierce, Bessie Louise. 1937. *A History of Chicago.* Vol. 3. New York: A. A. Knopf.

Platt, Harold L. 1991. *The Electric City: Energy and the Growth of the Chicago Area, 1880–1930.* Chicago: University of Chicago Press.

Pokagon, Simon. 1893. *The Red Man's Rebuke.* Hartford, Mich.: C. H. Engle.

Pooley, Siân. 2009. "Domestic Servants and Their Urban Employers: A Case Study of Lancaster, 1880–1914." *Economic History Review* 62, no. 2: 405–29.

Praetzellis, Mary, Adrian Praetzellis, and Marley Brown III. 1988. "What Happened to the Silent Majority? Research Strategies for Studying Dominant Group Material Culture in Late 19th-Century California." In *Documentary Archaeology in the New World,* ed. M. Beaudry, 192–202. New York: Cambridge.

Providence College. 2008. *Guide to the Anastase Vonsiatsky and Marion Ream papers, 1861–1970.* Vol. 2018. Providence, R.I.: Phillips Memorial Library, Special and Archival Collections.

Rand, McNally and Company. 1893. *New Indexed Miniature Guide Map of the World's Columbian Exposition at Chicago, 1893.* Chicago: Rand, McNally.

Ransom, Candice F. 2007. *Magician in the Trunk.* Renton, Wash.: Mirrorstone.

Rathje, William L. 1974. "The Garbage Project: A New Way of Looking at the Problems of Archaeology." *Archaeology* 27: 236–41.

———. 1979. Modern Material Culture Studies. *Advances in Archaeological Method and Theory* 2: 1–37.

Reed, Christopher Robert. 2000. *All the World Is Here! The Black Presence at White City.* Bloomington: Indiana University Press.

Reiff, Janice L. 2005. "The Worlds of Prairie Avenue." In *The Electronic Encyclopedia of Chicago.* http://www.encyclopedia.chicagohistory.org/pages/410056.html. Accessed February 21, 2018.

Rinehart, Melissa. 2012. "To Hell with the Wigs! Native American Representation and Resistance at the World's Columbian Exposition." *American Indian Quarterly* 36, no. 4: 403–42.

Reitzel, J. A. 1949. *The Flourishing Tree: A History of the Bowman Dairy Company, 1874–1949.* Chicago: J. A. Reitzel.

Roberts, Sir Charles George Douglas, and Arthur L. Tunnell. 1910. *The Canadian Who's Who.* London: Times Publishing Company.

Rollason, Christopher. 2002. *The Passageways of Paris: Walter Benjamin's Arcades Project and Contemporary Cultural Debate in the West.* http://www.yatrarollason.info/files/BenjaminPassagesYatraversion.pdf.

Rotman, Deborah L. 2007. "Public Displays and Private Tasks: Nineteenth-Century Landscape Utilization and Social Relationships at the Morris-Butler House, Indianapolis, Indiana." *Midcontinental Journal of Archaeology* 32, no. 1: 89–116.

Ruíz, Elena. Framing Intersectionality. In *The Routledge Companion to the Philosophy of Race,* ed. P. Taylor, L. M. Alcoff, L. Anderson, 335–48. London: Routledge.

Rydell, Robert W. 1978. "The World's Columbian Exposition of 1893: Racist Underpinnings of a Utopian Artifact." *Journal of American Culture* 1: 253–275.

———. 1984. *All the World's a Fair: Visions of Empire at American International Expositions, 1876–1916.* Chicago: University of Chicago Press.

———. 1993. "A Cultural Frankenstein? The Chicago World's Columbian Exposition of 1893." In *Grand Illusions: Chicago's World's Fair of 1893*, ed. Neil Harris, Wim de Wit, James Burkhardt Gilbert, and Robert W. Rydell, and S. Chicago Historical, 141–70. Chicago: Chicago Historical Society.

Sahlins, Marshall. 1972. "The Original Affluent Society." In *Stone Age Economics*, 1–39. London: Tavistock.

Saliga, Pauline. 2015. "Obituary: Seymour H. Persky (1922–2015)." *SAH Newsletter*, March 24. http://www.sah.org/publications-and-research/sah-newsletter/sah-newsletter-ind/2015/03/24/seymour-h.-persky-architectural-preservationist-dies-at-92.

Salmon, Lucy Maynard. 1987. *Domestic Service*. New York: Macmillan Company.

Scharf, Albert F. 1900. *Indian Trails and Villages: Centered to the North Branch, Chicago River, 1804, as Shown by Weapons and Implements of the Stone-Age*. Chicago: Albert F. Scharf.

Schlereth, Thomas J. 1991. *Victorian America: Transformations in Everyday Life, 1876–1915*. New York: HarperCollins.

———. 1992. "Columbia, Columbus, and Columbianism." *Journal of American History* 79, no. 3: 937.

Schoch, Leonard E. 1893. Leonard E. Schoch letter. World's Columbian Exposition Collection. Chicago: Chicago Historical Society.

Schrenk, Lisa Diane. 2007. *Building a Century of Progress: The Architecture of Chicago's 1933–34 World's Fair*. Minneapolis: University of Minnesota Press.

Schumpeter, Joseph Alois. 1942. *Capitalism, Socialism, and Democracy*. New York: Harper and Brothers.

Schuyler, Montgomery. 1893. State Buildings at the World's Fair. *Architectural Record* 3: 55–71.

———. 1895. Architecture in Chicago. *Architectural Record*, Great American Architects Series, 2, no. 17: 40–41.

Sears, Roebuck and Company. 1993. *1897 Sears, Roebuck Catalogue*. New York: Chelsea House.

Seligman, Amanda. 2005a. Gold Coast. In *The Electronic Encyclopedia of Chicago*. http://www.encyclopedia.chicagohistory.org/pages/524.html. Accessed February 21, 2018.

———. 2005b. Streeterville. In *The Electronic Encyclopedia of Chicago*. http://www.encyclopedia.chicagohistory.org/pages/1208.html. Accessed February 21, 2018.

Seyfert, Elizabeth H. 2006. "The Ohio State Pavilion at Philadelphia's 1876 Centennial Exhibition: Identification, Survey and Evaluation of 20 Types of Ohio Stone." Master's thesis, Historic Preservation. Philadelphia: University of Pennsylvania.

Shanks, Michael, David Platt, and William L. Rathje. 2004. "The Perfume of Garbage: Modernity and Archaeology." *Modernism/modernity* 11, no. 1: 61–83.

Shapiro, Dena Evelyn. 1929. *Indian Tribes and Trails of the Chicago Region: A Preliminary Study of the Influence of the Indians on the Early White Settler*. Master's thesis, Department of Sociology and Anthropology, University of Chicago.

Silkenat, David. 2011. "Workers in the White City: Working Class Culture at the World's Columbian Exposition of 1893." *Journal of the Illinois State Historical Society* 104, no. 4: 266–300.

Simpson, Pamela H. 1999. *Cheap, Quick, and Easy: Imitative Architectural Materials, 1870–1930*. Knoxville: University of Tennessee Press.
Singleton, Esther, and Russell Sturgis. 1916. *The Furniture of Our Forefathers*. Garden City, N.Y.: Doubleday, Page and Company.
Skiba, Katherine. 2016. "Obama Foundation Makes It Official: Presidential Library Will Go up in Jackson Park." *Chicago Tribune*, July 29.
Skidmore, Owings and Merrill Foundation. 1986. *The Charnley House*. Chicago: Skidmore, Owings and Merrill Foundation.
Smith, Andrew F. 2007. *The Oxford Companion to American Food and Drink*. Oxford: Oxford University Press.
Smith, Frank H. 1893. *Art, History, Midway Plaisance and World's Columbian Exposition*. Chicago: Foster Press.
Sprague, Paul, and John Vinci. 1975. Editorial. *Prairie School Review* 12, no. 3: 4.
Stamelman, Richard Howard. 2006. *Perfume: Joy, Obsession, Scandal, Sin: A Cultural History of Fragrance from 1750 to the Present*. New York: Rizzoli.
Stamper, John W. 1991. *Chicago's North Michigan Avenue: Planning and Development, 1900–1930*. Chicago: University of Chicago Press.
Stevens, Charles McClellan. 1893. *The Adventures of Uncle Jeremiah and Family at the Great Fair*. Chicago: Laird and Lee.
Stocking, George W. 1987. *Victorian Anthropology*. New York: Free Press.
Stone, David. 2005. *Chicago's Classical Architecture: The Legacy of the White City*. Charleston, S.C.: Arcadia.
Stone, May N. 1979. "The Plumbing Paradox: American Attitudes toward Late Nineteenth-Century Domestic Sanitary Arrangements." *Winterthur Portfolio* 14, no. 3: 283–309.
Storch, Charles. 1995. "Architecture Group Moves to Charnley Site." *Chicago Tribune*, February 14.
Stottman, M. Jay. 2000. "Out of Sight, Out of Mind: Privy Architecture and the Perception of Sanitation." *Historical Archaeology* 34, no. 1: 39–61.
Strasser, Susan. 1982. *Never Done: A History of American Housework*. New York: Pantheon.
———. 1989. *Satisfaction Guaranteed: The Making of the American Mass Market*. New York: Pantheon.
———. 2000. *Waste and Want: A Social History of Trash*. New York: Henry Holt.
Sullivan, Louis H. 1956. *The Autobiography of an Idea*. New York: Dover.
Sutherland, Daniel E. 1992. "Modernizing Domestic Service." In *American Home Life, 1880–1930: A Social History of Spaces and Services*, ed. J. H. Foy and T. J. Schlereth, 242–65. Knoxville: University of Tennessee Press.
Swenson, John F. 1991. "Chicagoua/Chicago: The Origin, Meaning, and Etymology of a Place Name." *Illinois Historical Journal* 84, no. 4: 235–48.
Tanner, Helen Hornbeck, and Miklos Pinther. 1987. *Atlas of Great Lakes Indian History*. Norman: University of Oklahoma Press.
Tarlow, Sarah. 1999. "Strangely Familiar." In *The Familiar Past? Archaeologies of Later Historical Britain*, ed. S. Tarlow and S. West, 263–72. London: Routledge.

Tarlow, Sarah, and Susie West. 1999. *The Familiar Past? Archaeologies of Later Historical Britain*. London: Routledge.
Tarrisse, Edwin. "1910. Odd Ways of Earning a Living; One Man a Human Alarm Clock." *Chicago Tribune*. March 27, p. E3.
Thomas, Seth E. 1876. *U.S. Patent No. 183,725*. Washington, D.C.: United States Patent Office.
Thompson, E. P. 1967. "Time, Work-Discipline and Industrial Capitalism." *Past and Present* 38: 56–97.
Thompson, William Y. 1956. "The U.S. Sanitary Commission." *Civil War History* 2, no. 2: 41–63.
Thoreson, Trygve, 1980. "Mark Twain's Chicago." *Journal of the Illinois State Historical Society* 73, no. 4: 277–90.
Tolmie, Clare, and Paula Porubcan Branster. 2018. Section 106 Archaeological Properties Identification Report. Obama Presidential Center (OPC) Mobility Improvements to Support the South Lakefront Framework Plan (SLFP), Cook County, Illinois. Technical Report No. 184. Board of Trustees of the University of Illinois and the Illinois State Archaeological Survey.
Trachtenberg, Alan. 1982. *The Incorporation of America: Culture and Society in the Gilded Age*. New York: Hill and Wang.
Trouillot, Michel-Rolph. 1995. *Silencing the Past: Power and the Production of History*. Boston: Beacon Press.
Trump, Erik. 1998. "Primitive Woman—Domestic(ated) Woman: The Image of the Primitive Woman at the 1893 World's Columbian Exposition." *Women's Studies* 27, no. 3: 215–58.
Tuley, Murray F. 1873. *Laws and Ordinances Governing the City of Chicago*. Chicago: Bulletin Printing Company.
Twain, Mark, and Charles Dudley Warner. 1873. *The Gilded Age: A Tale of To-day*. Hartford: American Publishing.
Twombly, Robert C. 1986. *Louis Sullivan: His Life and Work*. New York: Viking.
Upton, Dell. 1998. *Architecture in the United States*. Oxford: Oxford University Press.
U.S. Congress. Senate. Committee on the District of Columbia. 1902. *Report of the Senate Park Commission. The Improvement of the Park System of the District of Columbia*. 57th Congress, 1st session. Washington, D.C.: U.S. Government Printing Office.
Vale, Lawrence J. 2014. Up from Little Hell. *Chicago History* Fall: 18–33.
Van Arsdale and Massie. 1873. *The Inter-State Exposition Souvenir; Containing a Historical Sketch of Chicago; also a Record of the Great Inter-State Exposition of 1873, from Its Inception to Its Close; Names of Exhibitors, and Description of Articles Exhibited*. Chicago: Van Arsdale and Massie.
Van Meter, H. H. 1894. *The Vanishing Fair*. Chicago: Literary Art Co.
Vance, Packard. 1960. *The Waste-Makers*. New York: David McKay Company.
Veblen, Thorstein. 1899. *The Theory of the Leisure Class: An Economic Study in the Evolution of Institutions*. New York: Macmillan.
Voss, Barbara L. 2005. "The Archaeology of Overseas Chinese Communities." *World Archaeology* 37, no. 3: 424–39.

———. 2008. *The Archaeology of Ethnogenesis: Race and Sexuality in Colonial San Francisco*. Berkeley: University of California Press.

Wade, Stuart Charles. 1893a. *Rand, McNally & Co.'s Handbook of the World's Columbian Exposition*. Chicago: Rand, McNally.

———. 1893b. *Rand, McNally & Co.'s A Week at the Fair, Illustrating the Exhibits and Wonders of the World's Columbian Exposition, with Special Descriptive Articles*. Chicago: Rand, McNally.

Walker, Robert W. 2006. *City for Ransom*. New York: Avon.

Wall, Diana diZerega. 1991. "Sacred Dinners and Secular Teas: Constructing Domesticity in Mid-19th-Century New York." *Historical Archaeology* 25, no. 4: 69–81.

———. 1999. "Examining Gender, Class, and Ethnicity in Nineteenth-Century New York City." *Historical Archaeology* 33, no. 1: 102–17.

Weber, Max. 1968. *Economy and Society: An Outline of Interpretive Sociology*. New York: Bedminster.

Weimann, Jeanne Madeline. 1981. *The Fair Women*. Chicago: Academy Chicago.

Wells-Barnett, Ida B. 1893. *The Reason Why the Colored American Is Not in the World's Columbian Exposition: The Afro-American's Contribution to Columbian Literature*. Chicago: Ida B. Wells.

Wesemael, Pieter van. 2001. *Architecture of Instruction and Delight: A Socio-Historical Analysis of World Exhibitions as a Didactic Phenomenon (1798–1851–1970)*. Rotterdam: Uitgeverij 010.

White, Trumbull, and William Igleheart. 1893. *The World's Columbian Exposition, Chicago, 1893*. Philadelphia: P. W. Ziegler and Co.

Wiebe, Robert H. 1967. *The Search for Order, 1877–1920*. New York: Hill and Wang.

Wilcox, David R. 2016. "Going National: American Anthropology Successfully Redefines Itself as an Accepted Academic Domain." In *Coming of Age in Chicago: The 1893 World's Fair and the Coalescence of American Anthropology*, ed. C. Hinsley and D Wilcox, 413–54. Lincoln: University of Nebraska Press.

Williams, Susan. 1996. *Savory Suppers and Fashionable Feasts: Dining in Victorian America*. Knoxville: University of Tennessee Press.

Wilson, Mark R. 2005. "The Fair." In *The Electronic Encyclopedia of Chicago*, ed. J. L. Reiff, A. D. Keating, and J. R. Grossman. Chicago: Chicago Historical Society. http://www.encyclopedia.chicagohistory.org/pages/2656.html.

Wilson, Robert. 2007. *Great Exhibitions: The World Fairs 1851–1937*. Melbourne, Au.: Council of Trustees of the National Gallery of Victoria.

Wilson, William H. 1989. *The City Beautiful Movement*. Baltimore: Johns Hopkins University Press.

Wolf, Eric R. 1982. *Europe and the People without History*. Berkeley: University of California Press.

World's Columbian Commission. 1893. *The Annual Report of the World's Columbian Commission and Other Papers Relating to the Exposition*. Washington, D.C.: Government Printing Office.

Wright, Frank Lloyd. 1977. *An Autobiography*. New York: Horizon.

Wright, Frank Lloyd, Edgar Kaufmann, and Ben Raeburn. 1960. *Frank Lloyd Wright, Writings and Buildings*. Cleveland, Ohio: Meridian.

Wright, Gwendolyn. 1980. *Moralism and the Model Home: Domestic Architecture and Cultural Conflict in Chicago, 1873–1913*. Chicago: University of Chicago Press.

Wurst, LouAnn. 1999. Internalizing Class in Historical Archaeology. *Historical Archaeology* 33, no. 1: 7–21.

Yale University, ed. 1928. *Obituary Record of Yale Graduates, 1927–1928*. Vol. 87. New Haven, CT: Yale University.

Yandell, Enid, and Laura Hayes. 1892. *Three Girls in a Flat*. Chicago: Press of Kight, Leonard and Co.

Zorbaugh, Harvey Warren. 1929. *The Gold Coast and the Slum: A Sociological Study of Chicago's Near North Side*. Chicago: University of Chicago Press.

Zornado, Joseph L. 2000. *Inventing the Child: Culture, Ideology, and the Story of Childhood*. New York: Garland.

INDEX

Page numbers in *italics* refer to illustrations.

Adams, Henry, 5, 58
Addams, Jane, 156
Adler and Sullivan: Auditorium Building of, 72; Charnley family and, 47; Charnley-Persky House designed by, 3–4, 7–8, 10, 46–49, 76, 82, 102, 108, 160, 166–67; Transportation Building of, 11, 29, 32, 64, 76, *77*
The Adventures of Uncle Jeremiah and Family at the Great Fair (Stevens), 169, *170*
Affluence, 152
African Americans, 57, 68
Agricultural fairs, 23
Alarm clocks, 8, 57, *77, 78,* 79
The American Woman's Home (Beecher and Stowe), 86
Animal bones, 147
Anthropology, 61–62, 89
Arcades, Parisian, 127
Archaeology, 6; at Charnley-Persky House, 49–50, *50, 51,* 51–52, *52*; class and, 53; conspicuous disposal and, 148, 150–52; contemporary in, 9, 165–66; domestic material culture recovered in, 87–88; garbage and, 52, 148, 150–52, 158–59; on gender boundaries, 85; of Jackson Park, 6–10, 34, *35, 36, 37, 38,* 39, *40, 41, 42,* 49–50, 52–53, 70, 89, 98–99, 120–21, 123, 125, *128,* 129–30, 160, 163, 167–69
Artifacts: Charnley-Persky House, consumer, 8–11, 51, *52, 52,* 77, 119, 123, 125–26, *126,* 131–33, *134, 135, 135, 136, 137, 138, 139, 140,* 141–42, *142,* 143–44, *144, 146,* 146–48; Charnley-Persky House, diversity, geographical, of, 135, *136,* 137; class and, 125; food, 9, *139, 140,* 143–44, *144, 145, 146,* 146–48; from Jackson Park excavation, 39, *128,* 129–30; Victorian, 7, 22, 42
Art Institute of Chicago, 21, 108
Astor Street, Chicago, 11–12, 44; Adler and Sullivan on, 47–49; Charnley family and, 3–4, 46–47, 53, 104–5, 114, 133, 159, 167, 171; Charnley-Persky House and, 3–4, 56–57, 82, 102; landmarking of, 46. *See also* Gold Coast
Auditorium Building, 72

Beaudry, Mary, 85
Beaux-Arts: Sullivan and, 64, 76; in World's Columbian Exposition, 29, 64–65, 84, 88, 160
Beecher, Catharine E., 86
Benjamin, Walter, 122, 127
Binderton Apartments, 111, 132
Bluestone, Daniel, 45
Board of Lady Managers, World's Columbian Exposition, 12, 27, 66, 88
Boas, Franz, 61–62, 89
Bowman Dairy Company, 144, 146
Brands: in Charnley-Persky House, 6, 51–52, 119, 125–26, *134, 135, 136, 137, 138, 139, 140,* 141, 144, 146–47, 160; food and drink, 125–26, *139, 140,* 143–44, *144, 145, 146,* 146–47; fragrance, 119–20, 137, *139,* 141, 160; health, *138*; household, *140*; MacLaren's Imperial Cheese Company, 125–26, *139,* 146, *146*; No. 4711 cologne, 119, 160; toiletries, *138, 139*; Le Trèfle Incarnat perfume, 137, *139,* 141; Yacht Club salad dressing, *139,* 143–44, *144, 145,* 146

196 · Index

Britain: Crystal Palace Exhibition in, 21, 24–25, 61, 70, 122, 127, 141; fairs of, 21, 23–25, 61, 70, 121–22, 127, 141; industrial exhibitions of, 23–24; sanitation in, 152; vernacular houses of, 83; in World's Columbian Exposition, exhibition of, 63
Brown, Jack, 102–4
Buffalo Pan-American Exposition, 1901, 64, 80
Burnett, Frances Hodgson, 55
Burnham, Clara, 93, 127
Burnham, Daniel: for Charnley family, home designed by, 3, 47; City Beautiful movement and, 65; in World's Columbian Exposition, 3, 11, 28–29, 47, 65, 67, 91, 98, 167

Census, 114, *116*
Centennial Exhibition. *See* Philadelphia Centennial Exposition
Century of Progress International Exposition (Exposition of Progress) (1933–34), 19, 80–81
Chadwick, Edwin, 152
Charnley, Charles, 103–5
Charnley, Douglas, 3, 46, 103, 105–6, 133
Charnley, Helen, 3, 12, 101–2, 104; after Astor Street, 105–6, 133; before Astor Street, 46–47; parties hosted by, 53, 103
Charnley, James, 3, 12, 47, 101–2, 104; businesses of, 46; disease, death of, 4, 105, 133
Charnley family, 7, 12, 88; after Astor Street, 4, 105–6, 133; Astor Street and, 3–4, 46–47, 53, 104–5, 114, 133, 159, 167, 171; Burnham, D., and Root designing home for, 3, 47; in Charnley-Persky House, 3–4, 46–47, 53, 104–5, 114, *116*, 132–33, 167; scandal of, 4, 103–5; social life of, 53, 101–3, 105–7, 133
Charnley-Persky House, *45*, *73*, *75*, *163*, *169*; Adler and Sullivan designing, 3–4, 7–8, 10, 46–49, 76, 82, 102, 108, 160, 166–67; alarm clock from, 8, *57*, *77*, *78*, *79*; animal bones recovered from, 147; archaeology and, 49–50, *50*, *51*, 51–52, *52*; Astor Street and, 3–4, 56–57, 82, 102; brands in, 6, 51–52, 119, 125–26, *134*, *135*, *136*, *137*, *138*, *139*, *140*, 141, 144, 146–47, 160; Charnley family in, 3–4, 46–47, 53, 104–5, 114, *116*, 132–33, 167; Charnley family leaving, 105–6; consumption and, 8–11, 51–52, 112, 119, 123, 125–26, *126*, 131–33, *134*, 135, *135*, *136*, 137, *138*, *139*, *140*, 141–42, *142*, 143–44, *144*, *146*, 146–48, 156, 160; domesticity and, 11, 81, 102, 110, 113, 117–18; domestic space of, 8, 39, 42, 83–84, 88, 102, 112; durability of, 72, 102, 112; elite networks and, 49, 53; excavation of, 6, 9–10, *50*, 50–51, *51*, *52*, 52–53, 77, 83, 131, 133, 160; as familiar and strange, 166–67; food and drink in, 9, *139*, *140*, 143–44, *144*, *145*, *146*, 146–49; garbage from, 8–9, 17, 50, 52, 100, 117–18, 120–21, 131–33, 148, 152, 156, 158–59; Gold Coast and, 3–5, 44–45, 83; infrastructure of, 72, 82–83; McClurg family in, 106, *107*, 108–9; midden of, 6, 8–9, 17, 48, 50, 52, 100, 112, 117–21, 131–33, *134*, 135, *135*, 137, 148, 152, 158–59; modernity of, 5, 48, 56–57, 72, 76–80, 82–84, 88, 120, 148, 160, 164–65; as museum and landmark, 9–10, 46, 82, 161, 168; from 1969–86, 112; Ohio Building (1893) compared with, 39, 42, 52, 84, 102, 112, 117; party wall of, 48, 50, 111, 132; Persky and, 49, *107*, 113, 168; plan of, *74*; SAH in, 49–51, 82, *107*, 113, 117, 131, 168; servants in, 8, 83–84, 98, 113–15, *116*, 117–18; social life and, 101–2, 106, 133; SOM owning, *107*, 113; Stephens family in, 82, 106, *107*, 109–10, 114, *116*, 117–18; temporalities of, 56, 72, 76–80; Waller Jr. family in, 106–7, *107*, 110–12, 115, *116*, 132; waste disposal and, 9, 17, 83, 100, 120–21, 133, 148, 152, 158–59; Winterbotham family in, 106, *107*, 108; Wright and, 3–4, 8, 10, 48–49, 62, 72, *74*, 76–77, 82, 160, 166–67
Chicago Consolidated Bottling Company, 123
Chicago fire. *See* Great Chicago Fire
Chicago municipal device. *See* Municipal device, Chicago
Chicago Plan, 65
Chicago school of architecture, 71–72
Christianity, 86–87
City Beautiful movement, 64–65
Civil War, U. S., 153
Class: archaeological research and, 53; in Chicago landscape, 44; conspicuous

consumption and, 124–25, 130, 149–50; conspicuous disposal and, 149–51; consumption and, 124–25, 141–42; department stores and, 128; domesticity and, 85–87, 124, 144; food products and, 144; fragrances and, 141; garbage and, 85; infrastructural changes and, 87; leisure class, 123–24, 149; manicure and, 141–42; modernity and middle class, 164; working class, 21, 53, 67–68, 121, 141; World's Columbian Exposition and, 67–68. *See also* Elites
Clocks: alarm, Charnley-Persky House, 8, 57, 77, *78*, 79; in modernity, 77, *78*, 78–80
Clow Sanitary Company, 99
Codman, Henry Sargent, 28, 65, 91
Cologne. *See* Fragrances
Colten, Craig, 153–54
Columbus, Christopher, 63, 96
Conspicuous consumption, 159; class and, 124–25, 130, 149–50; Veblen on, 120, 124, 149–50, 162; world's fairs and, 150
Conspicuous disposal, 121, 149–52, 159
Consumerism: elites promoting, 123, 125; in World's Columbian Exposition, 120, 123–25, *128*, 129
Consumption: body and, 137, *138*, *139*, *140*, 141–42, *142*; Charnley-Persky House and, 8–11, 51–52, 77, 112, 119, 123, 125–26, *126*, 131–33, *134*, 135, *135*, *136*, 137, *138*, *139*, *140*, 141–42, *142*, 143–44, *144*, 146, 146–48, 160; class and, 124–25, 130, 141–42, 149–50; conspicuous disposal and, 149–51; department stores and, 127–29; dining, 130–31, 144; disposal and, 121, 130–32, 131–32, 149–52, 159; fairs, rise of, and, 23; food and drink, 9, 130–31, *139*, *140*, 143–44, *144*, *145*, *146*, 146–49; fragrance, 119–20, 137, *139*, 141; mass production and, 68, 121, 129–30, 149, 151; modernity of, 148; Philadelphia Centennial Exposition and, 26, 124, *126*, *126*; race, ethnicity, and, 126–27; trashmaking and, 69, 121, 132, 148–51; World's Columbian Exposition and, 6, 8–9, 11, 39, 120, 123–25, *128*, 129–30, 133, 137, 143–44, 160, 169; world's fairs and, 7, 26, 120–25, *126*, 126–27, 129, 141, 150, 159
Contemporary archaeology, 9, 165–66
Creative destruction, 17, 166

Cronon, William, 18, 46
Crystal Palace Exhibition, London, 141; consumer goods at, 122; infrastructure of, 21, 70; non-Western peoples in, 61; structure of, 21, 24–25, 127

Dairy industry, 144, 146
Defamiliarizing. *See* Familiar and strange
Dentures, *142*, 142–43
Department stores, 127–29
Depression, 1893–94, 1, 3
The Devil in the White City (Larson), 33–34, 80, 89
Dickens, Charles, 63
Dining, 130–31, 144
Disney, Walt, 59
Disney theme parks, 59, 62, 169
Disposal: consumption and, 121, 130–32, 149–52, 159; of modernity, 168. *See also* Conspicuous disposal; Waste disposal
Domesticity: in archaeology, material culture of, 87–88; Charnley-Persky House and, 11, 81, 102, 110, 113, 117–18; class and, 85–87, 124, 144; food products and, 143–44; ideologies of, 8, 84–88, 102, 110, 113, 117, 144; quasi-domesticity, 89, 93–96, 98–101, 117, 160, 167; social life and, 87; Victorian, 4, 72, 76; women and, 66–67, 85–87; in World's Columbian Exposition, 11, 66–67, 81, 89, 93–96, 98–101, 117, 160
Domestic spaces: Charnley-Persky House as, 8, 39, 42, 83–84, 88, 102, 112; future, 81; infrastructure and, 87–88; in Ohio Building, 1893, 8, 39, 42, 83–84, 88–89
Dostoyevsky, Fyodor, 25
Douglas, Mary, 148
Dr. J. Parker Pray Manicure Lotion, *139*, 141–42
Durkheim, Émile, 164

Elites, 42, 44; Charnley-Persky House and networks of, 49, 53; Chicago, networks of, 8, 10–13, 49, 53, 161, 171; consumerism promoted by, 123, 125; creative destruction of, 17; fragrances and, 141; Gold Coast and, 11–13, 132, 161; as leisure class, 123–24, 149; in World's Columbian Exposition, 11–12, 21, 27–28, 110, 123, 132, 161; world's fairs and, 124

England. *See* Britain
Ephemerality: conspicuous disposal and, 150–51, 159; of Ohio Building, 1893, 39, 42, 102; planned obsolescence, 33, 150–51; of White City, 6–7, 54–55, 80, 100–101, 166, 168–69; of World's Columbian Exposition, 6–8, 21, 33, 39, 42, 54–56, 69–72, 80, 100–102, 166–69, 171; of world's fairs, 21–22, 71
Eskay's Albumenized Food, *139*, 147
Eskimo Village, World's Columbian Exposition, 68
Eulalia (*infanta*), 12
European peoples, exhibition of, 62
Excavation: of Charnley-Persky House, 6, 9–10, *50*, 50–51, *51*, *52*, 52–53, 77, 83, 131, 133, 160; in Jackson Park, 6, 8–10, 34, *35*, 36, *36*, *37*, *38*, 39, *40*, *41*, 50, 52–53, 89, 98–99, 120–21, 123, 125, *128*, 129–30, 160, 168; of Ohio Building, 1893, 6, 8–10, 39, *40*, *41*, 52, 98–99, 121, 129–30, 160
Exposition of Progress. *See* Century of Progress International Exposition
Exposition publique des produits de l'industrie française (1798), 24, 122
Exposition Universelle, Paris: of 1855, 129; of 1867, 122; of 1889, 26, 29, 70; of 1900, 126, *126*

Fabian, Johannes, 60
Fairs: agricultural, 23; British, 21, 23–25, 61, 70, 121–22, 127, 141; French, 22–24, 26, 29, 70, 121–22, 126, *126*, 129; as modern, 59; national, 23–24, 121–22; sanitary, 23, 153. *See also* World's fairs
Familiar and strange, 9, 166–67, 171
Flag, Chicago, 19
Fogelson, Raymond, 60
Foodways: Charnley-Persky House artifacts and, 9, *139*, *140*, 143–44, *144*, *145*, *146*, 146–49; dining, 130–31, 144; mass production and, 129
Foucault, Michel, 100
Fragrances, 120, 161; Crystal Palace perfume fountain, 141; No. 4711 cologne, 119, 160; Le Trèfle Incarnat perfume, 137, *139*, 141
France: fairs in, 22–24, 26, 29, 70, 121–22, 126, *126*, 129; national exhibitions of, 23–24;

Paris, 65, 127–28, 167; Paris, Exposition Universelle in, 26, 29, 70, 122, 126, *126*, 129
French, Daniel Chester, 2, 31, *32*, 129, 161
Freud, Sigmund, 100

Garbage: archaeology and, 52, 148, 150–52, 158–59; from Charnley-Persky House, 8–9, 17, 50, 52, 100, 117–18, 120–21, 131–33, 148, 152, 156, 158–59; in Chicago, disposal of, 8–9, 133, 153–58; class and, 85; history of, 152–58; as landfill, 17–18, 153–54; from Ohio Building, 1893, 8–9, 121, 130–31; scavengers of, 148, 154–58
Garland, Hamlin, 57
Geismar, Joan, 151
Gender. *See* Women
Gilded Age, 68, 130, 163–64
Glessner, Frances, 67–68
Glessner House Museum, 102
Gold Coast, Chicago, 112; Charnley family and, 101–2, 106; Charnley-Persky House and, 3–5, 44–45, 83; elites and, 11–13, 132, 161; overview of, 42, *43*, 44–46; World's Columbian Exposition and, 11–12, 29, 45
The Gold Coast and the Slum (Zorbaugh), 42
Golden Doorway, 76, *77*
González-Ruibal, Alfredo, 165–66
Gothic styles, 87, 90
Great Chicago Fire (1871), 18–21

Harrison, Carter H., Sr., 11, 80
Harrison, Edith Ogden, 11–12
Harvey, David, 165
Haussmann, Georges-Eugène, 65, 167
Health products, *139*
Heritage movements, 63
Herrick, Robert, 161, 163
Hinsley, Curtis, 69, 126
The History of Shit (Laporte), 100
Homes: Astor Street, Adler and Sullivan designing, 47–49; Astor Street, Charnley-Persky House compared with, 3–4, 56–57; bottom-up approach to, 83–84; Chicago, World's Columbian Exposition and, 11–12, 29, 45, 111; concept of, 85–86; domesticity, ideologies of, and, 8, 84–88, 102, 110, 113, 117,

144; Prairie, 72, 76; Victorian, 3–4, 57, 72, 76, 90, 160, 167. *See also* Charnley-Persky House; Domesticity

Ho-o-den Palace, World's Columbian Exposition, 29, 32, 34, 62

House of Tomorrow, Exposition of Progress, 81

Howells, William Dean, 57

Hygiene, 9, 65, 83, 120, 122, 152

Ideology: of cleanliness, sanitation and, 156; consumerist, 125; of domesticity, 8, 84–88, 102, 110, 113, 117, 144; racial, 56–57, 59–63, 69, 126–27, 169; temporalities and, 56, 68–69; in World's Columbian Exposition, 56–63, 68–69, 125–27, 161, 168–69

Infrastructure: of Charnley-Persky House, 72, 82–83; of Crystal Palace Exhibition, 21, 70; domestic spaces and, 87–88; of Ohio Building, 1893, 84, 118, 150; of World's Columbian Exposition, 39, 55–56, 65, 70–71, 84, 88, 98–101, 118, 120, 150, 156, 161, 168, 171; in world's fairs, 70–71

Infrastructure, sanitary. *See* Sanitation

International Exhibition of Arts, Manufactures and Products of the Soil and Mine of 1876. *See* Philadelphia Centennial Exposition

Intersectionality, 165

Inter-State Exposition (1873), 20–21

Jackson Park, Chicago: archaeology of, 6–10, 34, *35*, 36, *36*, *37*, *38*, 39, *40*, *41*, 42, 49–50, 52–53, 70, 89, 98–99, 120–21, 123, 125, *128*, 129–30, 160, 163, 167–69; consumer goods excavated from, 8–9, 120, 123, *128*, 129–30; contemporary, 10, 88, 161–62, 167–68; excavation in, 6, 8–10, 34, *35*, 36, *36*, *37*, *38*, 39, *40*, *41*, 50, 52–53, 89, 98–99, 120–21, 123, 125, *128*, 129–30, 160, 168; after fire, reclamation of, 162; Museum of Science and Industry in, 10, 36, 71, 88; as Obama Presidential Center home, 9, 162–63, 168; Olmsted and, 64–65, 162–63, 167; Olympic bid, 2016, and, 167–68; South Park Commission and, 2, 55; staff remains in, 70;

stratigraphy of, 39; after World's Columbian Exposition, fires in, 2–3, 5, 32, 80, 161; World's Columbian Exposition and, 1–5, 7, 10, 28–29, *30*, 31, *43*, 64–65, 80, 167–68

Japan, 29, 62

Javanese Village, World's Columbian Exposition, 2, 62, 127

Jenney and Mundie, 111

Johnson, Matthew, 83–84

Joyce, Patrick, 100

Keck, George, 81

Kee & Chapell Dairy Company, *139*, 144, 146

Koselleck, Reinhart, 59

Lake Shore Drive, Chicago, 44–45, 47, 153

Landfill, 17–18, 153–54

Landscape: Chicago area, 13–15, 17–18, 44; World's Columbian Exposition, *30*, 31–32, *32*, *33*

Laporte, Dominique, 100

Larson, Erik, 33–34

Leisure class, 123–24, 149

Letters from an Altrurian Traveller (Howells), 57

Lomax, John Alfred, 123

London, England. *See* Crystal Palace Exhibition, London

Lowenthal, David, 63

Lynd, Helen Merrell, 5–6, 87

Lynd, Robert Staughton, 5–6, 87

MacLaren's Imperial Cheese Company, 125–26, *139*, 146, *146*

Manicure lotion, *139*, 141–42

Mason, Otis T., 61, 66–67

Mass production: consumption, world's fairs, and, 121; food, 129; Gilded Age consumption and, 68, 130; packaging in, 149; waste and, 151

Mäurer and Wirtz, 119

McClurg family, 106, *107*, 108–9

McKinley, William, 64

Meat, 147

Medicine, *138*

Melosi, Martin, 152

Midden, Charnley-Persky House, 48; consumer goods in, 6, 8, 52, 112, 119, 132–33, *134*, 135, *135*, 137; discovery of, 131; garbage in, 9, 50, 100, 117–18, 120–21, 133, 148, 152, 158–59; landfill and, 17; waste disposal and, 9, 17, 120–21, 133, 148, 152, 158–59

Middens, conspicuous disposal and, 151

Middletown (pseudonymous city), 5–6, 87, 99

Midway Plaisance, World's Columbian Exposition, 1, 6, 21, 28, 32, 163; American past on, 63; architecture of, 29, 31; ephemerality of, 55, 80; European peoples exhibited on, 62; Javanese Village on, 2, 62, 127; non-Western peoples exhibited on, 56, 59–62, 127

Millet, Francis Davis, 14, 28

Minton dinner plate, 135, *135*

Modernity: archaeology and, 165; of Charnley-Persky House, 5, 48, 56–57, 72, 76–80, 82–84, 88, 120, 148, 160, 164–65; clocks in, 77, *78*, 78–80; concept of, 164–65; department stores in, 127–28; disposing of, 168; as Frankenstein, 58–59; garbage in, 158–59; Gilded Age and, 68, 130, 163–64; vanishing in, 166–67; waste disposal in, 148, 153–54, 158–59; in World's Columbian Exposition, 58–59, 165

Mumford, Lewis, 164

Municipal device, Chicago, 13–14, *14*, 28

Munn, Nancy, 166

Museum of Science and Industry, Chicago, 10, 36, 71, 88

Native Americans: in Chicago area, 13–17, 19, 166; Potawatomi, 15–16, 19, 166; World's Columbian Exposition and, 60–61, 68, 166

Nature's Metropolis (Cronon), 18, 46

Neoclassicism, 64, 91–92

New York, antebellum, 166

No. 4711 cologne, 119, 160

Non-Western peoples, exhibition of, 56, 59–62, 127

Obama, Barack, 162–63

Obama Presidential Center, 9, 162–63, 168

Ohio Building, Philadelphia Centennial Exhibition (1876), 25, 90–91

Ohio Building, World's Columbian Exposition (1893), 92, *92*, *94*, *95*, 169; Charnley-Persky House compared with, 39, 42, 52, 84, 102, 112, 117; design, approved, for, 96, *97*; domestic spaces in, 8, 39, 42, 83–84, 88–89; ephemerality of, 39, 42, 102; excavation of, 6, 8–10, 39, *40*, *41*, 52, 98–99, 121, 129–30, 160; as familiar and strange, 167; garbage from, 8–9, 121, 130–31; infrastructure of, 84, 118, 150; quasi-domesticity of, 89, 93–96, 98–101, 117, 160; servants and, 8, 96, 98, 117–18, 129; social life in, 88–89, 96, 130–31; toilets at, 98–101, 117

Olmsted, Frederick Law: City Beautiful movement and, 64–65; Jackson Park and, 64–65, 162–63, 167; on Sanitary Commission, 153; in World's Columbian Exposition, 28, 64–65, 91, 153

Olympic Games, 2016, 167–68

Otis family, 111, 132

Packaging, 149

Palace of Fine Arts, Chicago, 10, 29, 32, 71, 88. *See also* Museum of Science and Industry

Palmer, Bertha Honoré, 12, 27, 66, 123, 133, 154

Palmer, Potter, 133; Lake Shore Drive and, 44–45, 153; World's Columbian Exposition and, 12, 21, 27, 123

Palmer Castle, 12, 44–45, 112

Panama-Pacific Exposition, San Francisco, 125

Paris, France: arcades, department stores in, 127–28; Exposition Universelle in, 26, 29, 70, 122, 126, *126*, 129; Haussmann restructuring, 65, 167

Party wall, 48, 50, 111, 132

Paxton, Joseph, 24–25

Perfume. *See* Fragrances

Persky, Seymour H., 49, *107*, 113, 168

Pharmacies, *138*

Philadelphia Centennial Exposition (1876), 4; consumption and, 26, 124, 126, *126*; state buildings of, 25, 89–91; Women's Pavilion of, 25, 27

The Pickwick Papers (Dickens), 63

Planned obsolescence, 33, 150–51

Plaster, 68, 70–71, 94. *See also* Staff

Platt, David, 152, 158–59

Pokagon, Simon, 166

Potawatomi, 15–16, 19, 166
Pottery companies, *134*, 135
Prairie homes, 72, 76
Pray, Mary Cobb, 141–42
Privy vaults, 100, 151, 153, 155

Quaker Oats, 124–25
Quasi-domesticity: familiarity of, 167; of Ohio Building, 1893, 89, 93–96, 98–101, 117, 160; toilets and, 98–101, 117

Race, 121; consumption and, 126–27; racial violence, 68; temporalities of, 59–63, 67; white, 60, 62–63; in World's Columbian Exposition, ideology of, 56–57, 59–63, 69, 126–27, 169
Rathje, William, 151–52, 158–59
Robie House, 72, 76
Root, John Wellborn, 3, 28–29, 47
Rydell, Robert, 58, 164

SAH. *See* Society of Architectural Historians
San Francisco Midwinter International Exposition (1894), 80
San Francisco Panama-Pacific Exposition (1915), 80
Sanitary Commission, U. S., 153
Sanitary fairs, 23, 153
Sanitation: archaeology and, 52, 148, 150–52, 158–59; in Britain, 152; Charnley-Persky House and, 9, 17, 83, 100, 120–21, 133, 148, 152, 158–59; Chicago, 8–9, 153–58; history of, 17, 99–100, 120–21, 133, 151–59; sewerage and water systems, 17, 39, 70, 98–101; toilets, 98–101, 117; World's Columbian Exposition and, 39, 65, 70, 83, 88, 98–101, 120, 156, 168, 171. *See also* Garbage; Waste disposal
Scavengers, garbage, 148, 154–58
Schlereth, Thomas, 22
Schoch, Leonard, 54–55, 168
Schuyler, Montgomery, 76
Sears, Roebuck and Company, 130
Servants: in census, 114; in Charnley-Persky House, 8, 83–84, 98, 113–15, *116*, 117–18; Ohio Building, 1893, and, 8, 96, 98, 117–18, 129
Seth Thomas Clock Company, 79
Settlement, early Chicago area, 13–17
Sewerage and water systems: history of, 17,

99–100; World's Columbian Exposition, 39, 70, 98–101
Shanks, Michael, 152, 158–59
Shovel tests, 36, *36*, 37
Skidmore, Owings and Merrill (SOM), *107*, 113
Smith, Hawley L., Jr., *107*, 112
Social life: on Astor Street, 11–12; Charnley family in, 53, 101–3, 105–7, 133; Charnley-Persky House and, 101–2, 106, 133; domesticity and, 87; networks of, 7–8, 10–13, 49, 53, 161, 171; in Ohio Building, 1893, 88–89, 96, 130–31; society pages on, 53, 82, 103; in state buildings, 93; in World's Columbian Exposition, 88–89, 93, 96, 130–31
Society for the Encouragement of Arts, Manufactures and Commerce, British (Society of Arts), 24
Society of Architectural Historians (SAH): in Charnley-Persky House, 49–51, 82, *107*, 113, 117, 131, 168; driveway of, 131; excavations and, 50–51
Society of Arts, British. *See* Society for the Encouragement of Arts, Manufactures and Commerce, British
SOM. *See* Skidmore, Owings and Merrill
South Park Commission, 2, 55
Staff (material), 70, 94
State buildings: Philadelphia Centennial Exposition, 25, 89–91; World's Columbian Exposition, 88–89, 91–93
Statue of the Republic, 2, 31, 32, 129, 161–62
Stephens family: in Charnley-Persky House, 82, 106, *107*, 109–10, 114, *116*, 117–18; divorce of, 82, 109–10, 117–18
Stevens, Charles McClellan, 169, *170*
Stowe, Harriet Beecher, 86
Strangely familiar. *See* Familiar and strange
Strasser, Susan, 148–49
Stratigraphy, 39
Streeter, George Wellington, 18, 44
Streeterville, Chicago, 18
Sullivan, Louis: Auditorium Building of, 72; Beaux-Arts and, 64, 76; Charnley-Persky House designed by, 3–4, 7–8, 10, 46–49, 76, 82, 102, 108, 160, 166–67; modernity of, 48; World's Columbian Exposition and, 11, 29, 32, 64, 76, *77*; Wright assisting, 48–49
Sweet Clover (Burnham, C.), 93, 127

Temporalities: of Charnley-Persky House, 56, 72, 76–80; in Exposition of Progress, future, 80–81; future, 63–67, 69, 80–81, 88, 167; ideology and, 56, 68–69; past, 59–63, 67, 69; present, 67–69; race and, 59–63, 67; spatialized, 59–60, 67, 166; at World's Columbian Exposition, 7–8, 56–69, 81, 88, 167, 169. *See also* Time

The Theory of the Leisure Class (Veblen), 123
Thomas, Seth E., 79
Thompson, E. P., 78
Time, 77, *78*, 78–80
Toiletries, *138*, *139*
Toilets, 98–101, 117
Tönnies, Ferdinand, 164
Trachtenberg, Alan, 58
Transportation Building, World's Columbian Exposition, 11, 29, 32, 64, 76, *77*
Trashmaking: conspicuous disposal and, 148–51; consumption and, 69, 121, 132, 148–51
Le Trèfle Incarnat perfume, 137, *139*, 141
Turner, Frederick Jackson, 18
Twain, Mark, 68–69, 163
Two Little Pilgrims' Progress (Burnett), 55

University of Chicago, 36, 50, 123, 162–63
Upton, Dell, 81, 86
Urban planning, 65

Vanishing, 166–69, 171
Vaux, Calvert, 64
Veblen, Thorstein, 163; on conspicuous consumption, 120, 124, 149–50, 162; on conspicuous waste, 149–50; on leisure class, 123–24, 149
Vernacular architecture, 83
Victorian period, 96; Gilded Age and, 163; homes in, 3–4, 57, 72, 76, 90, 160, 167; world's fairs and, 7, 20–22, 42

Wall, Diana, 86–87
Waller Jr. family: in Charnley-Persky House, 106–7, *107*, 110–12, 115, *116*, 132; servants of, 115, *116*
Walt Disney World. *See* Disney theme parks
Washington, D. C., 65
Waste: in landfill, 17–18, 153–54; mass production and, 151; Veblen on, 149–50

Waste disposal: archaeology and, 52, 148, 150–52, 158–59; Charnley-Persky House and, 9, 17, 83, 100, 120–21, 133, 148, 152, 158–59; Chicago, 8–9, 133, 153–58; history of, 120–21, 133, 152–59; modern, 148, 153–54; trashmaking and, 132, 148–51
The Web of Life (Herrick), 161
Wells, Ida B., 57
White City, World's Columbian Exposition, 4, 21, 63, 65; ephemerality of, 6–7, 54–55, 80, 100–101, 166, 168–69; plaster columns of, 68; race and, 57, 60; sewerage, toilets in, 99–101; whiteness of, 28, 57; after World's Columbian Exposition, closing of, 1–3, 54–55. *See also The Devil in the White City*
Wiebe, Robert, 164–65
Winterbotham family, 106, *107*, 108
Wohlfeil, Lowell, *107*, 112–13
Wolf, Eric, 60
Women: Board of Lady Managers, World's Columbian Exposition, 12, 27, 66, 88; domesticity and, 66–67, 85–87; in Philadelphia Centennial Exposition (1876), 25, 27; Women's Building, World's Columbian Exposition, 29, 32, 34, *35*, 56, 66–67
Women's Share in Primitive Culture (Mason), 66–67
World's Columbian Exposition (1893), 18; African Americans and, 57, 68; anthropology in, 61–62; Beaux-Arts in, 29, 64–65, 84, 88, 160; Board of Lady Managers, 12, 27, 66, 88; Burnham, D., and Root in, 3, 11, 28–29, 47, 65, 67, 91, 98, 167; Chicago homes and, 11–12, 29, 45, 111; after closing of, 1–3, 5, *32*, 54–55, 80, 161–62, 171; conspicuous disposal and, 150; consumerism in, 120, 123–25, *128*, 129; consumption and, 6, 8–9, 11, 39, 120, 123–25, *128*, 129–31, 133, 137, 143–44, 160, 169; context of, 20–22, 164–65; as cultural Frankenstein, 58–59; department stores and, 129; domesticity and, 11, 66–67, 81, 89, 93–96, 98–101, 117, 160; domestic spaces in, 8, 39, 42, 83–84, 88–89; elites in, 11–12, 21, 27–28, 110, 123, 132, 161; ephemerality of, 6–8, 21, 33, 39, 42, 54–56, 69–72, 80, 100–102, 166–69, 171; Eskimo Village of, 68; European peoples exhibited in, 62; excavation of, 6, 8–10, 34, *35*, 36, *36*, 37, *38*, 39, *40*, *41*, 50, 52–53, 89, 98–99,

120–21, 123, 125, *128*, 129–30, 160, 168; as familiar and strange, 166–67; fires in former, 2–3, 5, *32*, 80, 161; garbage and, 130–31; Gold Coast and, 11–12, 29, 45; Great Chicago Fire and, 19; Ho-o-den Palace, 29, 32, 34, 62; ideologies of, 56–63, 68–69, 125–27, 161, 168–69; infrastructure of, 39, 55–56, 65, 70–71, 84, 88, 98–101, 118, 120, 150, 156, 161, 168, 171; interest, popular and academic, in, 33–34, 80, 83; Jackson Park and, 1–5, 7, 10, 28–29, *30*, 31, 32, *43*, 64–65, 80, 161, 167–68; Javanese Village, 2, 62, 127; landscape of, *30*, 31–32, *32*, *33*; Midway Plaisance, 1–2, 6, 21, 28–29, 31–32, 55–56, 59–63, 80, 127, 163; modernity in, 58–59, 165; municipal device and, 14; Native Americans and, 60–61, 68, 166; neoclassicism of, 64, 91–92; non-Western peoples exhibited in, 56, 59–62, 127; Olmsted and, 28, 64–65, 91, 153; planning of, 26–29, 31; racial ideology in, 56–57, 59–63, 69, 126–27, 169; sanitation and, 39, 65, 70, 83, 88, 98–101, 120, 156, 168, 171; sewerage and water systems of, 39, 70, 98–101; social life in, 88–89, 93, 96, 130–31; staff used in, 70, 94; state buildings of, 88–89, 91–93; temporalities, future, in, 63–67, 69, 81, 88, 167; temporalities, past, in, 59–63, 67, 69; temporalities, present, in, 67–69; temporalities in, 7–8, 56–69, 81, 88, 167, 169; toilets in, 98–101, 117; Transportation Building, 11, 29, 32, 64, 76, *77*; Victorian period and, 20–22, 42; White City, 1–4, 6–7, 21, 28, 54–55, 57, 60, 63, 65, 68, 80, 99–101, 166, 168–69; women in, 12, 27, 29, 32, 34, *35*, 56, 66–67, 88; Women's Building of, 29, 32, 34, *35*, 56, 66–67; workforce of, 67–68. *See also* Ohio Building, World's Columbian Exposition

World's fairs, 4–5, 164; conspicuous consumption, disposal, and, 150; consumption and, 7, 26, 120–25, *126*, 126–27, 129, 141, 150, 159; department stores and, 127, 129; elites and, 124; ephemerality of, 21–22, 71; historical roots of, 22–23, 121–22; infrastructure in, 70–71; literature on, 33; overview of, 20–26; as Victorian, 7, 20–22, 42

Wright, Frank Lloyd, 168; Charnley-Persky House and, 3–4, 8, 10, 48–49, 62, 72, *74*, 76–77, 82, 108, 160, 166–67; Ho-o-den Palace and, 62; Prairie homes of, 72, 76; Robie House of, 72, 76; as Sullivan assistant, 48–49

Wurst, LouAnn, 125

Yacht Club salad dressing, *139*, 143–44, *144*, *145*, 146

Zorbaugh, Harvey, 42

Rebecca S. Graff is associate professor of anthropology at Lake Forest College.

www.ingramcontent.com/pod-product-compliance
Lightning Source LLC
Chambersburg PA
CBHW020822230426
43666CB00007B/1058